The land's end?

The Great Sale of Cornwall

BERNARD DEACON

CoSERG

(The Cornish Social and Economic Research Group)

Redruth

Published by The Cornish Social and Economic Research Group

54, Adelaide Road, Redruth, Cornwall

ISBN 978-0-9513918-1-5

Preface

Around a year and a half ago I was looking forward to a quiet early retirement. I was saying goodbye with no little relief to the tedious bureaucratic tasks and metrics which now curse universities. I was anticipating replacing them with the research and writing on Cornwall that I wanted to pursue. But any dreams of living the life of a leisured nineteenth century Anglican clergyman were soon rudely shattered.

They dissolved in early 2012 as I gradually became aware of the scale of Cornwall Council's obsessive drive for housing growth. Almost a quarter of a century ago I'd joined with Andrew George, now MP for St Ives, and Ronald Perry, to write *Cornwall at the Crossroads*. In that book we warned that the endless population growth we were locked into threatened the very things that made Cornwall such a special place. We might as well not have bothered. Here we were, 23 years later, and a panic-stricken Cornwall Council leadership was gripped by the same unsustainable desire to expand the urban areas of Cornwall.

This time around they echoed an equally panic driven discourse of growth emanating from the ruling elite in the Westminster village. As the UK economy slipped into what the media term 'negative growth' and what most of us would consider to be decline, all considerations of the environmental costs of growth or fears about climate change seem to have melted faster than that Arctic ice cap.

But the short-sighted parrot cries of the growth obsessives and the global super-rich for business as usual cannot hide a growing awareness that a system that demands endless compound growth is fast approaching a crisis point. As the world's population careers towards ten billion the signs of distress are becoming too obvious to ignore. Extreme weather events, the problems of maintaining food supplies and the ongoing mass extinction of species, as their habitats succumb to humans' demands, will not go away. Even though politicians prefer to bury their collective heads in the sand and yearn for the return of that comforting three per cent a year growth.

Here in Cornwall this broader crisis manifests itself in a population growth that's been running at a far higher rate than the UK average now for half a century. Our problem since the 1960s has hardly been lack of growth; it's been rapid population and housing growth in a context of peripherality. Fifty years should be enough time to have made it plain to all but the most blinkered growth fanatics that growth is not the simple panacea its enthusiasts claim. Yet our opinion-shapers appear to have learnt nothing and forgotten everything.

Now Cornwall is being subjected to a new wave of 'place-shaping'. A new class of regeneration technicians set about re-designing our landscapes with a will, sweeping away the old to accommodate the new. Seemingly oblivious to the lessons of the past half century, they are egged on by a political leadership now concentrated in one top heavy institution – Cornwall Council – and a series of even less democratic quangos that pursue a growth policy that for the most part is never discussed or debated in the media. In another sense, this is nothing new. Cornwall began to be sold to outsiders for holidays, relaxation and pleasure back in the early twentieth as its industrial period faded into history. The great sale of Cornwall has now entered a new, even more intense phase, as its 'offer' is packaged by the place-shapers, its landscape sold to developers and its buildings to newcomers.

My mixture of anger and frustration at the ongoing destruction of the Cornwall that I grew up in spilled over in three months of frenetic scribbling in the spring and summer of 2012. Irritation at having to fight the same battle for a saner alternative to mindless suburbanisation resulted in this book. It explains why I feel that present Council policy is not just mistaken; it's a disaster. I hope the arguments in it make you equally concerned, equally determined to stop the ongoing trashing of our land and equally resolved instead to hand on a better Cornwall to future generations of Cornish people.

However, having finished the first draft of the book I began to realise that things might not be as bleak as I thought they were when I started it. Back in 1988 when we were writing *Cornwall at the Crossroads* the demographic data seemed to point to an inexorable rise in the population as the result of an apparently bottomless demand to migrate here from upcountry. In contrast, the results of the 2011 Census point to a slow and unmistakeable downturn in Cornwall's long-term rate of population growth. We may at last be beginning to follow rural west Wales, where population growth rates in the 1970s were comparable to those in Cornwall but have now declined to near zero. Cornwall might just be joining them and setting out along the path to a more sustainable population.

It's clear that, unlike the 1980s, policy-makers now have an opportunity to work with the demographic trends and explore policies that could dampen down unsustainable growth and protect our environmental and cultural heritage from its worst ravages. This is now on the cards in a way that seemed impractical in the 1980s at the height of the growth mania of those years. In a context of a long term falling population growth rate it seems absurd therefore to be planning to increase the housebuilding rate from 41,320 in the 20 years from 1991 to 2011 to 42,250 over the next 20 years. Yet amazingly, this is exactly what Cornwall Councillors are stubbornly planning to do. On the contrary, the Council now has a real choice. It can continue with the costly, unsustainable and failed old policy of population-led growth. Or it can work with the grain and evolve a better, more sustainable strategy. Unfortunately, despite a change of personnel in October of 2012, Cornwall Council's increasingly divided leadership and its fractious politicians seemed ill-prepared to grapple with this decision. We await to see if a new administration put in place after the 2013 elections can come up with the innovative solutions required to counter the pressures creating the great sale of Cornwall. Ultimately, however, it's up to us to ensure our representatives change course. By constantly criticising, harrying and exposing the cosy Council/developer relationship we can help to ensure the future of Cornwall remains a live issue and our elected representatives take a stand on the issue of Cornwall's long-term future.

In writing this book I've received invaluable advice and encouragement from a number of people. Unfortunately, at least three of these do not want to be mentioned in dispatches as they fear their jobs at Cornwall Council will be put at risk if they are identified with this polemic. This is itself a very sad indictment of the supposedly democratic society we live in and a measure of the quiet anxiety that exists in our own mini-version of North Korea. It also makes it invidious to name those others who have provided advice and encouragement on earlier drafts. Nonetheless, they will know who they are so I dedicate this book to those anonymous friends, colleagues and councillors who have the wit to see that the emperor's new clothes are just the same old rags. I do owe a special debt of gratitude to the blogger Cornish Zetetics for allowing me to shamelessly plagiarise his or her blogs. However, needless to say, I remain responsible for the opinions expressed in the following pages.

Bernard Deacon, Redruth

May 2013

Contents

Introduction

At the end of September 2012, campaigners from the group Save Our Unspoilt Land (SOUL) at St Austell were celebrating the decision of Cornwall Council's Strategic Planning Committee to reject a scheme for 300 houses on 35 acres of green fields to the north of St Austell. Undaunted, within a month the developers – Okehampton-based WainHomes – were back with another application for 300 houses at Porthpean road to the south of the town. In the meantime Mercian Developments of Shrewsbury had come forward with a plan to cover 100 acres of green fields on the western edge of the town with a retail centre bigger than St Austell's new town centre. Not to be outdone, a month later developers Westcountry Land, originally from Devon but now with a Truro office, unveiled their own scheme for a supermarket, 400 houses, another hotel and a petrol station at Higher Trewhiddle farm to the south west of St Austell. That made a total of four possible supermarkets for St Austell as a wolf pack of developers circled the town.

The residents of St Austell were not alone in facing a blizzard of planning applications in 2012. Across Cornwall developers were keen to stock up their land banks, hopefully anticipating the next housing boom. For example, at Probus WainHomes were again to the fore with a project for 100 houses, and again on green fields. Over at Redruth, the inner by-pass was set to be transformed into an 'urban street' under plans for a first phase of 350 houses to be built on yet more green fields at Tolgus as the town prepared to spill over its original by-pass. In the same month, the Council gave permission for another 280 houses up at Bodmin. Not to be left out, down at Falmouth Taylor Wimpey were among those leading the charge to join Penryn to Mabe and Falmouth to Budock as an advancing urban sprawl threatened to gobble up pleasantly green countryside. Earlier in the year, councillors had given the go–ahead for the 'biggest ever housing development in Truro', as the INOX Group of Exeter was granted permission for 1,500 houses (and a hotel, restaurant, shops, care home and primary school) at Langarth west of the town (*West Briton*, 2 Aug

2012). And it didn't end there. Amidst this storm of activity, yet another developer unveiled its own grand plan for 3,750 houses over a 20 year period at Nansledan, Newquay. In this case the developer was none other than the Duchy of Cornwall. The Duchy is a feudal relic that raises money to support the Duke. This can't be the same Duke of Cornwall who in a speech in Scotland in 2008 informed listeners that 'we owe it to our children and grand-children not to wreck [this small island] through short-termism and fashionable obsessions', can it? (http://www.princeofwales. gov.uk/speechesandarticles/a_speech_by_hrh_the_prince_charles_duke_o f_rothesay_for_sust_162042425.html) But sadly it is.

All these schemes to make money out of selling Cornwall were symbolically capped in December 2012 when the Council's Central Sub-Area Planning Committee (an Orwellian title that perfectly fits the times) gave the green light to WainHomes (again) to build 82 houses and a park and ride on fields overlooking Fowey. What made these particular green fields special however is that between them and the A3082 stands the Tristan longstone. This stone commemorates the real Tristan of the sixth century who became the inspiration for the French twelfth century legend of Tristan's doomed adulterous love affair with Iseult. It's material evidence for what was Cornwall's greatest contribution to European literature. Perhaps embarrassed at plonking some houses and a car park right next to this iconic slice of Cornish heritage, on the advice of 'English' Heritage, the planning committee made its removal by the developers to an undetermined location a condition of granting permission.

Already moved at least three times since the eighteenth century, the last in 1971 to make way for a roundabout, the Tristan Stone was destined either to resume its peripatetic wanderings or be stuck on the edge of a nondescript housing estate plus car park. Clearly, our heritage continues to play second fiddle to the need to build houses, accommodate in-migrants and transport ourselves to and from the shops and restaurants. If nothing else, this incident showed that there'd been precious little progress since it was last moved. Such crass acts of symbolic vandalism tell us much about contemporary Cornwall and its priorities. Nothing shall stand in the way of the sacred right to make profits; nothing must stop the steady encroachment of houses, roads, supermarkets and hotels into our countryside. Nothing must halt the great ongoing sale of Cornwall.

Moreover, Cornwall Council, far from standing up and trying to stem this relentless onslaught of planning applications and suburbanisation, seemed to be actively encouraging it. As the senior planning officer stated, the impact at Fowey upon an Area of Outstanding Natural Beauty (AONB), the Heritage Coast and the protected status of the Tristan stone was outweighed by the provision of 'new homes and local housing need' (email communication from Phil Mason, 14 December 2012). Meanwhile, senior councillors stand on the sidelines and applaud. Mike Varney, chairman of the Council's Strategic Planning Committee was quoted as saying that the Langarth development 'will enhance Truro' (*West Briton*, 2 Aug 2012). Chris Ridgers, economy portfolio holder in the Council's Cabinet, was adamant that the Duchy's grandiose plans for Newquay would 'drive forward' the local economy (*Western Morning News*, 3 Oct 2012). Ann Kerridge, Lib Dem councillor for Bodmin, was reported as concluding that the benefits of adding another 280 houses to Bodmin 'outweigh the disadvantages' (*Cornish Guardian*, 30 Nov 2012). Even Councillor Bert Biscoe, staunch opponent of excessive housing growth hitherto, was quoted as approving the construction of a hotly contested new road between Camborne and Redruth. The road would, he claimed, 'breathe new life into one of the historic industrial powerhouses of the local economy', giving the area 'a much better chance of building the future it deserved' (*West Briton*, 29 Nov 2012). Local campaigners were more sceptical, pointing out that previously the Council had stated the road was critical in order to unlock land for another 5,000 houses.

Indeed, very little seems to have changed since Professor Charles Thomas issued a heartfelt plea to halt the ongoing 'spoliation' of Cornwall back in 1973 (Thomas, 1973). Almost forty years ago he had been scathing about a 'local government machine' that was 'committed to courses of action that could destroy Cornishness for ever'. The 'short-sighted actions of local councils, stuffed with builders, developers and those engaged in the tourist industry' that Charles Thomas railed against have sadly not disappeared in the fullness of time. We no longer have local councils, just one council in a stripped down caricature of democracy. But short-termism is still rife. The developers' lobby, oiled by the prospects of ever-larger financial gains, is if anything even stronger. And in 2012, hopefully the high point of short-termism and lack of vision, the current council, or rather its elected and unelected leadership, was happily committing itself to stoking up the rate of housing growth in Cornwall.

The day to day battles over individual planning applications were merely the tip of a very large iceberg. Down the Fal at Falmouth-Penryn the Council wanted to build 4,000 houses over the next 20-year plan period, 56% more than in the previous 20 years. Over at Camborne-Redruth the hope was that 5,500 more houses would be in place by 2030. This was the equivalent of adding a built-up area roughly the size of Redruth. At Hayle they were looking forward to another 2,000 houses (equal to a 51 per cent growth rate in just two decades). At Truro the plan was to up the building rate by 54% with another 5,500 houses. At that rate the population of greater Truro was set to double from 20,000 to 40,000 in just two generations. Meanwhile, north of St Austell another 6,000 houses were poised for delivery (even though in the clay area villages, local parish councillors have pleaded for a breathing space after a massive 40% population growth in just 20 years). At Liskeard the housebuilding rate was planned to grow by 82% while at Bodmin Cornwall Council seemed to have completely lost any sense of proportion and was telling us at one stage that ideally 5,000 houses were needed to guarantee prosperity for the town (an eye-watering 70 per cent growth in a mere 20 years). In the end they settled for 'only' 3,200 houses for Bodmin, although this was still 82% more than were built in the previous 20 years. All these targets were set out in Cornwall Council's Core Strategy, rather ambiguously re-branded in the summer of 2012 as Cornwall's Local Plan in response to yet another change in the planning framework set by central government.

The Local Plan: Blueprint for suburbanisation

Mention things like core strategies or local plans to people and their eyes are likely to glaze over as they suddenly remember that pressing engagement several miles away. But this really is critically important as it establishes the framework for planning and development over the next 20 years. It indicates how much growth is likely to occur in the built environment and suggests where the planners would like it to be put. Only 'suggests' as the actual building is done by private developers. Yet, by using phrases such as 'the Council has to make tough decisions and ... shape how Cornwall positively and pro-actively deals with change' or 'we need to set our own agenda which responds to the needs of Cornwall' (Cornwall Council, *Planning Future Cornwall, Our Preferred Approach (PA)*, Foreword and p.1) an entirely false impression is given that the Council, rather than developers and the profit motive, sits in the driving seat.

It doesn't. The vast majority of houses built in the UK result from developers spotting a chance to make a profit and then acting on it. This basic element of the process lurks in the background but is rarely explicitly acknowledged. The actual word 'profit' doesn't appear at all in the Council's documents. In its absence the strong impression is conveyed, sometimes deliberately, sometimes unwittingly, that property developers are keen to provide affordable housing for local people, acting out of some kind of philanthropic motive. The truth is a little different. The planners try to maximise the number of houses that are 'affordable'. But in order to do that, as I shall explain in Chapter 3, they have to accept the building of many more 'unaffordable' (for locals) houses that allow developers to make their profits. Developers build to provide houses that someone, whether local or not, can afford to buy. As long as there is an effective demand for houses, developers will build.

And there is obviously effective demand to buy houses in Cornwall. This demand has to an extent been created and fostered by Cornwall's image-makers over the past century. Developers are able to sell houses here more easily than elsewhere. This becomes particularly easy if they aim their sales pitch at the comfortably off in wealthier areas.

However, this is where local authorities are supposed to come in. To build, developers have to obtain planning permission in a process known as development planning. This takes place within a context of planning policy, which includes the Local Plan and the neighbourhood plans that will be based on it. These set the parameters for building. Development planning involves the day to day process of granting (or withholding) permission to build. The critical importance of the Local Plan is that it sets the overall total of houses to be built. The higher that figure the easier it becomes to obtain planning permission; the lower it is the more difficult it is for developers to get permission. Furthermore, the way new housing is planned also has consequences. If housing is concentrated in large blocks around towns big regional or UK based housing companies with the resources to initiate large schemes are likely to benefit; if housing is dispersed in small developments then a bigger share is likely to go to smaller, more local companies.

It comes as little surprise therefore that over the years, in the structure planning that predated the Local Plan, developers and the House Builders' Federation (now rebranded as the more cuddly Home Builders' Federation) were very interested in the number of houses being planned. They poured a lot of effort and resources into lobbying local authorities, both openly in planning consultations and examinations in public and less openly in direct contacts with planning officers, to ensure as high a housing target figure as possible. As we shall see later, property developers vigorously supported a very high housing target in the first round of consultations on the Core Strategy in early 2011. If evidence were needed, this in itself should be sufficient to puncture the claims of those councillors who disingenuously try to persuade us that somehow the housing targets in the Local Plan have no relationship to the number of houses built, which depend instead on the state of the housing market. Of course the actual decision to build does. But if the housing targets in Structure Plans and Local Plans were so irrelevant then why have developers been so consistently keen to demand as high a figure as possible? In this respect the developers appear to have a far better grasp on reality than some of our councillors.

Yet, despite its crucial importance to the future of Cornwall the Local Plan was virtually ignored. A campaign against the pasty tax proposed in the 2012 budget could within a week amass over 5,000 supporters on Facebook. A campaign to bin the Local Plan struggled to win 100. The Local Plan documents that set out the Council's 'vision' for our future caused hardly a ripple in the local media when they went out for what the Council like to call 'consultation'. Most people remained blissfully unaware of them. Equally, most elected representatives preferred to remain stubbornly silent and refuse to divulge their views on the matter. Even environmental pressure groups seemed paralysed in the face of them. There are of course some good reasons for this. As I shall argue, it's not exactly in the interests of developers or their close ideological companions on the Council or in central government to make the process of deciding planning policy either simple or transparent. Moreover, people might rightly be cynical about a 'consultation' process that seems to operate by consulting people only to entirely ignore their views.

Wozzon then? What this book is about.

In this book I want to try to achieve what may seem an impossible task. I want to make the decidedly anorakish Local Plan a little less impenetrable and a little more comprehensible. But more importantly, I want to argue that this is merely a symptom, the most recent manifestation of a much bigger plan to suburbanise Cornwall, an ongoing project which will end in the loss of the unique character of this land and its people. This book outlines the hyper-growth strategy that we have experienced since the 1960s in Cornwall and calls for an alternative if we want to stop ourselves stumbling into disaster.

The first chapter strips away the pages of flannel in order to expose the dark heart of the Core Strategy/Local Plan, which is the number of houses it proposes should be built in Cornwall by 2030. I will explain how the Local Plan deliberately chooses to lock us into a never-ending spiral of housing and population growth that is inexorably leading to a population of nearly a million by 2100. The fundamentally political nature of this project is disclosed by the fact that, despite recent data showing that Cornwall's runaway population growth since the 1960s is slowing down, the Council persists in its intention to increase the building rate and the speed of suburbanisation.

Despite trumpeting their 'vision' for Cornwall, the authors of the Local Plan have a curiously limited attitude to time. First, they fail to explore or reveal the long-term consequences of their own proposals. Put bluntly, these are likely to change Cornwall beyond all recognition if not wreck it entirely through, in the words of the depressingly hypocritical Duke of Cornwall, 'short-termism' (not to mention 'fashionable obsessions'). Second, they ignore the past. While their 'vision' stops abruptly in 2030, to be replaced by well-meaning utopian aspirations, their sense of history only extends back a few years. They seem completely unaware of the lessons of the past half-century. It's as if Cornwall was only 'discovered' somewhere in the early noughties.

Chapter 2 is a short interlude that explains how the planning system is biased towards developers and against objectors. Despite the insistence by the Tory/Lib Dem Government and the business lobby that planning is somehow holding back growth there is little actual evidence for this claim in Cornwall. In fact it's been the reverse as the planning system is increasingly used to generate high growth rates.

Chapter 3 sets out the reasons why the growth assumptions of the Core Strategy are fundamentally flawed. At the risk of depressing everyone, I'll set out the economic, environmental, social and cultural consequences of continuing on our current path. I submit that this path is selling off Cornwall's crown jewels irresponsibly in the pursuit of short-term growth and up-country profits. I will also reveal how the Council uses unsupported assertions, half-truths and partial evidence to justify its strategic planning approach.

One reason that environmentalists seem very quiet about the environmental effects of the growth strategy is that the Local Plan takes great care to shroud its central message in page after page of verbose greenwash. Chapter 4 shows how the 'greening' of strategic planning is actually a device to distract us from the truth and explains why a growth policy is deeply unsustainable. 'Sustainability' has become a word to be hauled out cynically in order to legitimate never-ending developer-led housing and population growth. Instead of cruelly deceiving the public in this way Cornwall Council needs to be a lot more honest about the future that they, together with the developers and landlords they work with, are mapping out for us. If they believe that doubling the population within three generations is such a good idea then come out into the open and argue the case for it. Stop hiding behind a torrent of greenwash. Stop treating us like idiots.

What do we mean when we talk about 'growth'? Like 'sustainability' the word is bandied around willy-nilly with little clarity. It tends to be used as shorthand for 'prosperity' or 'standard of living'. Yet the way economic growth is measured doesn't just count the things that make us feel prosperous. The gross domestic product (GDP) is the value of all the goods and services produced plus taxes. For example it includes the cost of treating drug and alcohol addiction or the value of the fast foods engineered to produce obesity which will then further add to the GDP by increasing the need for healthcare. Gross value added (GVA) is another measure of output but focuses on the difference between the cost of production and the price of the product.

So economic growth can include more houses and more consumption produced by the extra people who then live in these houses. 'Growth' can therefore mean a number of things – more income, more houses, more people, more jobs. One suspects that when Cornwall Council employs the term it is thinking primarily of growth in population and housing and hoping that this will produce the growth in consumption and output that will lead to a hoped-for growth in jobs. But as a growth in output requires a growth in inputs and as inputs includes such things as land and natural resources (energy, wood, metals etc.) growth raises questions of sustainability. This might be in the sense of sustaining those natural resources around us (see Chapter 4) or sustaining the process of growth itself. Sustainable growth in the latter sense can thus increase the pressure on sustainable growth in the former sense. Or even, as we shall in Chapter 4, make it impossible, as it dawns on a growing number of observers that growth is itself ultimately unsustainable (see for example Jackson 2009).

Chapter 5 turns to how the Cornish themselves are affected by the Council's growth strategy. What makes Cornwall Cornish is not its cliffs or beaches. Or its classy restaurants. Or its 'stunning' landscape. Or even its historical monuments. It's the presence of the Cornish people – a people that can trace their roots back more than a thousand years to a time before the English arrived on these islands. But the Local Plan and the growth strategy that it worships must have its sacrifices. And many Cornish people worry that the long-term sacrifice we have paid for the demographic changes experienced since the 1960s, and will pay as a result of the growth promised for the future, is the continuing existence of the Cornish people. How far, wittingly or unwittingly, does the Local Plan bring the prospect of a de-facto ethnic cleansing closer to reality? Less dramatically, I want to assess the effect of the Council's continuing adherence to its growth strategy on the Cornish as a group, something the Local Plan itself neglects to do. In doing so I shall argue that one reaction – demanding minority rights – may be mistaken and insufficiently ambitious.

The big question remains. Why is the ruling clique in Cornwall so fixated on population and housing growth? Why does the Council intend to pursue into the next two decades the exact same policies whose promised benefits we're still waiting for after 50 years of population–led growth? As we shall see, the majority of the population believe this growth is the biggest threat to the Cornish environment. So why does the Council choose to ignore them and stubbornly insist that growth on an even bigger scale will be such a good thing? If we are to oppose this juggernaut we need to understand the thinking behind it. Chapters 6 and 7 explore the dominant mindset that growth is good for us and teases out what drives it.

Chapter 6 follows the money. Are councillors wholeheartedly committed to the growth that leads inexorably to the million-plus Cornwall policy because of a background that predisposes them to housebuilding and population growth? The chapter then asks who gains financially from a growth policy. It also outlines the pressures local councillors come under to guarantee the flow of profits to developers. In short, Government bullying in favour of a blatant predisposition to growth combines with developer lobbying.

Chapter 7 then follows the policy and identifies the ideological context that makes growth the only game in town. It spells out some factors that help us explain an inability to avoid the million-plus scenario. For example some councillors appear to be ignorant of the way the housing market works. Others are unable to imagine an alternative. Councillors and planners alike seem to be easily seduced by the attractions of the latest big idea. But in a more abstract fashion the taken-for-granted assumptions that lie behind the way our economy is organised work to make the deeply irrational rational.

Moreover, in Cornwall we have an extra factor - the insidious effect of deeply ingrained stereotypes and myths produced and reproduced by tourism that ensure we remain locked into a spiral of population growth. Tourism is such a critical element in reproducing population pressure and leading us on to the ultimate extinction of Cornish Cornwall that it deserves a chapter all to itself. The danger of raising reasonable questions about continuing to build over our countryside for the purpose of attracting more and more people to come and play in Cornwall is that it inevitably raises the objection that somehow we are burying our heads in the sand and objecting to 'progress'. We are living in the past. We want to return to those days when we sent our sons down the mines and put our maids into service as we munch contentedly on our pasties and spin dialect tales to each other. Those who wish to protect the countryside from the vandalism of profiteers are pilloried as nimbys (usually by people who themselves live nowhere near the place they're so keen to 'transform') or, in a curious reversion to Victorian terminology, 'naysayers'. However, this is a shallow and hackneyed response. In reality those who have doubts about what's happening to Cornwall seem to have a better handle on modern social change than those who resort to easy stereotypes and witter on about 'progress', equating it mindlessly with endless population growth. In fact, Cornwall entered on a period of change in the 1990s. A 'new' Cornwall has emerged. However, this 'quality Cornwall', with its emphasis on gourmet restaurants, luxury housing, air travel and suchlike turns out on closer inspection to be just the old Cornwall repackaged. It feeds off the same old stereotypes that have circulated since the end of the nineteenth century. Worse than that, it reproduces them in ever more exaggerated form. It's no new solution but the familiar problem, as Chapter 8 will point out.

It's all very well moaning but what can we do about this growth strategy? The final two chapters start to sketch out some preliminary proposals. Preliminary as they need to be developed through open debate and discussion among those who are becoming increasingly concerned about the direction in which we're being taken. But first in Chapter 9 I need to explain why I think Cornwall has suffered a crisis of democracy since the turn of the century. The last quarter of a century hasn't been a great time for democracy in the UK generally but in this respect as the UK has sneezed we've really gone down with a bad cold. Our political institutions have been centralised and 'streamlined', in the process conveniently reducing the points at which popular pressure can be applied. The number of elected representatives has now shrunk to the point where the people of Cornwall are the least well represented in western Europe. While the quantity of elected representatives has fallen, the quality shows little sign of improvement. Indeed, the vast majority of councillors on Cornwall's unitary authority have shown no inclination at all even to express an opinion on the Local Plan, let alone provide any sort of lead on it. Political parties are feeble or in hock to their regional or London-based masters and mistresses.

While our elected representatives dither, the quango state in Cornwall spends our money on dubious projects with little democratic oversight and even less public participation. It's hardly an exaggeration to conclude that Cornwall resembles a one–party state with no effective opposition to the growth strategy of its closeted elite. While Cornish democracy withers, the media, understaffed and uncritical, is in no position to offer a check, preferring to concentrate on the trivial rather than the significant, and on shallow surface events rather than underlying structures. No wonder that politics has become a dirty word. Encouraged by a parochial press that resolutely bypasses the big picture, people harbour a deep scepticism about the political process in general. Scepticism can easily become cynicism which then teeters on the borders of complete alienation from a politics corrupted by financial influences and Machiavellian manipulation. Unfortunately, this state of affairs perfectly suits those who are quietly pushing forward the growth agenda.

Having identified the political paralysis, what are the remedies? Chapter 10 sketches out some general principles for restoring democracy to Cornwall and challenging the growth consensus. Changes to our political institutions will have to come about from the bottom up. Attempts to enter and change centrally-directed political parties that have no inkling of Cornwall's needs have failed. If we rely on elected representatives who collude with the growth strategy then we're in danger of waiting until doomsday. If our elected representatives provide no lead then they must either be by-passed or replaced. The flowering of local groups protesting against unwanted building projects hints at a growing anger about the ongoing great sale of Cornwall. That anger needs to be joined up; pressure has to be applied on Cornwall Council. If the developers' lobby has captured Cornwall Council's bureaucracy and leadership then we need equally to recapture our elected representatives. But this requires organisation to build a movement which cannot be ignored.

Ultimately our political institutions need to be reformed or rejuvenated so that short-term policies which lock us into an unsustainable future are replaced by properly sustainable policies that respect the

Cornish people and build on the unique heritage of our built and natural environments. To do this I offer in the final chapter my own three simple steps to sustainability. I do not claim to have all the answers – or even most of them – but I've written this book in the hope that others will be able to take up the challenge and chart a way out of the mess we're in. We live in a great place. Let's not go on destroying it. Let's build a Cornwall that future generations can be really proud of.

Chapter 1

The drive to a million: Planning to double the population

I want to begin by examining the central element of the Local Plan, its housing target. Throughout 2012 Cornwall Council was insisting with growing desperation that we needed to build at least 49,000 houses in the two decades to 2030 (in fact we had already started to do so well before the ink was dry on the draft plan). By December 2012 it looked as if a combination of growing pressure from campaigners and rising unease among councillors would reduce this figure to 38,000. However, councillors voted in February 2013, by 58 to 33 with two abstentions and 28 not voting or not present, to increase this again to 42,250. But 42,250 is a thousand more houses than were built in the previous twenty years and basically means a business as usual target. It moderates some of the ridiculously high targets that the Council was bandying around during the process of writing its Local Plan. But it does little to postpone that inevitable crunch point when we eventually realise that we've sold our land and heritage so that developers can make a quick buck. By then it'll be too late. Cornwall will have become an over-crowded congested hellhole, a soulless suburban sprawl indistinguishable from most of the places in southern England.

Houses are built for people to live in. So in this chapter I'll start by asking who these houses are being built for. I shall look a little more closely at the Council's claims and demonstrate that they never did justify 49,000 houses. Indeed, using the most up to date statistics available to us we find that the Council might easily have made a case for a far lower target. However, it chose not to. For the truth is that this is not a technical matter of accommodating demographic change or local housing need at all. On the contrary, it's an irrational political decision to return to the failed policy of housing-led growth. But expanding the built environment in this way also increases the number of people who live in Cornwall. So I will move on to extrapolate the proposed rate of growth in housing and see where current growth rates lead us. The frightening answer is that we're well along the road to doubling the Cornish population to a million by the end of the century. The chapter finishes by comparing past rates of population growth in Cornwall with other places. As a result of this comparison I shall suggest that we are overdue for some fair treatment when it comes to 'accommodating' population growth.

Inevitably, this chapter rests heavily on numerical evidence. But none of it is too complex, so bear with it and you'll find the conclusion is sadly that the Council, deliberately or otherwise, inflated the requirement for houses and hid their real end use behind a deluge of dubious data. What we discover is nothing less than an exercise in mass deception, one blatantly designed to push forward a housing growth project that, as I shall explain in Chapters 3-5, holds dire consequences for Cornwall and its people. But let's start by establishing the big picture. In 1961 there were 132,000 houses in Cornwall. By 2011 there were just under 260,000 houses (Census, 2011). In other words the built environment had doubled in less than two generations. At the same time population grew steadily, from 342,000 in 1961 to 532,000 in 2011, an increase of 56 per cent (Figure 1.1). If the planned 42,250 houses target is adopted and then maintained through to 2060 the built environment will expand again by another 40 to 50% in just half a century.

Happiness and housing: the Council's vision

The Local Plan consultation documents originally amounted to 366 pages of paperwork plus supporting documents. The pre-submission *Local Plan Strategic Policies* document published in March 2013 has been slimmed down to a more manageable 152 pages. The original document was decorated on the cover page with pictures of a happy young new-age family, deserted countryside, solar panels, a builder and a car. By 2013 the new-age family was still there but the countryside and the car had been replaced by photos of a brutalist innovation centre, a train and a bus, which I guess is symbolic of something. The document makes a nod towards Cornish distinctiveness as the foreword is provided both in English and in revived medieval Cornish (*Local Plan Strategic Polices* (LPSP), p.5). Yet, whichever language is used, both the original 366 pages and the slimmer 152 pages were basically devices to distract attention from the central element of the housing target.

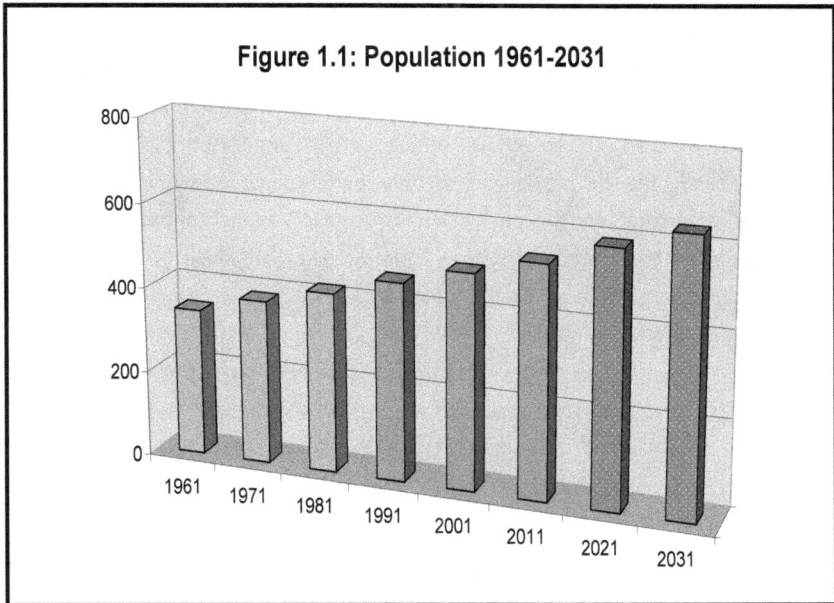

Figure 1.1: Population 1961-2031

It's the Council's equivalent of busily shifting the deckchairs around as SS Kernow drifts majestically and inexorably towards the iceberg. Up on the bridge the Captain enthusiastically urges us onwards, ever onwards, as Chief Stoker Kaczmarek slaves away below decks shovelling coal into the boiler as fast as he can. The Captain and his officers insist the iceberg is a figment of our imagination and will magically melt in front of our eyes. Meanwhile, a handful of the crew, powerless to intervene, frantically jump up and down, as they try to draw attention to the looming iceberg. But most of the rest ignore it. Instead, they squabble over whether this particular deckchair should be placed here rather than there, or there rather than here. Meanwhile, the majority of the passengers party on, oblivious to the approaching disaster. A small minority gaze out across the water, horrified by the approaching iceberg. But even they seem paralysed into inaction. Truly, a ship of fools.

In the Introduction to its preferred approach to 'Future Cornwall', the Council's message was robust and uplifting, confident and can-do. We were told it 'has to make tough decisions' as it shapes 'how Cornwall positively and pro-actively deals with change' which will, it goes without saying, be done 'in the most sustainable way'. What it failed to mention however is that, stripped of all the verbiage about visions and sustainability, the Council was not only planning to continue the growth rate we've suffered for the past half-century but wanted to give it a bit of a shove. For at the heart of 'Future Cornwall' was the desire to build more houses than were built in the 1990s and 2000s.

The housing target is the core of the Local Plan. This is the number of houses the Council expect to see built over the twenty years from 2010 to 2030. The basic number the Council had originally set its heart on was 49,000. Say it quickly and 49,000 is a fairly meaningless number out of context. What does it mean? It means adding another 19 per cent to the stock of 257,000 or so dwellings in Cornwall in 2010. Let's return for a moment to that bigger picture. Back in 1961 there were just 132,000 houses in Cornwall. It had taken us nearly 1,530 years after the Romans left Britain to reach that figure. But we'll have doubled it in just over 50 years. And the Council wanted to continue that rate of growth and then add some more to it. Cllr Kaczmarek claimed that the original minimum housing target of 48,000 houses in 20 years 'is less than the previous two decades' (*Western Morning News*, 20 March 2012). Either Cllr Kaczmarek couldn't count or he was deliberately misinforming us. In its *Housing Growth Discussion Paper v.4* the Council states that 41,320 houses were built in the 20 years to 2011 (p.26). As is often the way with the Council's statistics, this figure can't easily be reconciled with others. For example, their statistics of *Housing growth by parish 1991-2010* inform us that 43,092 houses were built in the nineteen years to 2010. If we add in the 2,046 dwellings completed in 2010-11 we have a twenty year growth of 45,138 houses. But most people would conclude that 48,000 is more than either 41,320 or 45,138.

Originally, the Council was planning to build even more, up to 57,000 houses (a whopping 38 per cent increase on the recent rate). In 2011 a consultation on these numbers resulted in all parish and town councils who responded asking for 48,000 or fewer. But their pleas were ignored as the Council stubbornly decided to stick to 54,000. That was a minimum as there were also plans in the pipeline to top those up by another 8,500 at Bodmin and Saltash if necessary. And if that didn't prove to be enough there were additional ideas for a network of eco-communities. Even the Council's own Planning Policy Advisory Panel found this proposed growth rate too much to swallow. But only just. At its meeting in August 2011 by a very narrow margin of six votes to five its members recommended reducing the housing target to 40,000. This was very close to the actual total built in the previous plan period, although still excessive and far from sustainable in the long term. But it was to no avail. In the end, the Council's Cabinet rather typically ignored the advice of its own advisory panel and decided to go for 49,000. The Planning Advisory Panel met again in September 2012 and, by the somewhat more convincing margin of six votes to three with one abstention, voted to reduce the target to 38,000. Despite the replacement of the growth obsessed Leader and the culling of his cabinet a month later, the new Cabinet duly bowed to its planning officers once again by overruling its own panel and restoring the 49,000 target in November. In January 2013 the Advisory Panel reiterated its determination to reduce the target to 38,000, which maintained business as usual and entailed a rather slower rate of environmental and cultural destruction. By this time planning officers, having argued just weeks earlier that 49,000 was the lowest acceptable figure necessary to avoid all sorts of terrible trials and tribulations, now felt the magic (though constantly mutating) number was 45,400. While ignoring their officers' changing recommendations, the full council, in a process more akin to horse-trading than strategic planning then promptly added another 4,250 houses to the provision in Bodmin, Newquay and Falmouth to bring the total back up to 42,250.

So why do we need to go on steadily suburbanising our towns and villages and building over more and more of our countryside? Underlying rapid housing growth is rapid population growth. In the old days of structure planning the planners adopted what they described as a 'predict and provide' approach. The excess of births over deaths (or vice versa) was calculated and the likely net migration predicted. Change in the size of households was factored in and the number of houses required was then provided. However, there was always a glaring problem with this approach. It simplistically assumed that houses follow population. Neither planning policies, nor the marketing strategies of private companies, nor the activities of estate agents or the property pages of newspapers, not to mention the type of houses being built, had any effect on that population growth. Put technically, it focused entirely on the demand side – more people want houses so let's build them. The supply side disappeared entirely from view.

Those in charge of the Local Plan persist in lecturing us that the demand to move to Cornwall exists and must be accommodated. But they decline to inform us what produces this demand. One major factor is the way Cornwall is packaged. Almost every week the property or travel pages of the broadsheet press run lifestyle features selling Cornwall and its 'attractions' to an up-market demographic.

To take one example from a constant deluge of pieces, the *Daily Telegraph* on 9 June 2012 ran a 'Westcountry special' in its property section. 'There has never been a better time to buy a weekend retreat in the westcountry', it told its readers. The geographically challenged *Telegraph* in fact focused not on the West Country but on Cornwall. Here was a chance to 'snap up your own slice of this gorgeous corner of England'. 'A second home here is still a lifetime pass to an idyll far removed from London's sweat and smoke' it enthused while providing examples of Cornish property for sale at the knock-down prices of

£495,000, £695,000 and £835,000. It provided examples for others to emulate. One couple had moved from ('sweaty and smoky'?) Hampshire to buy not just one but three 'rundown' properties and convert them into 'charming cottages'. Now they were intending to sell two of them off for £475,000 and £725,000 while keeping the third as a holiday let.

The *Telegraph*'s Cornwall is a geographically restricted one stretching from Launceston past Tintagel down as far as the Camel estuary. This is also Cameron's Cornwall, Knightsbridge-on-sea. In this idyll the 'natives', when they get a mention, are reported to have 'a bit of a reputation for being brusque with second-homers'. But fear not. The *Telegraph* assured its readers there was no prospect of any Straw Dogs scenario here. 'Far from being cold-shouldered by the locals, Elizabeth says she and her husband were welcomed from the start'. So 'whether you're looking for a glorious holiday home for a young family, a buy-to-let beach house, or a rundown cottage to renovate, the westcountry [sic] is studded with gems'. But if you're looking for an affordable home in order to stay in the land of your birth then forget it.

Be that as it may, the planners make a virtue out of necessity by arguing that population growth was good for Cornwall anyway. More people means more demand for goods and services and thus more jobs. Even better, although a little patronisingly, we are informed that dynamic in-migrants would lift local people out of poverty. Unfortunately it turned out that more people also mean more demand for jobs and the resulting increased competition in the labour market drives down wages. Yet some years ago, researchers discovered that the income of in-migrants tended to drift down to the level of the host community instead of dragging them up (Williams and Chapman, 1998). This was easily explained when it was remembered that other researchers had previously discovered that a lot of in-migrants weren't exactly dynamic, as many planned their move to Cornwall as a halfway house to retirement (Perry et al., 1986).

The con(juring) trick of assessing housing need

The *Local Plan Strategic Policies* document says little about why we need to build this particular number of houses. Admitting that 'there is no precise measure to predict what level of housing need we need to plan for', it merely states that 'we must plan for the housing needs of our future communities' while meeting 'housing need and demographic change' and of course 'supporting economic growth' (LPSP, p.22).

In its consultation documents of 2011 the Council was a little more forthcoming, explaining where the 'need' for houses came from in the following terms.

> the level of need ... comes from the number of new households that come from our existing communities, young people leaving home, family breakup, older people living longer, and through an expected level of migration into or back into Cornwall (*Our Preferred Approach (PA)*, p.8)

The first four of these five factors basically amount to the same thing – an increase in the number of households. We now live in smaller households than our parents or grandparents did. Household size fell dramatically over the course of the twentieth century as families became smaller, divorce was made easier, children left home at an earlier age and people lived longer. By 1991 the mean household size was 2.4 persons. Even if there was no net migration into Cornwall new households would be generated. The only issue was how many.

The Council confidently predicted that the number of households would grow from 190,000 in 1991 to 236,200 by 2010, an increase of 46,000. They were still sticking to this assertion as late as July 2012, which was a trifle odd to say the least as a few weeks earlier the results of the 2011 Census had showed that the actual number of households in 2011 was 230,400. This was below both the Council's prediction and that of central government, which had gone even further over the top and forecast 232,000 by 2008! (Department for Communities and Local Government (DCLG), Live Table 406) In fact, starkly contradicting the forecasts of the planners, mean household size in Cornwall has been virtually stable since 2001. Here are the figures.

Table 1.1 Households and household size 1991-2011

Year	Number of households	Mean Household size
1991	190,000	2.400
2001	215,700	2.285
2011	230,400	2.272

Undeterred by the discovery that the forecast number of new households was overstated in the past, Cornwall Council's planners stuck to their assumption that the mean household size would dramatically resume its downward path and sink to 2.10 by 2030. This was despite the new data clearly indicating the fall in household size had slowed to a crawl. This allowed them to reach the bizarre conclusion that 'the number of households in Cornwall could increase by between 45,000 and 65,000 between 2010 and 2030 (*Household Growth Discussion Paper, v4*, p.14) even though the actual increase over the previous 20 years was only 40,000 and in the previous ten years just 15,000. It's difficult if not impossible to see how this conclusion could be reached on the basis of the available evidence.

I will demonstrate later how many additional houses would actually be required if we were to adopt a more rational assumption of mean household size based on the reality of the last 20 years. But let's turn to the second factor cited by the council – that of in-migration. Now what was it they said again?

> the level of need ... comes from the number of new households that come from our existing communities, young people leaving home, family breakup, older people living longer, and through an expected level of migration into or back into Cornwall (*PA*, p.8)

'And'? One could be forgiven for thinking from this that migration is the least important factor as it looks like an afterthought, something topping up the numbers of houses already needed by the existing population. This is far from the case.

Oddly, in all the 366 pages of the Core Strategy documentation the critical role of in-migration was mentioned just twice. In *Local Plan Strategic Policies* it's not mentioned at all as such, although the planners do admit that 'migration rates' are 'a major component in housing need' (LPSP, p.22). Occasionally at other times too the veil slips. The Council itself in its own 'evidence base' admits that natural change in Cornwall without factoring in in-migration would lead to a lower population (*Housing Issues Paper*, p.5). And at other unguarded moments the planners are forced to admit the truth: 'The housing projections ... are primarily driven by migration' (*Core Strategy Options Paper 1, Introduction*, p.1). The Council also knows full well that in-migration is the single greatest driver of population change as it states this bluntly in its internal documents (*Population and Household Change v.2,* p.5). Actually, even this understates things. In fact in-migration provides **all** of the increase in expected population according to the Office for National Statistics (ONS). Yet for some reason Cornwall Council didn't care to draw attention to this quite important 'evidence' in their consultation paperwork. Instead, they deliberately blurred the issue of exactly what proportion of the proposed new housing was 'needed' for in-migrants and how much for the existing population.

Although we would never guess it from the Local Plan or the exhibitions that trundled around Cornwall to justify it, the main reason we have to keep building lots more houses seems to be that we have to house lots more in-migrants. If net migration were zero – if the numbers of in-migrants equalled the number of out-migrants – the required housing target for the next twenty years would not be anything like 42,250. Instead, even on the Council's own, now hopelessly outdated, figures it would be somewhere between 10,000 to 12,000 houses. In fact, with the benefit of the more recent Census data we can see that it would be more like 3,000. Let's put it another way; even the Council admits that almost three quarters of the houses that they wanted to see built were going to be sold or rented to people currently living outside Cornwall. 'Future communities' turns out therefore to mean communities that will be present in Cornwall by 2030 but currently reside elsewhere. So we are sacrificing more and more of our countryside to sustain a high level of continuing in-migration. This is a fact. Though, curiously Cornwall Council's planners were reluctant to give it its proper weight in its press releases and other statements.

Inflating the numbers; ignoring the evidence

But how do we know how many in-migrants will descend on Cornwall over the next twenty years? Here, the ONS population projections are now the Holy Grail. Every couple of years the ONS forecasts what it thinks will happen to population in the future. The latest projection, which appeared in 2012, used a 2010 base. It predicted a population in Cornwall by 2030 of 616,000, an increase of 84,000 (resulting from another 90,000 net in-migrants) on the actual Census population of 2011. This became the magic number the Council must then accommodate in its Local Plan.

Hang on though. Although the planners treat the ONS predictions as close to the absolute and unadorned gospel truth they are essentially the result of intelligent guesswork. As the ONS itself admits, predicting future population trends isn't an exact science. Fortunately however, we can check their past performance by comparing their predictions with what has actually happened. Their 2008 projection based on 2006 predicted that the Cornish population would be 674,000 by 2030. Then in 2010 they reduced this to 631,000. This was reduced yet again by another 15,000 in 2012 to 616,000. Such large decreases from one prediction to the next don't look like very 'robust' evidence and might provide some food for thought. If we check the ONS population predictions back a few years a curious phenomenon occurs. It seems that the ONS consistently over-predicts population growth in Cornwall.

Table 1.2: The ONS population predictions for Cornwall compared with reality

	Predicted population in 2011	Actual population 2011	Difference
2003 base	548,100	532,300	+15,800
2004 base	552,200	532,300	+19,900
2006 base	554,900	532,300	+22,600
2008 base	544,200	532,300	+11,900
2010 base	541,000	532,300	+ 8,700

Rather strangely, the predictions became more wildly inaccurate as the time period shrank up to 2006. This tendency to over-predict was bluntly displayed when the results of the 2011 Census were published. Just a year before, the ONS had estimated Cornwall's resident population in 2011 to be 541,000. In fact it turned out it was 532,300. So even the predicted figure in the most recent 2010-base prediction (published **after** the Census results appeared) had already over-shot by nearly 9,000. Either that or the census enumerators seem to have rather carelessly lost a town the size of Liskeard or Launceston. One can be forgiven for thinking we might as well pay a fortune-teller for the use of their crystal ball than rely on such inaccurate predictions. But this is the 'robust and credible' evidence on which the Council was basing its housing targets!

If relying on forecasts that consistently over-estimate Cornwall's population wasn't bad enough another reason for the inflated population projections adopted by Cornwall Council lies in its resort to consultants who for some reason come up with bizarrely inflated growth forecasts. For example, Peter Brett Associates of Exeter are employed as a consultant by the planners who then uncritically accept their calculations. Peter Brett Associates concluded in 2011 that the 'long term growth trend' in the 2000s was 3,920 a year. In fact, population growth turned out to be a more modest 3,230 a year. Yet oddly, the higher figure still served as the basis for the planners' predictions as late as July 2012 when such data had been comprehensively shown to be nonsense (*Housing Growth Discussion Paper, v4*).

Peter Brett Associates, a merger of Roger Tym Partners and Baker Associates, engages in 'planning, economic and technical consultancy' and provides 'trusted advice' (Peter Brett Associates website, at http://www.peterbrett.com/). That's the key. The Council seeks advice from those it can trust to come up with the right answers, those that fit the political objective of increasing housing and population growth. As a result of this trust Peter Brett Associates were paid a total of £142,810 from July 2011 to March 2012 by Cornwall Council for its consultancy work on the (now abandoned) eco-town, 'countryside' (for Highways) and, ironically enough, the 'green infrastructure strategy' (see Cornwall Council payments to suppliers at http://www.cornwall.gov.uk/default.aspx?page= 26474). It's strange that despite all the fanfare about a university campus in Cornwall the Council still has to resort to Exeter for its demographic data. Surely, there's someone who could provide more accurate data in our brand-new, gleaming university research and innovation centres. In the same way that Peter Brett Associates would be fully aware of the answers their paymasters expect, so the technicians who do the number-crunching at County Hall know what results their masters in the Chief Executive's Office and the Cabinet desire. It would be foolhardy in the extreme to face the facts when the message coming over so strong and clear is that 'growth' is the main priority. Give us the 'facts' that fit the policy; we're not interested in policies that might fit the facts.

So on a simple predict and provide approach based on demographic change the Local Plan seriously over-estimated the 'requirement' for houses because of its reliance on flawed ONS evidence and consultants' 'advice'. The 'evidence base' the Council sets so much store by turns out to be just dodgy data derived from dubious assumptions and built on sand. But of course growth is not just a technical matter of providing housing for a certain level of in-migration plus the real needs of the existing population. It's part of a political decision to emphasise housing and population-led growth as a solution to Cornwall's problems while facilitating the ability of the construction industry and others – from upcountry planning consultants and architects to local estate agents and landowners – to make a lot of money out of the great sale of Cornwall.

The mystery of the missing houses: Cornwall's Boscoppa Triangle

So do these two factors – a slowly falling household size and in-migration – account for all the houses built recently in Cornwall and being planned for the next 20 years? Well, here's the strange thing. It appears not. With the benefit of recent 2011 Census data we can calculate what proportion of the extra houses built was accounted for by each component in the last ten years. Table 1.3 shows the results.

Table 1.3: Housing growth and demographic change 2001-11

	Houses built	Number required for falling household size of 2001 population	Number required for in-migrants	Unaccounted for
2001-11	24,940	1,250	14,350	9,340

A very large proportion – 37.4 per cent of all the houses built in the last decade – is unexplained. It seems we have stumbled across our own version of the Bermuda Triangle here. Let's look at this mystery in other ways. According to the 2011 Census the number of households in Cornwall rose in the previous ten years by 15,581 but the number of 'household spaces' (houses and flats) by 28,264. According to the Census we seem to be building almost twice as many houses as might be predicted by 'housing need'. Moreover, **in Cornwall for every 1,000 rise in the population we build 765 houses. In Wales they build 517 houses and in England just 421 for every extra 1,000 people.** So why do we need to use up our countryside at a relatively more profligate rate than elsewhere?

In what we might call our own home-grown Boscoppa Triangle houses are apparently built for no real reason, only to disappear without trace, unoccupied by all those extra households produced by factors like longevity, which the Council are so keen to remind us about, or even by the in-migrants that they're not so keen to mention. In 2012, Council apologists made much of the rising number of students and the need for student dwellings. But the number of these according to the 2011 council tax base data amounted to just 166 in halls of residence and 969 other properties occupied only by students. If we assume that all of these were built since 2001 (an unlikely assumption as anyone with a knowledge of Falmouth could tell us) then even that can only account for a maximum 1,135 of our missing 9,340 to 13,000 plus houses. Which still leaves over 8,000 to 12,000, or 33 per cent to 43 per cent, unexplained.

Here's another table that might just shed some light on this mystery.

Table 1.4: Second homes and holiday lets

	1991	2011	change
Second homes	4,000	14,100	+10,100
Holiday lets	7,600	7,000-12,000	-600 to +4,400

Sources: 1991 Census; 2011 Council tax base, business rates lists and letting agency data.

So it transpires that the equivalent of one in three of the houses built in Cornwall in the last decade leaked away into the second home/holiday let market. We can't be sacrificing our countryside at a rate almost twice as fast as in England merely to accommodate the growth of second homes and holiday lets, can we? But indeed, it seems we are. 'Future communities' in fact turns out not only to mean communities not at present resident but who will be resident by 2030 but communities not currently resident and who still won't be resident in 2030! This also helps to explain why the thrust of current policy is to concentrate housing around the inland towns of Cornwall. The rural and coastal areas have to remain attractive for second home owners and the holiday trade. But in the context of a growing population, in order to maintain this attractiveness the poor and dispossessed must live in flats overlooking traffic-choked roads and busy roundabouts.

So there we have it. In the last decade just one in twenty houses was required for the much cited reasons of household change due to increased longevity and the like. Another 11 or 12 of the 20 were needed to accommodate in-migrants. But six or seven out of every 20 were being built to feed the voracious demand for second homes and from the holiday industry, something I'll return to in Chapter 8. Perhaps not surprisingly, Cornwall Council makes hardly any mention of this aspect of housing need in its public pronouncements. Indeed, 'second homes' are mentioned just five times in the *Local Plan Strategic Policies* document. Contrast this with the four pages given over to 'affordable homes' (LPSP, pp.24-27).

From dodgy data to more robust evidence

Having solved the curious mystery of the missing houses we are now in a position to assess exactly what a real housing target might be, given no change in policy but assuming that we no longer cater for the scandalous growth in second homes. The Council's method for working out their target is basically simple and goes like this:

1. forecast the likely population growth (migration plus or minus natural change)
2. estimate what the mean household size will be and therefore the number of expected new households
3. decide how many more houses those households will need

So let's do the same. But instead of relying on what is essentially grossly distorted and subjective guesswork designed to meet the hyper (housing and population) growth strategy adopted by Cornwall Council's leadership clique, I intend to rely on the actual historical evidence. We don't know what might or might not happen over the next 20 years; we do know what happened in the last 20. Therefore, a much more sensible and soundly based strategy would be to calculate where the long-term trends are taking us and apply them to the plan period.

First, what's the likely population growth? For the last half century, the rate of natural increase in Cornwall, that is the difference between births and deaths, has been negative. This means that, left to its own devices, with no net in-migration, the population of Cornwall would slowly decline. But it hasn't. Here is the actual growth of population since 1961 and the latest population growth projections for the next twenty years.

Table 1.5: Population change in Cornwall 1961-2031

Year	Population (thousands)	Absolute change (thousands)	Percentage change
1961	340		
1971	382	+42	+12.4
1981	424	+42	+11.0
1991	466	+42	+ 9.0
2001	499	+33	+ 7.1
2011	532	+33	+ 6.6
2021	573	+41	+ 7.7
2031	610	+37	+ 6.5

Source: Population censuses 1961-2011 and ONS population projections 2012 (recalculated to allow for over-estimated 2011 population)

Note that growth during the 1990s and 2000s was a lot less than in the 1960s, 70s and 80s. Indeed, the last 50 years have seen a (painfully slowly) declining population growth rate over the long term. If we extend this long term falling trend we discover the likely population rise over the

next 20 years will be 53,000, rather than the 78,000 assumed by the ONS
(in fact once we allow for the inbuilt bias of the ONS figures this isn't that
far from their projections). While still far too high this might form a more
realistic basis than the inflated figures adopted by Cornwall Council.
We therefore have the following projection.

Table 1.6: Population change in Cornwall 1971-2031

	Population (thousands)	Absolute change (thousands)	Percentage change
1971	382		
1991	466	84	+22.0
2011	532	66	+14.2
2031	*585*	*53*	*+10.0*

But how many houses does this population growth translate into? At
present about 9,000 people are living in institutions, mainly residential
care homes. So if, like the Council, we assume this number doesn't rise
(although surely it ought to if longevity is as important as the Council
claims) we can expect a household population of 574,000 by 2031. We
now need to find out what the mean household size is likely to be. Again, if
we apply a trend line to the data for the last 50 years we can forecast that
it will decline to 2.24 by 2031. So let's apply that to the figures in Table
1.6.

Table 1.7: Household change 1991- 2031

	Household population (thousands)	Mean household size	Number of households (thousands)
1991	456	2.40	190
2011	523	2.27	230
2031	*574*	*2.24*	*256*

This predicts a 26,000 increase in the number of households by 2031. If
each new household requires a new house then this would mean a housing
target of 26,000. But in their planning, the Council assumed that each

household would only require 0.7 houses. I find that difficult to justify but it would reduce the housing requirement to 18,200.

Even if we added in more houses to cope with a growing housing crisis it's very difficult to see why we would need any more than 30,000 even if continuing to accommodate the anticipated level of in-migration in the absence of policy change. This gives us a target far below the Council's 49,000. Or indeed 38,000. But even a rate of 18,000 or 26,000 over the next 20 years is still unsustainable in the long run. The population of Cornwall is, as we shall see in Chapter 4, already too high. It urgently needs stabilising. If this were to happen and we built solely for the housing needs of the existing residents then the number of extra houses required drops to just 3,400, or 2,400 if we adopt the Council's formula of 0.7 houses for every new household.

Of course, the Local Plan defenders are likely to respond, as the Council regularly does, by referring us to the HomeChoice Register, which we used to know as council house waiting lists. But as there are no council houses any more, and the present government is following the same policy as the last one and effectively destroying social housing (see Minton 2012, p.114), the name has had to be changed. As the Council's justifications for its 49,000 house target became ever more threadbare it resorted, its needle stuck firmly in the groove, to parroting the climbing numbers registering on the waiting lists and then sitting back smugly. In fact, this looks like the only rational line of argument left to it, but it is of course nothing of the kind. Like all the talk of natural change or local needs, references to affordable housing and the HomeChoice Register serves as a very convenient smokescreen to mask the essential fact. Which is that the council wanted a large increase in the building rate. The issue of affordable housing is too important to ignore however, so I intend returning to it in Chapter 3.

As we have seen, the basic fact is that demographic and housing projections are not a technical matter at all; they're fundamentally political. The idea that planning future housing targets is somehow merely a technical issue of predicting population growth or economic change or affordable housing requirements is a device to fool the public (and councillors), producing a huge dust storm designed to blind them with a blizzard of data. Such a strategy is even more effective given the wider context where standards of numeracy have become so appallingly low that virtually any statistical sleight of hand can be foisted onto the great British public.

For example, In its Core Strategy Options paper 1, p.3, a planning officer stated that the purpose of the 48,000 houses proposed was 'to meet the needs of the population which is set to rise potentially due to natural population growth (i.e. the number of births exceeding deaths) as well as inward migration from outside of Cornwall'. This is referenced to another Council-produced document, *Population and Household Change in Cornwall* (January 2011).

If we look at the latest version (1.4) of this 'Demographic Evidence Base' we find the following 'key message'.

> Natural change (total births minus total deaths) increasingly accounts for a larger proportion of Cornwall's population growth.

This is a downright mendacious conclusion. In fact the number of births did indeed rise in the noughties but in the last year cited (2010) natural change was still **minus** 159 according to Eurostat. That means that natural change was contributing precisely nothing to Cornwall's population growth. In fact it means that if net migration had been zero (in-migrants equal to out-migrants) Cornwall's population would have fallen.

The council uses ONS population estimates as the basis for its calculations and these are now predicting a period when births will exceed deaths. Yet what it didn't tell us is that the ONS is also predicting that deaths will again exceed births by 2030. This in turn means that over the next ten years even the flawed ONS projections are predicting a growth as a result of natural change of around **zero**. The unpalatable truth is that no amount of massaging the figures can hide the fact that all of Cornwall's population growth stems from in-migration and is likely to continue to do so throughout the plan period.

Spurning the opportunity to slow down population growth

Meanwhile, let's re-state the argument. As Table 1.5 above tells us, the decadal growth rate was over 10 per cent from 1961 to 1981. But in the 1990s and 2000s it fell back to between 6.5 and 7.0 per cent. While this was still a far from sustainable rate, it does suggest that, as we might expect given the growing congestion and environmental degradation we suffer from in Cornwall, the demand to move here seems to be slowing down. Even the consistently inflated ONS projections have been scaled down since 2008.

At last, the data provide us with a golden opportunity to argue for a slowdown in population growth. Instead of assuming that population will go on rising by between six and seven per cent a decade it seems clear that, when we compare the growth rates of the 1970s and 1980s with those of the 1990s and 2000s the trend is most definitely downwards. Yet Cornwall Council is adopting planning policies that at best continue this rate and at worst push it up again. If policy decisions can be taken to *increase* population growth from its long-term trend then equally we could adopt policies that aim to *reduce* growth to below its long term trend. Here's the chance for Cornwall Council to take advantage of the recent demographic trends by actively planning to slow down this still unsustainable rate by another couple of percentage points. However, it seems reluctant to do this. Rather bemusedly, it admits that 'the population figures for Cornwall [in the 2011 Census] are lower than expected' but merely says that 'the Council will be looking to better understand the reasons behind the apparent slowdown' (Cornwall Council, *2011 Census at a Glance*, 2012, p.1). Planning officers have claimed that the census data are somehow 'unsound' and that their validity ought to be questioned (Cornwall Council Cabinet papers, 7 Nov 2012). While disputing the measurements of the Census, the Council's planners bizarrely prefer to accept the guesswork of the ONS and its own consultants. Clearly a case of the messenger being shot for the message.

Originally, the Local Plan contained now outdated proposals to build sufficient houses – 48,000 or 49,000 – supposedly to meet the inflated estimates in its 'demographic evidence base' of an additional 93,000 people over the next 20 years – a full third higher than the growth actually experienced in the last 20 years. But surely, as the population projections are being steadily reduced then the housing target should also decline? Even on the flawed ONS figures these could safely be scaled back by a fifth. In other words, even meeting the ONS's latest inflated projections and accepting the 'logic' of continuing to 'accommodate' in-migrants and a growing second home market requires around 38,000 houses, many fewer rather than the 49,000 originally proposed. In addition, if the council were to accept the message from the real world, that mean household size is likely to be nearer to 2.24 than 2.10 in 2030, then even that 38,000 should be further scaled down. As we have seen, if we could stabilise the number of second homes and holiday lets, we would only require from 18,000 to 26,000 houses. And if we could stabilise the Cornish population, housing need would plummet to just 3,000 give or take a few hundred. In February 2013 an amendment to reduce the housing target to a more reasonable figure of 29,000 (though still excessive for actual needs even including in-migration) received just 20 votes from Cornwall Councillors, with the other 100 voting against or not present, a sad indictment of the ability of councillors to understand or engage with our growing environmental and cultural crisis.

But building to meet local needs only. or even in-migration plus local needs, is not what the Council wants. Far from it. In stark contrast, Cornwall Council is planning to build more houses in the next 20 years than were built in the past 20. Even though the long-term trend of population growth is falling! It is no longer reluctantly planning to meet past trends – itself a short-sighted approach – but has now reverted to the failed 1980s policy of housing-led growth as it effectively seeks deliberately either to encourage a higher population growth, which means actively encouraging more in-migration, or to encourage more second home ownership and empty properties. In fact, as the latter expand the council tax base but make fewer demands on services or the competition for jobs, according to their logic expanding the proportion of second homes looks the better bet.

Beam us up (to a million)

As the next Table reminds us, despite the clear evidence of a slowdown in the rate of population growth in the past two decades, unfortunately Cornwall Council's planners prefer to assume an increase in the absolute rate of growth and even an increase on the percentage growth rate.

Table 1.8: Population change in Cornwall 1961-2031

Year	Population (thousands)	Absolute change (thousands) per 20 year period	Percentage change
1961	340		
1971	382		
1981	424		
1991	466	+84	+ 22.0
2001	500		
2011	532	+66	+ 14.2
2021	573		
2031	610	+78	+14.7

And remember – this is a minimum. In fact the Core Strategy originally provided options for another 8,500 houses at Bodmin and Saltash and an unstated number of extra houses at eleven 'eco-community' sites. If their preferred scenario had happened then we could have been looking forward to another possible 35,000 people over the next twenty year period, on top of that 78,000 being planned for. That equates to a maximum possible population growth of 113,000, back to a truly eye-watering twenty year growth rate of 21.2 per cent. A Cornwall Councillor who read this last sentence in an earlier draft described it as 'scare-mongering'. However, it's hardly 'scare-mongering' to point out that the planners seemed perfectly comfortable with such a ridiculous level of growth when they wrote the Core Strategy consultation documents in 2011. Indeed, they had no problem in describing even that level of growth as 'sustainable'.

The Local Plan has two obvious shortcomings. Both emanate from an apparent inability to think in terms of extended periods of time. First, despite all the grand words about 'vision', this is a vision that extends only as far as 2030. Our planners live in a little bubble of time – peering just twenty years into the future. We are left entirely in the dark as to what's likely to happen thereafter. Will the predicted rate of population growth then suddenly stop? Will it slow down? Will it go on at the same rate? And if it is going to stop or slow down then how precisely will that happen? In short, given the uncertainties surrounding climate change, food and water security or peak oil, does the Council have an exit strategy to back up their current 'business as usual' policies?

The second flaw is that, if this myopic vision weren't bad enough, the planners don't appear to possess a rear-view mirror either. The lessons of the past half-century are completely ignored. It's as if Cornwall has no recent history. With no rear-view mirror and blind when it comes to the future, the Local Plan fails to spell out the demographic prospects for the coming century. These are kept at a very safe distance so as not to frighten the locals.

Let's transcend the short-term approach and extremely limited timeframe of the Council for a moment and speculate on what the future will bring us if we continue along the road mapped out in the Local Plan. Figure 1.2 sets out the minimum scenario for the future population growth of Cornwall.

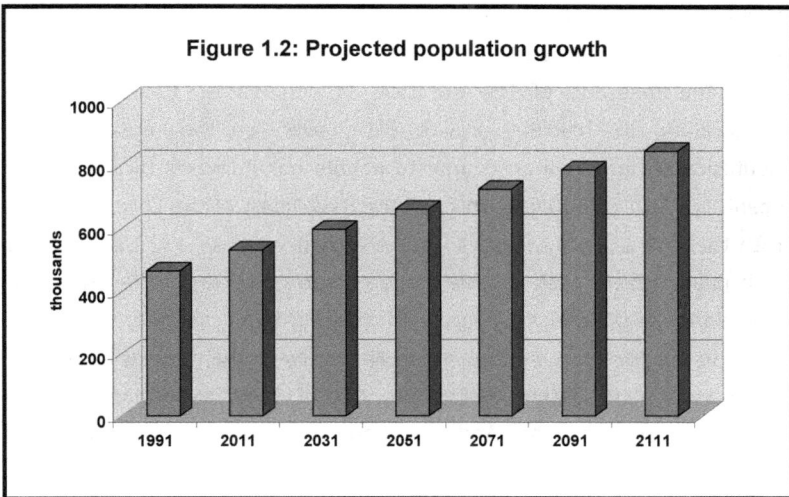

Figure 1.2: Projected population growth

This projection is based on some very conservative assumptions. First, it assumes that population growth will bear the same relationship to the number of houses built as it did in the 1991-2011 period, even though one in five of the houses built in that plan period disappeared into the second home/holiday lets sector. If all houses built in Cornwall were actually lived in, population growth would be even higher, in fact around a fifth higher. Second, it factors in a continuing reduction in mean household size, assuming this will go on declining at the rate it did in the last decade. We can see that, even on these very conservative assumptions, the current plan for 42,250 houses will still result in a population in Cornwall by 2111 of around 845,000. That's an increase of 318,000 on the current 532,000. In 1961 the population was only 350,000 in total. Moreover, even this very conservative prediction involves building the equivalent of twelve St Austells or Penzances, or fourteen Truros, or more than fifteen Newquays, or more than 22 Bodmins, or nearly 35 Liskeards, or 19 Saltashes **in not much more than the period of one lifetime**. Allow for 'temporary residents' and tourists and we'll be knocking on the door of a million by the end of the century. If the highest growth plans of the Council had been adopted then the situation would have been even more horrific, taking us well over a million and quarter.

The message of the numbers is undeniable. If we carry on heading along the current growth path, even on the most cautious computation we are well on course to double our numbers by the end of the century. This is the bleak truth at the dark heart of the Local Plan, but a truth that the Council fails to mention anywhere in its 152 pages. Their growth policy means that for every one person now living in Cornwall our grandchildren will have to cope with two. Without some very radical changes to our lifestyles this will mean almost twice the present amount of built-up area, cars, litter, congestion, out of town supermarkets, dog walkers, day trippers etc. And the Council describe this prospect as 'sustainable development'!

Excuse me, but I don't remember ever being asked whether I would like my grandchildren to live in such a Cornwall. Yet this is the future that's being insidiously foisted upon us by those who claim to lead us at County Hall. Not only have they given up resisting the future being effectively mapped out for us by their private developer chums. They are now actively encouraging this drive to double the population.

This leaves us with a very intriguing question. Are the planners and the leaders of the Council actually aware of the inevitable consequences that flow from current rates of growth? As the plan only takes us to 2030 do they seriously think that everything will suddenly grind to a halt somewhere around then? If this is the case then don't our policy-makers have a duty to explain to us how exactly this will happen and what policies they intend to adopt to help stop the 600,000 people of 2031, which they clearly believe is perfectly sustainable, becoming 850,000 by the end of the century? Or perhaps they're not naïve at all. Perhaps, unlike me, they're not at all alarmed by the prospect of an increasingly urbanised and over-developed Cornwall. If they welcome doubling the population and truly believe this is the road to everlasting prosperity then why not take the opportunity to present the arguments for long-term growth more openly and honestly? Unfortunately they do neither. They refuse to divulge what long-term action they may have in mind that will help drive down growth pressures. But they also fail to defend the scenario of over 800,000 people within three generations. As a result Cornwall Council seems open to the charge of a dereliction of duty, acting extremely irresponsibly in the face of massive, unprecedented and irreversible change to Cornwall's built and natural environment and to its society.

There is some evidence that the planners at least, if not their supposed masters (and mistresses), have a glimmer of realisation of the inevitable market-led outcomes. On page 2 of the *Preferred Approach* they rather vaguely and optimistically called on us to 'change our behaviour as a society; how or when we travel'. Although there is precious little evidence of any real planning to encourage this behavioural shift, changing our behaviour is not a luxury, it's essential if we are to survive the million-plus strategy. The only possible way we can double the population yet at the same time 'save natural resources, reduce waste, and reduce greenhouse gas emissions' (*PA*, p.3) is by speeding up a massive change towards lifestyles that tread a lot more lightly on this earth. Moreover, the central aim of the Local Plan – increasing the rate of population growth – makes this change even more essential. And even more impossible, as I shall explain in Chapter 4.

Of course, a more responsible plan might recognise the problems which current growth rates stoke up and explore the possibilities of engaging in damage limitation. We could seek ways of slowing them down further rather than speeding them up while passing the buck and calling on everyone else to change their behaviour. Such a plan might replace irresponsibly encouraging unsustainable population growth with the precautionary principle in order to make that necessary behaviour change much easier to achieve. But the Local Plan doesn't. Hell for leather, helter-skelter, by proposing 42,250 houses, and implicitly giving the green light to another 78,000 people in just two decades, it takes Cornwall not only well beyond the crossroads, but past the point of no return.

Blinkered vision, blind to the past

If Cornwall Council finds it impossible to look beyond 2030 and realise the consequences of its short-term infatuation with housing and population growth then it also seems unwilling or incapable of looking backwards and assessing the lessons of the past half a century. Sometimes it seems from the pronouncements of planners, planning consultants and councillors that growth is some brand-new, never-tried-before policy. Some, having only 'discovered' Cornwall recently, may have the excuse of allowing stereotypes of a sleepy and sparsely populated western periphery to get the better of them. (In fact the rural density of population in mid and west Cornwall is higher than most rural parts of the UK outside the south-east.) Others however cannot beg this excuse.

Some have demanded that Cornwall takes its fair share of the counterurbanisation process, as people ripple outwards from the suburbs of south-eastern England. But in our case the ripple has been more like a tidal wave for some time now. If we look at how population growth in Cornwall since 1961 compares with that elsewhere we discover that our population has grown three times faster than that of England, four times faster than Wales and fully 73 times faster than Scotland. The combined growth of the other Celtic countries has been just five per cent in half a century, that of Cornwall a whopping 57 per cent.

Even if we compare the Cornish experience with that of English counties we find we've already taken a lot more than our 'fair share'. There are 46 counties in England (assuming the 1973 definition of counties). Cornwall has grown at a faster rate than 39 of them, including all those in south west England. Devon's population growth has been 36 per cent, Cornwall's 57 per cent. Just seven English counties have seen a faster population growth than we did. Five of those are on the northern and western fringes of the London labour market – Buckinghamshire (although having a new town in the shape of Milton Keynes might be a factor here), Cambridgeshire, Northamptonshire, Berkshire and Bedfordshire. And the others are West Sussex and Wiltshire. Even the most geographically-challenged might notice that Cornwall seems a mite unusual. Here's a peripheral region with population growth rates more like well-heeled and high-wage parts of south east England than similarly peripheral areas such as Cumbria, which has seen a growth rate of just seven per cent over the same period. And keep in mind that, as we build more houses for every extra thousand people than these other places do, our relative rate of building and loss of countryside is actually higher.

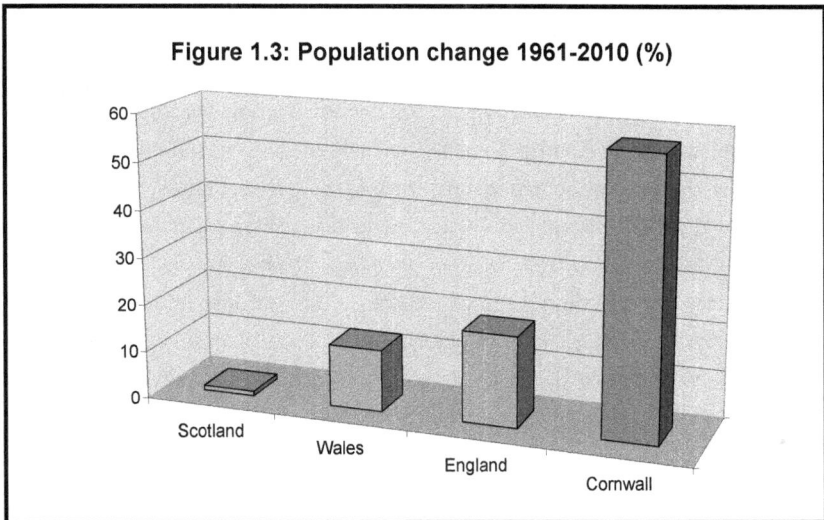

Figure 1.3: Population change 1961-2010 (%)

By all means let's have some fairness when it comes to population growth. If Cornwall had taken the same proportional share of in-migrants as Devon our population would now only be 462,000 rather than 532,000. If we had had the same growth rate as England our numbers would be 410,000. Put another way, we have had unfair excess growth of somewhere between 70,000 and 120,000 depending on whether your benchmark is Devon or England. On the basis of the history of the past 50 years we therefore have a very strong case to demand to be treated a little more fairly in the coming 50 years.

So why is our Council ignoring this argument? Why does it prefer not merely to go on accepting an unfair rate of population growth but does its best to stoke it up even further as their little bubble of time – oblivious to the future, forgetful of the past – floats merrily onwards? And why, having planned for an excessive population growth not justified by the most recent data, do we then have to build even more houses than everywhere else, houses which effectively end up empty?

We have seen in this chapter that in Cornwall in the 2000s we had to build houses and concrete over our countryside at a rate 84% higher than that in England to accommodate the same population rise. The reason for this was that over one in three of the extra houses are snapped up as second and holiday homes. Despite the Council's assertion that our houses are for the 'needs of our future communities' we find that some of these communities will never be permanently resident in Cornwall. We have also seen how the planned housing target of 42,250 still equates to continuing population growth, even though we have already seen growth since the 1960s at levels far above most of the rest of the UK. Before trying to explain how we got ourselves so hopelessly locked into this policy dead-end we need to look a bit more closely at the Local Plan and ask ourselves what's so wrong with these projected levels of growth. But before doing that I intend to set out in the next, short chapter the context for the Local Plan. What does planning aim to do and does it provide a level playing field? If you already know how the planning system works you can skip the next chapter and move straight on to Chapter 3.

Chapter 2

How the planning system creates a developers' paradise

As we saw in Chapter 1 the Local Plan translates what effectively turns out to be a long-term million people strategy into short-term planning policies. But what's the larger planning context for this Local Plan? How does planning work these days? This chapter takes us on a brief detour into the planning world and reflects on the current rules of this particular game with the help of one or two examples. A quaint idea still does the rounds that the planning system provides some kind of balance between the desire of developers to build and make profits and the need to conserve and safeguard the environment, local communities and the interests of residents. But how far is this the case? How far do we have a level playing field when it comes to planning? In pursuing this question we shall meet such exciting things as the predetermination rule introduced by the Labour Government, supposedly to guarantee unbiased and open-minded decision-making by councillors. And then there's the presence of planning gain. How do these phenomena affect planning outcomes? And finally, the Tory/Lib Dem Government's new National Planning Policy Framework decisively tips the balance towards the developers who are poised to take advantage of it by building up their landbanks even if they have no intention of actually building anything. I conclude that the main function of the planning system is not (if it ever was) to ensure some sort of 'balance'. Instead, it is there to legitimate growth. This clearly became the case when the referee, in the shape of Cornwall Council, began openly to take up the cudgels on behalf of one side only – the developers.

Michael Heseltine in 2012 stated that 'The idea we have local government ... is a fiction' (*Guardian*, 1 March 2012). If *local* government in England is a fiction then so is the idea of a democratically accountable planning system. Central government now prefers to call town and country planning 'development management'. Formerly, it was known as 'development control'. This re-branding is significant. It coincided with a gradual change of the planners' role from honest broker (always honoured more in theory than in practice however) to a mere tool for economic growth, managing it rather than controlling it.

To most of us planning is an arcane arena. Like any profession it's evolved its own specialised language. This jargon then works to make it difficult for outsiders to join in discussions about planning matters which are conducted in an impenetrable phraseology. Consequently, we only try to understand its mysteries when it either prevents us doing something or imposes something on us that we don't want. Otherwise, planning is left to a privileged circle of 'experts', operating in the background of our lives. It's a bit like the fuel distribution network or waste collection services. We only notice them when they break down. Most people wouldn't have the time nor the inclination to take an interest in the intricacies of day to day planning, much of which is left to officers. Indeed, decisions on much of development planning – extensions to individual properties, the building of one or two houses and the like – are delegated to planning officers rather than determined by councillors answerable to the electorate. Around 96 per cent of planning decisions are in fact delegated to officers these days in Cornwall (the figure for England is 91 per cent) and not made by elected councillors at all.

In the case of the vast majority of planning decisions this seems acceptable as they are uncontroversial. However, this attitude has unfortunately spilt over into planning policy, the planning that sets the broader boundaries and parameters of 'development'. Although this is precisely the area where planning ought to respond to democratic input, little real effort is made to involve people in strategic planning. Consultations are often a sham with partial data used to confuse and defuse potential opposition, or evidence cynically selected and designed to produce desired outcomes. It doesn't come as too much of a surprise then that planning in the UK is often presented as a purely technical matter, best left to planners. Which of course suits the interests of those who benefit from the way the planning process works. By ensuring that planning is seen as technically difficult and/or boring, decisions about how much to build and where to build are for the most part kept safely away from the public gaze.

In more contentious applications, councillors will decide, but are heavily dependent on advice from their planning officers. The fiction is that this advice is always disinterested and neutral. In reality planning officers, involved in day to day negotiations and interactions with property developers, construction companies, planning consultants and the like, share a broader culture with those interests. At its worst this results in their capture by the developers' lobby. At best it means that they come to share the assumptions of developers which are then taken for granted and uncritically presented to councillors as objective advice. As a result democratic scrutiny is eroded, worn away by a blizzard of 'technical' advice.

Predetermination or gagging?

Level playing fields have never existed in planning. It's always been biased towards those who wish to build and have the financial resources to see their plans through the system. In recent years the slope of the playing field has become even more steeply pitched against objectors. Take for instance, the strictures introduced by the last Labour Government against 'predetermination' by councillors. Under these rules councillors involved in planning decisions were not supposed to express an opinion on an application before meeting to determine it. If they did so they were barred from voting. If they arrived safely at the planning meeting without expressing an opinion then they had to base their decisions only on the 'disinterested' advice provide by supposedly neutral planning officers. The Government told us this was designed to ensure that councillors had an 'open mind'. In fact it was a gagging mechanism, stopping councillors representing the opinions of those who elect them and curtailing the power of communities to lobby those who are supposed to represent them. The Tory/Lib Dem Government's Localism Act has now modified the rules on predetermination to make it less far-reaching but councillors and, more importantly, planning officers and developers, still appear to act as if predetermination was the law of the land.

More specifically, in Cornwall the planning playing field has assumed a dizzily vertical aspect in recent years. This is because of the abolition of district councils and the concentration of decision-making in one local arm of the central state – Cornwall Council. Under the old two-tier system there was at least a division of power when it came to planning. The county council decided on strategic matters - how many houses to be built and broadly where – while district councils were involved in the day to day business of development policy, granting or withholding permission to build.

Both elements could of course still be captured by developers' interests and district councils were more or less susceptible to their pressure. North Cornwall District Council for example went through a phase where permissions were readily doled out in rural areas, especially to those farmers acquainted with local councillors, while Restormel Borough Council appeared to be a soft touch for developers. But at least in theory, the division of powers made it more difficult for developers to over-influence the system. But now planning policy and development planning are both decided by the same body. Cornwall Council plans how many houses should be built and then goes on to grant the actual permission. This makes it much easier for the developers' lobby to exert pressure. At the same time, this centralisation of planning makes the objectors' task more difficult as the councillors who ultimately make decisions are drawn from wider areas and become less susceptible to local pressure. This can be illustrated by the close vote to allow WainHomes to build right next to the Tristan stone at Fowey. The proposer and seconder were councillors from St Agnes and Falmouth, well away from Fowey.

Planning gain or bribery?

Meanwhile, the power of the developers' lobby grows. We find the last Labour Government urging local authorities to go for fewer big housing schemes instead of a plethora of small-scale projects. The logic was that big developments with hundreds or even thousands of houses were more likely to be delivered. From the councils' viewpoints this had another advantage. The big regional or UK-wide construction companies and developers who would deliver such schemes had the financial reserves to provide lots of what's called 'planning gain' or Section 106 money which could be used to finance a range of other facilities. Planning gain is a morally dubious scam whereby a property developer or a supermarket offers large inducements as the price of getting planning permission – for example new roads, schools, workshops and community centres (for all the new people) or green public spaces (to replace the existing green spaces that they want to build on!)

Take the example of the new Sainsburys supermarket given permission at Penzance. Sainsburys agreed to pay £152,000 to subsidise parking in Penzance town centre and another quarter of a million on other 'improvements' and a town centre coordinator who would promote the town. This was on top of £1.2 million for a park and ride scheme, £115,000 for bus stops, £130,000 for a crossing on the A30, £25,000 on subsidising bus fares and £50,000 for other transport links (*Cornishman*, 26 Apr 2012). A couple of years earlier over at Helston, Sainsburys and Tesco had stumped up £400,000 each towards the costs of a town centre manager who would manage the inevitable decline of the town centre caused by ... two massive supermarkets on its outskirts! (*This is Cornwall*, 24 Jun 2010).

But even planning gain does not always produce the promised outcomes. At Wadebridge, Sainsburys offered £800,000, which local town councillors and business leaders thought was going to be used to mitigate the effect of another out of town store and benefit the town centre. Not so. Two former mayors of the town who were involved with the initial negotiations concluded that the eventual agreement was 'totally against the wishes of the original negotiations where the expected outcome was to see subsidised parking in the town centre with no obligation to go to the store first. We see this having a wholly negative outcome for the retailers in the town.' Instead of aiding town centre traders, the 'planning gain' turned out to be gains for Cornwall Council and Sainsburys itself, with a good proportion of the cash going to help people get to the store more easily. Predictably, a Cornwall Council spokesperson defended its deal with Sainsburys and lamely responded that the 'planning obligation met all the criteria' and would 'help the town centre' (*Cornish Guardian*, 13 Mar 2013).

Since the 1980s local authorities have been strapped for cash to build things for themselves so they've come to rely on the cash cow of 'development' to obtain the 'improvements' that their electorates then see visibly sprouting around them. However, what this means is that local authorities have to wait for developers to come forward with their plans. Which they will only do if they can make a profit. If a locality doesn't attract 'development' then it doesn't get the goodies that go with it. Politicians thus have little control over where the planning gains occur. Planning gain could also be viewed as a legitimised form of bribery, with larger offers of section 106 money working to persuade otherwise reluctant councils to grant permission. The obvious and more equitable alternative to relying on planning gain would be to tax development projects so that local authorities could themselves decide where best to spend the money instead of relying on locating them only where developers want to build. But to utter the word 'tax' these days is akin to committing a mortal sin.

And a final point. Relying on planning gain for public projects increases dependence on large building firms and large developments, as only these command the resources to deliver the goods. Big construction companies tend not to be based in Cornwall and the smaller ones find it more difficult to compete against them. As a higher proportion of houses is delivered by the industry's giants, conversely a lower proportion is built by smaller, less well financed local firms. Upcountry non-Cornish companies take the bulk of the revenue; local firms do not benefit so much from the building bonanza. Profits are more likely to flow out of Cornwall and a smaller percentage of the income from housebuilding is likely to be retained.

Planning in practice: the example of Langarth, Truro

The 'debate' over a stadium for Cornwall is a classic example of this link between massive housing development and other infrastructure. These days it's difficult to obtain public funding for something like a sports stadium as local authorities are unwilling or unable to take on the cost of borrowing and face the fury of local council taxpayers if they are seen to have raised the council tax in response to a particular special pleading (although money is spent on special pleading all the time). Even at the very earliest Internal Officers' Group (IOG) meetings about a stadium for Cornwall officers were already thinking in terms of Truro. It was reported that there were several options 'linked to development schemes in Threemilestone, Treliske and within Truro, such as the sale of Richard Lander School' (IOG minutes, 5 Jan 2010, formerly accessible on Cornwall Council website but now removed).

Inconveniently, a previous consultants' report in 2007 had concluded that the site with the 'greatest suitability' for a stadium was near Camborne. Other sites were suggested, notably Carn Brea (IOG minutes, 30 Mar 2010). Carn Brea, unlike Threemilestone, had the advantage of direct rail access. This was important because the 'robust' criteria first proposed by the consultants and officers stated that 'proximity to rail access' was the most important element of its transport factors – with a 40 per cent weighting as opposed to just 15 per cent for 'proximity to A roads'. The stadium consultants then looked at 27 possible sites for a stadium, from Launceston in the east to Treswithian Junction west of Camborne. These were whittled down to four. Their site evaluation, involving a 'robust' matrix of criteria designed to give a spurious objectivity to the exercise, resulted in this ranking

1. Maiden Green, Truro
2. Willow Green, Truro
3. Langarth, Truro
4. Cattle Market, Truro

Amazingly, the consultants had scored Carn Brea lower than Langarth for accessibility. This was too much even for some officers. A planning officer for instance questioned it at the 6th July 2010 IOG. He rightly considered that the scorings were 'anecdotal'. At the next meeting he was still 'not comfortable with the score for Carn Brea' (IOG minutes, 21 July 2010).

But powerful pressures were pointing to the inevitable rejection of Camborne-Redruth and a site in Truro. At the 21st July 2010 IOG the Cornwall Development Company noted that 'commercial operators are only interested in Truro, Cornish Pirates wish to be located in Truro, developers are also biased towards Truro'. As Cornwall Development Company is closely related to Cornwall Council its enthusiastic lobbying for growth in Truro should come as no surprise but its reference to the Pirates' preference on 21st July is odd. Because just two months earlier at the stakeholders meeting of 20th April the Pirates themselves had explicitly stated they 'felt that Camborne, Pool, Redruth was the area of preference as it is the rugby heartland of Cornwall [although] if the stadium is attractive to users, we don't mind where it is'. The consultants' report, produced over the winter of 2010/11 transformed this less than enthusiastic endorsement into 'the Pirates have expressed a strong preference for Truro' (p.22). 'Strong' seems to overstate things and if this was the case it was a very late conversion on the road to Langarth.

By November 2010 Langarth was the only game in town. The IOG was told that Langarth was the chosen site as the 'site mix would create synergies [that magic talismanic word of the modern project class] with the nearby colleges and hospital, as well as providing financial viability'. In December the Steering Board agreed that Langarth was best because it was next door to the park and ride and close to a main road. (The rail access deemed so important six months earlier was quietly and conveniently dropped!) Furthermore, there were already 'negotiations with landowners' and in any case it was 'part of a Masterplan'. This secretive 'masterplan' existed in a parallel universe which involved the building of 1,500 houses right next to proposals for another 1,000+. It was clearly the key to the decision.

On 24th March 2011 the Stakeholders' Group was assured that Langarth was preferable because of

- the commercial appeal of Truro
- adjacency to park and ride and
- link to hospital and colleges

Strangely enough there was no mention at all here of the 'masterplan'. No matter; the Cabinet had in any case already endorsed the Langarth recommendation on 16th March.

At the same time the consultants' report summarised the reasons for Langarth. One was the Pirates' preference for Truro (which as we have seen was a tad reluctant), but clearly more critical was 'the greater appeal of Truro to the private sector and resulting greater potential to deliver enabling development and be financially viable'. But was this 'enabling development' more than just a background factor? Was the stadium plan merely being used as a smokescreen to legitimate the housing? Despite the later denial by the developers INOX that they had any intention of putting money directly into the stadium it stretches credibility to believe that there was never any link between the preferred site for the stadium and the housing suburb. At the end of the day Langarth was chosen because of its connection with the surrounding massive house building schemes. The only thing left was to crank up the Media Manipulation Machine to sell the message that there was absolutely no alternative.

Despite increasingly hysterical protestations to the contrary, it's crystal clear that the location of Cornwall's putative stadium was driven by the location of anticipated housing developments rather than decisions about where best to maximise attendances or minimise the environmental costs. The connection may not have been direct, but it was always there, at the least as an unstated assumption framing the discussions of local planning officers and other 'stakeholders' (which group strangely didn't include – or not until a very late date – elected representatives of local people). At the end of the day the private sector couldn't find the cash for the stadium and Cornwall Council's Cabinet refused to step into the breach, having claimed all along that no public money would be involved. Well, no more than was needed for various planning consultants that is. So at the time of writing we get the 1,500 houses but no stadium.

The new national planning framework: creating a developer's paradise?

If a unitary authority, the predetermination gag and the lure of planning gains weren't enough, the new National Planning Policy Framework introduced by the Tory/Lib Dem Government tilts the planning system even further towards property developers. The government has responded to criticisms from businesses that obtaining planning permission is a bureaucratic nightmare. It uncritically accepts this and has introduced a 'presumption in favour of sustainable development' although cunningly omitting to define 'sustainable'. Reducing the planning framework from over 1,000 pages to just 52 is not just a bonfire of regulations. It makes gaining planning permission easier by whittling away the possible grounds on which objectors might object. And it also promises windfall revenues for a whole gang of lawyers as the slimmed down regulations get tested in the courts.

For developers, although not objectors, also have the right to appeal if they are not granted permission. This weapon was used to bludgeon Cornwall Council into submission at Wadebridge after they had had the temerity to refuse planning permission for new Sainsburys and Morrisons supermarkets in January 2011. Threats of costly legal appeals served to concentrate minds wonderfully at the Strategic Planning Committee and later in the year it approved a second planning application from Sainsburys (much to the annoyance of Morrisons) even though to a layperson this was very difficult to distinguish from the one originally put forward and rejected.

And while writing this chapter I was entertained over my toast one morning by a news story about the Government's plans to 'simplify' the planning system (BBC Radio 4, 27 Mar 2012). The BBC introduced this story from Osbaldwick near York, where plans for a development containing 50 per cent affordable homes had apparently been delayed for ten years. The implication was plain. We have a cumbersome and over-bureaucratic planning system that proceeds at a snail's pace, thus frustrating all those developers eager to build affordable housing, plus putting the brakes on 'growth'. Strangely, the BBC, so keen to put the developers' and the Government's case for them, didn't tell us how typical this sort of delay actually is. To find out, let's look at some major planning applications in Cornwall in the year 2011. For example, Truro's eastern urban extension took just nine months from start to finish (application PA11/04599 dated 14 June 2011 determined 8 Mar 2012). Taking eight other major schemes agreed by the Strategic Planning Committee in 2011, I find that the average length of time was around six and a half months. A solar farm at St Ervan (PA 11/00760) was submitted on January 25th 2012 and determined before the end of March. Even the longest (the Sainsburys supermarket at Penzance Heliport and the ING development on Hayle's South Quay) took ten months rather than ten years.

It seems that the Osbaldwick case is nowhere near the norm, at least in Cornwall. Later in the same news story Greg Clark, Conservative Minister for Planning, was wheeled on to defend the presumption in favour of 'sustainable development' which will become part of the Government's new planning framework. Sustainable, he explained, exchanging an ill-defined term with an indefinable one, means 'in the public interest'. Ah, that makes it so much clearer. In the Government's mind it's not much to do with the Brundtland Commission's widely accepted 1987 definition of sustainable development as 'development that meets the needs of the present without compromising the ability of future generations to meet their own needs.' Instead, it's simply what's 'in the public interest', an altogether looser and infinitely more malleable definition.

Clark did however go on to claim that the planning system's role would still be to maintain the environment 'for future generations' and that there was no contradiction at all between this protection and growth. Of course, he didn't actually point to the ultimately finite aspect of natural resources, or to the pressures caused by a population increase of 17 per cent to 73 million people in the UK by 2035 (ONS projections).

The government constantly claims that its 'radical reform' of the planning system is giving new powers to communities and neighbourhoods. But these are powers to build rather than to stop building. In fact the power it guarantees is that of well funded development companies to make a lot more money by building lots of houses everywhere, while further curtailing the ability of objectors to object. Andrew George, MP for St Ives, has warned that the new rules risk turning

> places like Cornwall into a developer's paradise and stop stone dead any chance of us ever meeting our desperate local housing need ... the planning system is fuelled by greed rather than by need ... simply allowing developers to set the planning agenda doesn't provide the long-term answers for the local community' (St Ives Lib Dem website at http://stiveslibdems.com/andrew-george-mp/andrew-george-warns-against -turning -countryside-into-developers-paradise/).

However, the government that Andrew George supports turned a deaf ear to most of the critics, even though they included Tory traditionalists as well as conservation groups and the odd Liberal Democrat MP.

Moreover, just months after introducing the new National Planning Policy Framework, the Government suddenly discovered that even its slimmed down policy framework didn't go far enough. In September 2012 Cabinet ministers proposed further changes aimed at making it even easier for developers to get planning permission and hoard land while increasing central powers to force recalcitrant councils into line. According to planning gauleiter Eric Pickles this centralization was 'muscular localism' (*Guardian*, 6 Sep 2012). No matter that the interim report of the Barker review in 2003 had discovered that house builders were deliberately constraining supply (Minton, 2012, p.118). Or that even the *Financial Times* (7 Sep 2012) pointed out that removing planning restrictions was not going to produce the hoped for building boom. Or of course that the previous building boom must carry a large share of the blame for the economic crash in the first place. The Tory/Lib Dem Government's policy aim is plain – transfer decisions on when and where houses will be built from democratically accountable local authorities to private developers.

The result of all this is that planning becomes even more just an exercise to legitimate growth. The planning system is designed not to plan future development but to give an acceptable gloss to growth driven, as Andrew George says, by greed not need and by the pursuit of profit rather by the provision of decent housing for all. Individuals can object to planning applications, although this right is already so constrained that it has become little more than a joke. For example, objectors to planning applications that come in front of Cornwall Council's area planning committees are allowed just three minutes, rigidly enforced, to put their case. And there is no right to respond to the pages of advice from planning officers, which are often based on questionably subjective interpretations. While the right to protest against individual applications is carefully policed and a travesty of democratic participation, the consultation process for strategic planning is similarly widely regarded as a joke. The consultation on the initial options for the Local Plan in February-April 2011 was hardly noticed with little coverage in the media. The same went for the public consultation on the draft documents in January-March 2012. Even had someone become aware and attended one of the exhibitions they would have been little the wiser. Questions about why so many houses were needed were met with bland responses of 'to meet the needs of the local population'. That this 'local population' included the current residents plus an expected 70,000 plus in-migrants was only reluctantly conceded on further questioning.

I'll return to the disingenuous way the Local Plan is packaged in later chapters. But the context for it doesn't end with a central government that is committed to a mantra of 'growth' narrowly equated to building more houses for an ever-growing population. For the role of Cornwall Council itself has changed markedly since its transformation into a unitary authority in 2009. Put simply, Cornwall Council no longer, if it ever did, remotely resembles an honest broker balancing the drive for private profit against the public good. To adopt another metaphor, it's no longer the gamekeeper but has turned poacher. For the Council now not only responds to the building agendas of developers but actively encourages them. For example, it was Cornwall Council that brought together Waitrose and the Duchy to build an urban extension east of Truro. The Council uses our council tax to pay consultants (usually from well beyond the Tamar) to come up with grandiose schemes to build thousands more houses in places like Bodmin or Saltash. The Council invites landlords to offer sites for so-called 'eco-communities' in rural areas in order to attract even more people to come and live in Cornwall. (In practice some of the proposed eco-community sites turned out to be on Council-owned land. But that's another story.)

We are now left with the bizarre situation where Cornwall Council applies for planning permission to itself, a state of affairs that even the most benighted banana republic might have second thoughts about but is accepted as perfectly normal practice here. In short, Cornwall Council now combines the roles of strategic planner, development planner and developer. Little surprise therefore that it wants to increase the number of houses to be built in Cornwall. Which brings me back to the Local Plan.

Chapter 3

Housing our huddled masses? Or the comfortably-off classes?

As we discovered in Chapter 1, finding a clear answer in the Core Strategy/Local Plan paperwork to the question of why we need over 40,000 houses in the next two decades turned out to be surprisingly difficult. As we discovered, the demographic data pointed towards falling rather than rising growth rates. Those defending a high housing target had to resort to the need to solve the local housing crisis caused by the lack of affordable homes. Yet, even according to the Council almost three quarters of all the net extra houses are actually required for in-migrants. Although some of these will be return migrants and have a connection with Cornwall or be Cornish, this is unlikely to amount to more than a third. And in reality, as we have seen, as much as a third of the additional housing stock in the 2000s was not even being used for permanent residence. Instead those houses become second homes or are otherwise empty. In this chapter I will first discuss the complicated issue of affordable housing, before moving on from how many houses to build to where to put them. I will demonstrate how the Council has changed its policy from one of dispersal to one of concentration around Cornish towns, although it remains oddly reticent about admitting this change. The second half of the chapter turns to the claimed benefits of boosting population growth. Does population-led growth really bring with it all the economic and social advantages that the Council claim? I conclude that even the alleged economic advantages of high population growth are open to some debate, although this is a debate that rather predictably we've not actually had.

Affordable housing – the only game in town

Councillor Mark Kaczmarek, Cornwall Council's Planning and Housing portfolio holder, was very keen to talk about affordable housing. In his introduction to *Planning Future Cornwall: Our Preferred Approach* he pinpointed the issues he wanted to tackle, which include 'affordable housing'. The phrase 'affordable housing' was then used 24 times in the 27 pages of PA. But we can hardly criticise him for that. After all, relying on the market to provide everyone with decent housing would indeed involve a long and fruitless wait. Like any market, the housing market is fine and dandy if you enter it with plenty of disposable cash. There's considerable choice and sooner or later you'll find what you want. But, again like other markets, if you haven't got the money then you don't get the choice. Indeed, you can't even enter the market because there's nothing available at your price. Now when it comes to yachts, Ferraris, iPads or plasma TVs this is hardly a disaster. We do without. But we all need to be housed. Which is why our great-grandfathers had the very good sense to realise that the housing market needed supplementing by subsidised housing (resulting in lower than market rents) if all our people were to be housed to a minimum standard. Unfortunately, their grandsons and daughters threw this overboard in the 1980s, and adopted the dangerous ideological nostrum that we all had to be home owners. Home ownership became good and council housing (as it was) most definitely bad. As happened everywhere, a large chunk of Cornish council housing was promptly sold off into private ownership, resulting in the current shortage of social housing.

In the 1980s council housing was redefined as social housing. But now even social housing is far less likely to be subsidised directly by the taxes of the better-off. That most logical and elegant solution was sacrificed to appease the tax-avoiding greed of the middle and upper classes. (Although taxpayers forked out a huge amount of housing benefit instead which went straight into the pockets of private landlords). Now if you can't afford a house you can – theoretically at least – either rent from housing associations or buy into various shared equity schemes or buy at a discounted rate. But even here the message is that renting is a temporary, second-best solution. Which is why even at a time when we're told 'we have no money' the Tory/Lib Dem Government was willing to push the right-to-buy discount up to £75,000 for those in social housing so they can buy their houses and we can reduce the proportion of social housing even further (BBC News, 11 Mar 2012).

The market works least well in places where there's lots of demand from those who can afford houses but low incomes for the majority of local residents who then cannot afford to pay the prices inflated by all that demand. Cornwall is such a place. The demand to move here, a demand that as we shall see is deliberately ramped up by our own political institutions, has gradually raised prices well out of the reach of a population that 'enjoys' the lowest wages in the UK. 'Regeneration' schemes also pump public money into encouraging private sector investment which invariably has the aim of raising property prices. The hope is that the rising value of assets will somehow trickle down to the local communities. It doesn't. Instead, it displaces the original community and creates a segregated patchwork of housing areas. Moreover, we're trapped in one of those classic double whammies. The comfortably-off move to Cornwall and inflate house prices and once they're here they compete for jobs and deflate wages.

So what's the answer? The Home Builders Federation and the developers' lobby would have us believe it's just a simple matter of building more houses. Increase the supply and prices will fall, they chirrup. However, such a touching faith in market mechanisms is doomed because of the level of latent demand to move to Cornwall. We'd have to be building hundreds of thousands of houses to make any perceptible impact on the price of housing. After all - think about it for a moment - as Chapter 1 showed we've had one of the highest building rates in the UK. But we've also had one of the fastest rises in house prices. Patently absurd in the Cornish context, it's been pointed out that even on a wider scale 'introducing the market into every aspect of housing has not worked, fuelling a national housing shortage and the creation of ghettoes of poverty' (Minton, 2012, p.127). Of course the property developers want as many houses to be built as possible. That's how they make their money. But their 'arguments' need to be treated with extreme scepticism as they have a vested interest in the outcome.

Meanwhile, the Tory/Lib Dem Government is quietly undermining the social housing or affordable rented sector. Social housing companies or Registered Social Landlords can now charge up to 80 per cent of 'market rent'. In reality, they have little choice but to do so as grants are being cut alarmingly. This blurs the distinction between social housing companies and private developers, Indeed, Westward Housing, a social housing company operating in Devon and Cornwall, was recently advertising for a development manager. In their advert they stated 'in addition to our affordable homes programme we have a new commercial company which will develop homes for open market sale' (Inside Housing, online at http://www.insidehousing.co.uk/jobs/Development-Manager/443259.job). Meanwhile, in Cornwall 'market rents' are being calculated on the basis of like for like (new) property rather than the general local rent. Which results in rents creeping ever upwards at the same time as housing benefit is being reduced. Yet the only stale old option offered by Conservative thinktanks is to focus on building more houses for sale in order to drive down prices (see Policy Exchange website at http://www.policyexchange. org.uk/publications/category/item/ending-expensive-social-tenancies).

The changes wrought by the Government's vicious Welfare Reform Act of 2012 now make it easier for housing associations to charge higher rents and enforce shorter tenancies on their tenants. At the same time, the Localism Act of 2011 frees councils from the responsibility to house all the homeless and allows them, in Cornwall Council's ominous words, to 'make it easier for existing social tenants who do not fall into Reasonable Preference groups to move through direct allocation outside of the allocation scheme' (Cornwall HomeChoice Allocation Scheme Review Consultation, at http://www.cornwall.gov.uk/default.aspx?page=

32954). Couple this with cuts in housing benefit and the 'bedroom tax' and social housing tenants are rapidly becoming second-class citizens, subjected to growing discipline from the state.

Effectively social housing is being squeezed and the responsibility for housing the poor handed over to an unregulated private rented sector. This completes the privatisation project initiated by Margaret Thatcher's government in the 1980s and taken further by New Labour. It also goes hand in hand with a steady attrition of the ability of local authorities to control private developers. In 2004 the Labour Government quietly removed the concept of the 'public good' from planning legislation. Now, the National Planning Policy Framework replaces this with the notion that 'significant weight should be placed on the need to support economic growth through the planning system' (DCLG, 2012).

Although somewhat surprisingly continuing to support the Government, Andrew George, Liberal Democrat MP for St Ives, has explained how building even more houses actually makes it worse for local buyers.

The planning system is fuelled by greed rather than by need. This would give a massive hope value on virtually every piece of green space. The Government knows that you can't build affordable housing with inflated land prices, which would be an inevitable consequence of the Government's policy.

Cornwall can provide the evidence of why this policy will not work. We are not NIMBY (Not In My Back Yard) folk in Cornwall. We've grown faster than almost anywhere else in Britain – the housing supply has more than doubled in the last 40 years. Yet the housing problems of local people have got dramatically worse. So we have learnt that simply allowing developers to set the planning agenda doesn't provide the long-term answers for the local community.

It sounds counterintuitive, but the best way to meet local need is to stop or restrict development and then to only allow developments to go forward as an 'exception' where it meets a local need in perpetuity. We have been doing this for the past decade or so where planners have successfully restricted development.

The Government has got this one wrong and must be made to think again (Andrew George, St Ives Lib Dem blog, 8 Aug 2011).

The two aspects – a lack of housing and inadequate access to housing – are in fact separate issues. Although perhaps connected in their causes, they require something more than merely building a lot more houses. As Andrew George points out, they require *policy aimed at delivering certain types of housing*.

Which is where an affordable housing policy comes in. In 2008 the former Cornwall County Council adopted a Cornwall Sustainable Communities Strategy in which 'affordable housing' was one of the four strategies. In 2010 Cornwall Council's Cabinet signed up to an affordable housing policy in principle although at the end of the day this was not actually adopted. Across Cornwall it would have aimed at ensuring that 40 or 50 per cent of new housing was 'affordable'. This has now re-appeared in the Local Plan (LPSP, p.25). Affordable housing in this instance doesn't just mean cheaper housing as it would be difficult if not impossible to build houses cheap enough for local workers to afford. It means social rented housing (around 70 per cent of the proposed affordable housing) with intermediate shared equity, part sold/part rented properties and houses at discounted prices making up the rest. It's important to note how widely 'affordable housing' is defined. For example, to qualify for shared equity part-bought housing you have to have an household income of under £60,000 a year, which effectively means that well over 90 per cent of first time buyers in Cornwall could be defined as in need of affordable housing. And yet, at the 2011 Census found that only 12.8 per cent of our housing stock was 'affordable housing'. This gap between the need for affordable houses and the supply of them appeared to provide a get-out-of-jail-free card to those arguing for more housing (and indirectly for more population growth).

The proportion of housing completions that were affordable has risen steadily in the last few years as the following figure illustrates.

Figure 3.1: Affordable houses as % of total

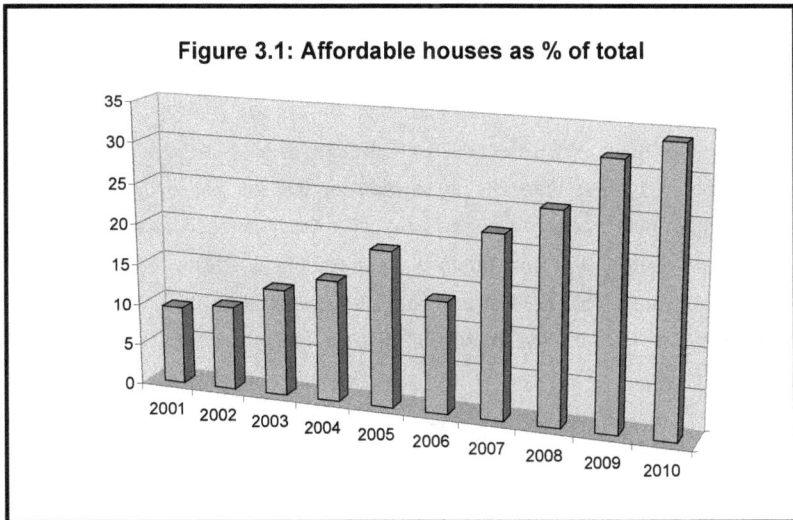

But let's not get too carried away. It turns out that only 20 per cent of the permissions handed out by Cornwall Council as of January 2012 were affordable. So it looks as if the proportion of affordables in the pipeline will drop as soon as the housing market starts to recover. There's a fundamental problem here which Cllr Kaczmarek tended to skate over in his public statements. For each affordable house we have to build some unaffordable ones. This is because affordable houses are delivered not by the public sector any more but by private developers (and housing associations). And private developers have to make their profits from unaffordable housing. The danger is clear. To increase the supply of affordable housing for local buyers we must rely on developers' willingness to build them. And that means allowing developers to build a sufficient number of unaffordable houses for non-local buyers. In fact none of the larger housing projects approved in the last few years came anywhere near offering 50 per cent affordable housing. Only a few offer as much as 40 per cent. Instead we find 25 per cent at a development at Pool, 25 per cent at Looe and 25 per cent at Falmouth (Cornwall Council, *Annual Monitoring Report Planning Policy* (AMR) 2010-11, pp.92-93). More recently, a report tabled at the Planning Policy Advisory Panel meeting of 31st January 2013 detailed 55 schemes. Only four in ten offered 40 per cent affordable housing or higher and the median proportion of affordables was 35 per cent (PPAP 4, Appendix 7, 31 Jan 2013).

Moreover, the proportion of affordable housing is always prone to being pushed downwards by 'renegotiation' between developers and planners. The temporarily abandoned mid-Cornwall eco-town was a good example. When it was first mooted the outline application promised 40 per cent affordables. Yet the first and maybe last detailed plans offered only 25 per cent. This is why the planners' original preference was for 54,000 or 57,000 houses rather than 48,000 as they knew that a high proportion of affordable houses would be difficult to maintain. What we're being offered is truly a policy of despair. In order to solve our housing problems within the constraints of the market we're being told we have to increase population growth and in doing so destroy large swathes of the countryside. It's a bit like that American soldier in Vietnam who said that in order to save the village they first had to destroy it.

The number of affordable homes 'needed' is also subject to alarming exaggeration. As we saw in Chapter 1 the actual number of extra households created from the existing population from 2001 to 2011 was 1,250. This implies that the demand for extra affordable homes could be met by building 125 houses a year. Yet, the Council appears to have convinced itself that 1,200 affordable homes were required across Cornwall every year for the next ten years to meet the backlog and new need from the roughly 2,000 newly formed households a year that they were expecting. But we now know that there aren't anything like 2,000 new households a year. In fact it was more like 1,500 a year in the 2000s, over

90 per cent of which result from the in-migration of households, not the creation of new households within the present population. Is the Council seriously suggesting that 80 per cent of these households, which include the households of in-migrants some of whom surely bring with them equity from the sale of houses upcountry, all require affordable homes? If so we have a real problem if we also have to build three or four open market houses for every 'affordable' one. On the basis of more up to date figures, CoSERG calculates that to meet *all* the housing needs of the currently resident population from changes in household formation would require a maximum of just 3,400 houses over the next twenty years – which is equal to 170 houses a year. But some of these households could enter the private market and would not require affordable housing at all. As the need for affordable housing from the current population is somewhere below 170, why does Cornwall Council conclude we need seven times that number? Part of the answer is that the Council is basing this requirement on outdated demographic data. Another part is that it includes a requirement for affordable homes for in-migrants in order to reach its total. What precise proportion of affordable need arises from the resident population and what proportion from future in-migrants is uncertain as their methodology is hardly crystal clear. Similarly, we remain in the dark about how many so-called 'affordable' houses are actually let or sold to in-migrants. Or indeed used for second homes or holiday lets.

Moreover, the Council's calculation of 1,200 affordable homes a year was made before changes were mooted to Cornwall HomeChoice, the system for allocating rented houses. Because of central government 'reforms', the Council is proposing to tighten up the role of local connections in allocating houses and making it more difficult for people to register for HomeChoice. Logically therefore, this should entail a reduction in the number of houses required to meet local needs. But that reduction has mysteriously not been factored into its Local Plan, which somewhat disingenuously quotes the numbers on the about to be changed HomeChoice Register and then equates this cavalierly to 'housing need'. Tightening up the necessity for local connections also begs the question of how loose this was previously. While conditions are often imposed on permissions to build affordable housing, demanding a local connection of some kind, no data seem to exist on how often these conditions are relaxed or removed if suitable tenants cannot be found. Anecdotally, stories abound across Cornwall of affordable housing being occupied by recent arrivals from upcountry. However, no reliable data exist that would allow these stories to be verified.

Once we dive into the murky waters of affordable housing need, calculations of disposable income, mean household size predictions and the like we're in great danger of drowning from too much detail. The whole 'debate' then gets shunted into a technical siding and the context - **the requirement to accommodate a population rise caused almost entirely by net in-migration** - is lost to sight. The basic assumptions – that we have to rely on the market to supply the bulk of our housing, that most affordable houses are provided by private developers in a location of their choice rather than ours, that we have to sacrifice swathes of Cornish countryside in order to accommodate prospective in-migrants, that we must allow for houses to be built that will then disappear into the second and holiday home sector – all go unquestioned. So does the danger that a continuation of present policy risks creating a segmented housing market - one for locals and one for incomers - and thus wider social inequalities. However, these are all political issues rather than technical matters, and require political solutions. Restricting the debate about house numbers only to how many affordable houses we need (whether for locals or for future locals) neatly avoids addressing the bigger issue, which is why Cornwall Council is so keen to talk about affordable housing even though well over four fifths of houses (both affordable and unaffordable) would be built for incomers and as second home owners and not for local need at all?

Let's remind ourselves what we found in Chapter 1. In the ten years from 2001 to 2011 25,087 houses were built in Cornwall. Yet population growth was just 32,300. Something looks very wrong here. The very small reduction in household size wasn't the reason for all those houses, as that required a mere 1,250. The growth in population accounted for another 14,350 on top of that. Which adds up to 15,600 houses. So over a third of the net extra houses were unaccounted for. Where did all these extra houses go? If we investigate comparative statistics for English counties we find that only five have a higher rate of unaccounted for houses. Three of these, Merseyside, Northumberland and Durham, have far lower population growth, or even decline. The other two are Cumbria and the Isle of Wight, which points strongly to the second/holiday home market as the common factor. And as we have seen, the number of second homes in Cornwall has grown steadily since 1991.

The result is that in Cornwall we have to build more houses – and consume more valuable green fields – to achieve any given rate of population growth. Between three and four in ten of the extra houses being built in Cornwall appear to be leaking into the second/home home sector or are otherwise unoccupied and Cornwall has one of the highest housebuilding rates in the UK for its size of population (exceeded in the 2000s only by Cambridgeshire, Lincolnshire and Wiltshire, all of which experienced population growth in that decade around twice as high as Cornwall). As Cornwall Council now wants to push population growth up again the implication is that we must get used to an even more profligate sacrifice of our land.

The unavoidable facts are these:

- **On the evidence of the past decade the bulk (around three quarters) of the 42,250 houses proposed in the Local Plan will be bought by or rented by in-migrants and are not required by the population currently residing here**

- **This locks us into an ongoing population spiral that is will produce a near million-people Cornwall by the end of this century**

▪ **We are subjected to much hand-wringing about affordable housing but the need to build houses for the second and holiday home sector is hardly mentioned.**

Don't get me wrong. We have a real and urgent need for more affordable housing. But too often it seems to be used as a smokescreen to divert attention from the central facts of unsustainable growth. At its most banal, this is seen in the mindless incantation of the numbers registered on Cornwall's HomeChoice scheme. The impression is fostered by politicians and media alike that somehow the 26,886 households registered on 30th September 2012 were all homeless or in desperate housing need. In fact, even under the old legislation on homelessness, 11,000 of these were deserving of a 'reasonable preference', and classed as Bands A to D on the basis of need. Fully 56 per cent of those on the HomeChoice Register in 2012 were categorised as Band E, most of whom are described as 'adequately housed'.

I'd go further. Simplistic referencing to the HomeChoice Register was being deliberately employed to persuade gullible local politicians there was a need to build a high number of houses and create guilt among those who wish to halt the ongoing suburbanisation of our land. Portraying opponents of the Council's growth strategy as selfish and comfortably-off nimbies is the Council's preferred approach to debating the housing target in its Local Plan (see the comment by a 'senior planner' in response to CPRE concerns – *Western Morning News*, 7 Feb 2012). Or routinely dismissing those concerned about Cornwall's future with that curiously antiquated word 'naysayers' (*Western Morning News*, 1 Aug 2012). Insults are much easier than reasoned debate. Avoiding the latter is also why the phrase 'affordable homes' or 'affordable housing' is used 24 times in the 27 pages of the *Preferred Approach* whereas the words in-migrants or in-migration don't appear at all and the word migration crops up just twice. Or why four pages of the *Local Plan Strategic Policies* document is given over to affordable housing whereas the 'need' to accommodate second homes owners is hardly mentioned. This is not merely a coincidence. It deliberately massages the message to obscure the central fact that the great majority of the housing is being built for the needs of the comfortably-off rather than the homeless.

The HomeChoice register is, moreover, only one measure of housing stress. Another is overcrowding. The ONS define this as having insufficient bedrooms available for the number of people in a household. By that measure, in 2011 2.6 per cent of Cornwall's households were overcrowded. But this is a lower overcrowding rate than in England or south west England and only half that in Bristol and Bournemouth. Strangely, both these latter places have had their Local Plans approved as 'sound' by government inspectors despite their containing lower pro rata housing targets than that being proposed by Cornwall Council. Cornwall Council's planners also made much of the over 4,000 caravans and other temporary housing stock in Cornwall. However, closer inspection of the census data reveals that although the numbers of caravans had indeed risen by around 500 in the 2000s, the number of occupied caravans had actually fallen by 300. All those additional caravans that the planners were so keen to crow about turn out to be empty! They turned out to be just another example of the distinctly dodgy data that seems endemic to the planners' case for housing and population growth.

Moving the deck chairs: concentrating people not minds

However, despite the ambiguous evidence, the Council still decided we need at least 42,250 houses to accommodate in-migrants, supply the second/holiday home market and deal with new household formation. The next problem they faced was where to put them. And here again sadly we find more sleight of hand. The Council claims that it is continuing past practice and their 'approach is based around a dispersed strategy' (*PA*, p. 4). Not so. Instead, their strategy concentrates housing in and around the main towns. Furthermore, this has been the implicit planning preference since at least the 1980s (and for good reason as we shall see later). Currently just over half (52 per cent) of Cornwall's people live in its towns.

Yet the Local Plan proposes to build over 67 per cent of the extra 42,250 houses in and around those towns. Just over a quarter (26 per cent) of people live in the five urban areas of Bodmin, Camborne-Redruth, Falmouth-Penryn, Newquay and Truro. But the Plan allocates 36 per cent of the housing to those five towns. This isn't a dispersal strategy at all; it's a concentration strategy. When Cllr Kaczmarek said 'if you break it down into towns and parishes it (the target housing) is not a great deal' (*This is Cornwall*, 20 Mar 2012) he was again being just ever so slightly economical with the truth. This can be demonstrated by looking at the change in the building rate that the Local Plan will bring.

Table 3.1   : Housing growth for selected towns

	Houses built in last 20 years	Houses proposed for next 20 years	Change
Camborne-Redruth	3688	4000	+ 8%
Newquay	2606	3000	+15%
Hayle	1028	1300	+26%
Falmouth & Penryn	2069	3200	+55%
Bodmin	1452	3000	+107%

And this is described by Cornwall Council as 'not a great deal'?! What sort of population growth rates does this level of urban housing equate to? Assuming two persons per house we get the possible population changes on Table 3.2 on the next page. Seven out of these eleven towns are set to see their already high growth rates of the past two decades get even higher as a result of the Local Plan. And at least three of the towns where the growth rate is set to fall will still grow at a rate that is unsustainable in the long run.

So why has Cornwall Council exchanged its dispersed strategy for one of urban concentration? Basically, it has little choice if it wants to ensure the rural areas remain fit for new permanent residents, second home owners and tourists. As population growth continues, the danger

from the Council's perspective is that we reach the point where the already
relatively densely populated rural areas become over-developed and their

Table 3.2: Population growth for selected towns

	Population growth in last 20 years	% growth 1991-2011	Estimated possible population growth in next 20 years	% growth 2011-31
Saltash	2,280	16%	1,500	9%
Penzance/Newlyn	760	4%	2,800	13%
Camborne-Redruth	5,210	12%	8,000	16%
Truro & Threemilestone	3,620	17%	4,400	18%
Liskeard	1,760	23%	2,000	21%
Falmouth & Penryn	3,810	15%	6,400	22%
Launceston	2,750	43%	2,200	24%
Wadebridge	1,430	27%	1,600	24%
Newquay	2,950	17%	6,000	29%
Hayle	1,680	23%	2,600	29%
Bodmin	2,185	17%	6,000	41%

environmental quality slides below the point of acceptability. Acceptability
that is from the point of view of a vociferous and over-represented tourist
lobby. Although it should by rights shoulder a lot of the blame for this state
of affairs (see Chapter 8), it would no doubt start screaming about the loss
of Cornwall's natural attractions. Marketing an increasingly suburbanised
and over-populated Cornwall would become even more difficult than it
already is. So the Council is forced to ensure that rural areas are protected
from the worst of the population growth and remain prime destinations for
the better off segment of the market. To guarantee this they have to shift
people into the towns and indulge in some social and cultural engineering.
This has the added advantage of making the necessary 'behavioural
change' a little more possible (although as I shall argue in the next chapter

this is wishful thinking) as they hope people will then use their cars less, public transport more and may even, heavens above, walk to the shops. That is if their local shops are able to survive the competition from out of town supermarkets.

There is of course another possible dimension to this. The towns will in absolute terms get the bulk of the cheaper and more 'affordable housing', enclaves suitable for the less well off, which is likely to mean the Cornish. We, or our children, must vacate the prettier areas and crowd into the higher housing densities of the towns. By doing so we're doing our bit to enable the process of population growth to continue a little longer before its inevitable contradictions become too great to ignore. We also help make rural and coastal Cornwall safe for gentrification and ensure it remains a haven for the better-off (or in some cases as at Rock, Fowey and on the Helford for the super-rich).

The Council's concentration strategy is therefore the inevitable result of an inability to confront the population growth we've been locked into since the 1960s. But the Council leadership these days shows no inclination that they want to confront that growth. Or any inkling that it might be a problem. Quite the opposite. They think it's a jolly good thing. We may have been taking the same medicine now for the past 50 years but although we may be utterly sick of it they're giving us even more. It's kill or cure time. Cornwall Council is now thoroughly wedded to a population growth strategy, using woolly claims about affordable homes and job creation to distract our attention from its central components or its longer-term consequences. But what's actually wrong with population growth? What's the problem of a million-people Cornwall? I would suggest a number of unacceptable consequences flow from this extremely short-sighted policy, especially as it's been adopted implicitly, with no open debate and with no democratic mandate.

Prosper through housing? The economic consequences of the Local Plan

Cornwall Council claims that we can 'prosper through housing, employment and infrastructure' (*PA*, p.5). Housing and the associated population growth is not something being reluctantly forced upon us. Far from it; from the Council's perspective it's become the key to growth, regeneration and the pursuit of that promised land that always for some odd reason lies just around the corner but is never actually reached. It also helps it avoid the unpalatable truth that it's building 30,000 houses more than is needed for the local population or that it wants to ratchet up the rate of population growth we've had to endure for the past half century. After all, neither building to accommodate in-migrants and more second homes nor building more in the future just because we've been building lots in the past look particularly convincing reasons for sacrificing familiar chunks of countryside or asking people to live in a congested rabbit-warren. So we are instead informed that 'development is necessary' to 'meet the needs of Cornwall's communities for homes, businesses, jobs and access to our daily needs' and in order to 'improve our economic prospects' (*PA*, p.4). As we have already seen affordable homes receive much attention whereas the larger number of unaffordable homes are passed over hastily without so much as a backward glance.

On closer examination the economic justifications for population growth are as spurious as the demographic and local need justifications for housing growth. They dissolve into groundless assertion rather than 'robust evidence' on little more than a cursory glance. Lazy assumptions about growth bringing prosperity turn out to be untenable on two levels. First, we have the actual evidence of the past 50 years of population growth to test them against. Although the planners seem to possess no historical awareness the recent history of Cornwall ought to make us question their claims. Second, there is a more fundamental problem underlying the Council's growth strategy. It's this – 'a world in which things simply go on as usual is already inconceivable' (Jackson, 2009, p.13). The Council fail to provide any answer to the rather fundamental 'question of how a continually growing economic system can function within a finite ecological system' (Jackson, 2009, p.14). I'll be returning to this central dilemma of growth at more length in Chapter 4.

But first, let's restrict ourselves to the Council's narrow definition of 'prosperity' and ask how their claims about the benefits of growth match up to the facts. Their reliance on stepping up housing and population growth to achieve 'prosperity' can be simply checked by looking at what's happened up to now. As we saw in Chapter 1 Cornwall has endured one of the highest population growth rates in the UK since the 1960s. Such a level of growth should surely have guaranteed prosperity beyond our wildest dreams. It's certainly the case that those few parts of England that have had growth rates as high as Cornwall include some of the wealthiest counties outside Greater London. Yet strangely, Cornwall isn't one of them. In fact our GDP/GVA per head was so hopelessly low that we slipped into the basket-case category back in the 1990s and qualified for the highest level of EU grant aid. And that was after almost three decades of 'growth'. Another decade of growth later, with the milk and honey of Objective One and then Convergence money having flowed into Cornwall, and it appears we're still so poverty stricken we remain eligible for continuing high amounts of grant aid (*West Briton*, 22 Mar 2012).

In 2012 in a letter to the *Guardian* (15 June) it was claimed that Cornwall 'has done very well' out of EU funding. That may be so in terms of grants received but how much does the European dividend actually amount to? In 2006 per capita GDP in Cornwall peaked at 18,600 PPS (purchasing power standards that allow for currency and price differences between countries) a year – 78 per cent of the EU average. In the last year's data available we had fallen back to 16,900 – and that was then only 72 per cent of the EU average. When we look at the more meaningful disposable income of private households (i.e. the amount of money we have to spend) we find that in the ten years from 2000 to 2009 it fell in Cornwall by 1.8 per cent, almost identical to the fall in Cumbria, which did not get European funding on the same scale. Furthermore, the years of fastest growth occurred in the first half of the decade before the effects of European grant aid were being felt.

According to the latest Eurostat statistics Cornwall's economy has contracted since 2007. From 2003 to 2007 disposable income per head grew by 12 per cent. But this was only one percentage point higher than the growth in Devon, which did not receive Convergence funding. Then, from 2007 to 2009 it fell by 14.9 per cent in Cornwall, 15.7 per cent in Devon, Pouring grants into iconic large scale ventures such as the Eden Project which was in 2011 almost £2 million in the red, the Combined Universities in Cornwall project, or Newquay airport, which has drained over £70 million from the UK taxpayer, does not seem to have had a great effect.   Unfortunately, despite more than a decade of European funding there appears to have been little independent academic research or critical examination of the effectiveness of such grant aid. The capacity for critical reflection on the consensus growth strategy appears to be absent. Self-criticism within the narrow circle of policy-makers is buried under self-congratulation.

As an example, just before Christmas 2011 it was revealed that Cornwall's economy, as measured by gross value added (GVA) per head, had shrunk by 2.9 per cent in 2009, which was the worst performance in the UK. It seems that the Cornish economy was hit more seriously by the bankers' crisis than most other places. But the Convergence Partnership Office, which spends our money churning out half a dozen press releases a week, was curiously silent about this relative stagnation. On the 14th December, the same day as the sub-regional GVA figures were being announced by the ONS, the Convergence Office instead pumped out a feel-good press release about the £16 million government grant towards yet another road between Camborne and Redruth (Convergence press release, 14 Dec 2011). Needless to say, that press release was then dutifully reprinted virtually word for word in the *West Briton*. Shamefully though, the paper didn't think it necessary to inform its readers that this was actually a press release from the Convergence Office and therefore might be providing just a very slightly rosy picture. Let alone seek to provide some 'balance' - such an old-fashioned concept in these post-modernist times.

There's something very strange going on here. It just doesn't compute. One of the fastest housing and population growth rates in the UK and yet one of the weakest economies! If we compare population and deprivation at a lower, sub-Cornwall, level the answer is the same. Those wards that experienced the highest population growth from 1961 to 2011 were not automatically the wards that had the lowest levels of multiple deprivation. In fact, statistically, there was no correlation at all between population growth and low multiple deprivation. On the contrary, there's a very weak negative correlation between the two, meaning that if anything population growth is associated with higher levels of deprivation, not lower. But not to worry. This utter lack of evidence that population growth has caused rising relative prosperity in the past half-century in Cornwall hasn't prevented those who like to think they make the decisions about such things assuring us that yet another dose of population growth will this time do the trick.

We should therefore not be surprised when we encounter the same old injection of even more population growth underpinning all the much-hyped regeneration projects that have sprouted up over the past decade or so. Take Pool, between Camborne and Redruth, which has over the past few years been subjected to an exercise in 'place-shaping'. Supposedly designed to regenerate the area, this might equally be viewed as ensuring a better class of people will be attracted to buy the 4,000 houses planned for the district between now and 2030. Puzzled by the existence of two town centres only four miles apart, CPR Regeneration's task from the start was to re-centre the district on Pool, thus tidying up this inconvenient geography.

It first tried to rename Camborne-Redruth CPR. This failed but it was fortunate to win a Heritage Lottery grant that resulted in the Heartlands Project. This placeless centrepiece for more population growth has been imposed on part of the old Crofty mine site. Whatever one might think of Heartlands or the value for money achieved for the £35 million spent on it, its marketing plumbs hitherto unimagined depths of puerility that are truly embarrassing. Especially as it's supposed to be part of a World Heritage Site.

We are invited to

'Go See, Go Play, Go Wow'

as we are reduced to drivelling imbecility by the

'19 acres of cultural candy'

on offer.

This asinine and infantile marketing goes hand in hand with a project class geared to assume Cornwall is a shallow leisure periphery. Go see. The film's not bad but the marketing is incredibly banal.

And it's not just me saying that population growth hasn't had the economic growth effects so widely touted by its supporters. The Cornwall and Isles of Scilly Local Enterprise Partnership (LEP) commissioned a study by Cambridge Econometrics on the Cornish economy, published in April 2012 (available at http://www.cornwallandislesofscillylep.com/strategy. html - see 'Evidence Base 4'). That study also concludes that 'there is little evidence of the "gap" [between the Cornish economy and the UK] closing – after progress between c.1995 and c.2005, the economy now appears to be moving in the "wrong direction"' (p.7). Cambridge Econometrics point out that 'Objective One and Convergence programmes have not been able to shift the trajectory of GVA per job'. Indeed they think that it will actually get worse – declining relative to the UK in the 2010s and 2020s (p.4). In similar fashion, they state that the UK economy was 'less severely affected' by the global bankers' crisis than was Cornwall.

Despite relatively high population and housing growth being associated with this failure however, the LEP rather ominously and illogically concluded that 'overall, he projections reinforce the need for a strategy focusing on economic growth' (p.7). So what sort of strategy are we supposed to have had up to now? The danger here is that this gives the green light to purely quantitative housing and population growth, adding to the 57 per cent growth we've had since the 1960s. If that growth has brought us to our current predicament then why does the LEP believe that more of it will somehow get us out of it? Incidentally, why also did the LEP waste public money paying people in Cambridge to tell them something anyone in Cornwall with a passing acquaintance with the economic datasets could have told them? Shouldn't the LEP be doing all it can to create employment in Cornwall rather than Cambridge?

Not that evidence seems to have much impact on the growth clique who steer our economy. For instance, is the Convergence Office deliberately stoking up the crisis of unsustainable population growth? There's certainly little evidence that its leadership cadre is in touch with reality. Carleen Keleman, the Director of Convergence, lauded the 'significant investments to build on the steady economic growth that we have experienced under the previous Objective One programme' (*Convergence Focus* issue 1, 2009, p.13). Except that it didn't, as this 'steady growth' had come to a grinding halt, as we have seen, in 2004/05 well before Convergence had begun.

But what does the Convergence Office think about population growth at the current level? Its Operational Programme states that 'there is a consensus that the population will continue to grow rapidly, with population growth relocating to the area to take advantage of the attractive lifestyle offer' (Convergence Operational Programme 2007, Executive Summary, p.3). (As have an unknown number in the Convergence Office presumably.) Let's put aside the more recent data that suggest this growth has been slowing down. So is rapid population growth good or bad news? 'The increase in population ... has increased GVA, although no progress has been made with regard to GVA per worker, the key measure of productivity' (p.1) and 'the growth in population and economic activity will place increasing pressure on the transport infrastructure' (p.1)

When it comes to the environment that supplies that 'attractive lifestyle offer', the Convergence Office remains trapped within the same old contradictions that imprison most of Cornwall's project class and decision-makers. The quality of the environment is a 'unique asset', a 'major draw' for tourists, economic migrants and businesses (p.10). Yet 'there will be a range of issues, e.g. brownfield vs greenfield, to be tackled to meet the aspirations and challenges of sustainable development' (p.30). Versus? The fact is we don't have anything like enough real 'brownfield' land in Cornwall to accommodate even the population growth projected for the next ten years let alone for another century. The Convergence Office very ambiguously states that 'environmental concerns will ensure that the issues surrounding sustainability are maintained as a policy-making priority' (p.3). The issues? Or sustainability itself? What does that opaque utterance actually mean??

Given the Convergence Programme's complacent and uncritical acceptance of the 'forecast population and employment growth over the next ten or twenty years' (p.9) plus its irresponsible fostering of the myths that drive in-migration (and see Chapter 8) we can assume that it shares the policy-makers' consensus that we must double the population of Cornwall, totally failing to realise that population growth may in fact be undermining its own economic objectives.

Bringing jobs. And job-seekers

Whenever the Council comes up with another scheme to build a few thousand more houses it's always dressed up with assertions about how many jobs will be created. These claims appear to have been conjured up via a mechanism akin to peering at the tea leaves in the bottom of some bureaucrat's afternoon cuppa. Take the Camborne-Redruth area. In 2007-08 it was being proposed to blight this area by building an astonishing 11,000 houses in the next 20 years (nearly tripling the current building rate). As there were only 22,000 houses in Camborne-Redruth in 2010 this was indeed a hefty increase. But we were assured it would create 8,000 jobs. By April 2010 someone had noticed how swivel-eyed this plan was. Soon-to-be-elected Tory MP George Eustice rightly dubbed it as 'bonkers' – so the figure was scaled down to 6,000 houses. But we were then told that would create 6,000 jobs (*This is Cornwall*, 15 Apr 2010), Each house had mysteriously acquired more job-creating capacity! In December 2011 this particular wild guess was changed again as the media meekly repeated the Council's assertions of 'expert' predictions that 6,000 houses would create 5,500 jobs. (*Western Morning News*, 15 Dec 2011).

Undeterred the Core Strategy stated that 'We will be seeking the equivalent of one job per new home' (*PA*, p.9). That this may not quite be so easy in practice is hinted at by other 'experts' on the Council who conclude that in the years from 2006 to 2011 for every new house built only 0.62 jobs were in fact created (*AMR* 2010-11, pp.6, 44, 46).

There is nonetheless a grain of truth hidden away in all this. More people do create more jobs in what's known as the multiplier effect. More people will consume more goods and services, thus raising demand. If that demand is met locally, as opposed to leaking out of the economy through online shopping for example, then jobs are created. So far so good. That's why the regeneration project class assured us that the proposed mid-Cornwall eco-town was supposed to 'give the people of St Austell and the China Clay community unprecedented access to thousands of new jobs and career opportunities' (*Convergence ESF Framework* 2009, p.8). However, there's one tiny problem with relying on housebuilding and a growing population to create jobs. In order to consume, people need an income. And most of them acquire that income by selling their labour. So more houses don't just produce new jobs. They also introduce new job-seekers. Tucked away in the CNA discussion paper on Camborne-Redruth the Council admitted this, though turning it into a positive benefit – 'housing growth will support the area's aspiration for economic growth [though they seem to have forgotten to actually ask the area first] by helping to provide the necessary supply of labour' (*CNA, Vol 1*, p.66).

What the planners disingenuously omit to do is to bring these two arguments together. How many of the new jobs will be taken by the new jobseekers? Instead, facile flannel about houses bringing jobs is used to fool our councillors. As at Bodmin, where Lib Dem town councillor Phil Kerridge was quoted as saying 'I'm not in favour of 5,000 houses, I'm in favour of new jobs for Bodmin which require 5,000 new houses' (*Cornish Guardian*, 8 Feb 2012). Then Cornwall Councillor at Bodmin,

Lance Kennedy agreed enthusiastically; 'we need more houses', although 5,000 in just twenty years might seem a trifle over-enthusiastic. Meanwhile, one of the other two Cornwall councillors at Bodmin, Lib Dem Ann Kerridge, had already gone on record in the initial consultation on the Core Strategy as saying 'I wish to record my support for a high level of [housing] growth in Cornwall'. As the third Bodmin councillor, Lib Dem Pat Rogerson, also said that she was 'in favour of the higher number of new homes' Bodmin's councillors appear to have fallen lock, stock and barrel for the argument that houses bring jobs while ignoring the fact that they also bring jobseekers. If it's that easy then no wonder the planning officers continue to wheel out the jobs argument.

But what are the facts? If we look at the headline number of employee jobs (excluding the self-employed) in Cornwall then perhaps the Council has a case. The number of jobs rose from 1995 to 2008 faster than the number of people aged 16-64.

Table 3.3: Jobs and jobseekers

	jobs	change	potential jobseekers	change
1995	143,000		293,000	
2008	194,000	+50%	329,000	+37%

This suggests that the Cornish economy performed relatively well in the area of job creation. And this was borne out by a reduction in the unemployment rate. Consistently and chronically higher than the general UK rate since before the First World War, by the late 1990s unemployment in Cornwall had fallen below the UK average. This was a welcome development. However, note that the shift coincided with the slowing down of in-migration seen after the 1980s. (Moreover, it also predates European grant aid.)

But let's take a closer look at the data. It seems that half of the new jobs created have been part-time. Part-time jobs accounted for 37 per cent of the total in 1995; by 2008 they were 40 per cent, almost 10 per cent higher than in Britain as a whole (Nomis official labour market statistics at https://www.nomisweb.co.uk/). This partly explains why incomes are so low in Cornwall. But even when like is compared with like hourly rates of pay in Cornwall were running in 2011 at a level over 26 per cent below the average. And this gap in pay between Cornwall and the rest of the UK has widened. In 1975-78 men in Cornwall earned 84 per cent of the general pay rate and women 88 per cent. By 2005-08 men were only earning 75 per cent of what the average British employee was taking home and women 83 per cent (data from *Regional Trends*). In-migration may well have helped to create more jobs, but many of those jobs were filled by the same in-migrants and the extra competition in the labour market has helped to push Cornwall firmly to the bottom of the wages league and keep it there.

The evidence for population growth bringing more jobs is therefore a lot more ambiguous than the enthusiastic claims of the Council or the project class might lead us to believe. In addition, more recent data suggest that, despite their assertions, the Cornish jobs market is not at all robust. Look at what's happened more recently.

Table 3.4: Employment and labour market changes 2004-10

	Total in employment (including self-employed)	change	Population 16-64	change
2004	235,700		318,800	
2011	245,600	+9,900	328,700	+9,900

Population growth has once more begun to overtake job creation. This is reflected in unemployment which has increased faster in Cornwall than in Great Britain as a whole.

One of the problems faced everywhere in the UK as online shopping booms is the decline of town centres outside a few mega-shopping centres. Sometimes, growth enthusiasts imply that more people will somehow turn around our town centres, bringing more money and allowing them to buck this trend. But again, the evidence hardly bears this out. For example, Liskeard has been one of the fastest growing towns in Cornwall since the 1960s. Its population rose by 110 per cent from 1961 to 2011, a rate exceeded only by Bodmin, Helston, Saltash and Wadebridge. Yet in 2012 Liskeard became one of twelve 'derelict town centres' across Britain that received grant aid from the Government's 'Portas pilot scheme' (*Daily Telegraph*, 26 May 2012). It was described as having a 'troubled high street'. But with a doubled population? How could this misery possibly happen if, as the Council assures us, housing will 'bring prosperity' and massive population growth rejuvenate our town centres? Something isn't adding up here.

All this implies that, even on its own terms, claims that population growth automatically produces material prosperity seem to be stretching the point somewhat. Yes, it brings some jobs. But it also brings people to fill those same jobs. It has also resulted in lower wages and salaries than everywhere else and has failed to insulate the Cornish labour market from wider difficulties – if anything it seems just as fragile as it was back in the 1970s. Despite groundless assertions in the Local Plan, growth is no magic panacea for Cornwall's economic problems. If it were then it becomes a bit of a puzzle why 50 years of relentless housing and population growth that has already doubled our built-up area has failed to have the expected results.

At bottom, the Council's approach seems to amount to crossing its fingers, indulging in some wishful thinking and trusting that by providing even more of what we've been getting for the past half century everything should turn out fine. While the medicine continues to be doled out the collateral damage from a rate of growth that's been four times faster than that of the UK generally is best not thought about too deeply. All in all, Cornwall Council appears to nicely fit Einstein's definition of insanity: 'doing the same thing over and over again and expecting different results'.

There are no limits: Consume! Consume!! Consume!!!

There is a much bigger problem with the Council's million-people growth strategy, yet this is one about which our planners and council leaders appear to be blithely unaware. The fundamental problem that the Local Plan ignores is that, while it assumes population expansion and material growth can be unlimited, its resource base isn't. Ecological resources and the regenerative capacity of ecological systems (their ability to maintain biodiversity, protect wildlife, maintain air and soil quality and the like) are under pressures that would have been unimaginable a century or so ago. Our resource base - the environment that ultimately supports us - is finite. The dilemma of growth is that it ultimately at some point therefore becomes unsustainable. Sooner or later infinite growth meets the limits of a finite world.

Tim Jackson (2009, pp.14 and 50) has written about the 'collective blindness of politicians and policy-makers', unwilling or unable to contemplate 'the stark reality' of constant growth. Growth produces what he terms an impossibility theorem – an incompatible combination of growing ecological instability and growing material consumption. But it's even worse than that. We are unable to think beyond a consumption-driven growth-based economy, where stability is only guaranteed by endless growth. Since the crisis caused by unregulated bankers' greed and casino capitalism in 2008 the world's political and economic leaders have panicked and rushed back to the comforting apron strings of growth. This is because our economic system has just two states – constant expansion or collapse, with little in between. This is Jackson's 'dilemma of growth' (p.65). The growing environmental costs makes growth unsustainable but stopping growth produces instability and collapse. Jackson's answer is clear. We need to seek less destructive ways of achieving prosperity. If it can't be done through increasing the size of the cake then we have to distribute that cake a little more equally.

While policy-makers on a global scale refuse to contemplate this impossibility theorem our policy-makers in Cornwall remain equally determined to avoid confronting the basic constraint of a finite environment. They act as if Cornwall had no limits at all. Jackson (p.88) concludes that 'running faster and faster to escape the damage we're already causing is itself a strategy that smacks of panic'. By this definition Cornwall Council must be in a rare old state of panic. As I have argued they're desperate to avoid spelling out the long-term consequences of their strategy, not daring to admit the million-people population that flows inexorably from it. They're so blinded by the simple talisman of housing and population growth that they can't do the sums. These reveal the stark truth of the future numbers we will have to cope with if 'business as usual' remains the watchword for the rest of the century.

Defenders of growth argue that its continuation is compatible with reducing the impact on the environment. This is supposed to occur through 'de-coupling'. Each unit of production and consumption involves less use of resources. If anyone thinks this will be the case just read Jackson's book, where he convincingly points out how the sums can't by any stretch of the imagination support this. If global population and economic growth both rise in the way they're predicted to, the greater efficiency of resource use required to reduce our impact becomes 'arithmetically impossible' (Jackson, pp.80-81). We can translate this into the Cornish context. From 2005 to 2010 the total carbon emissions per person in Cornwall fell by 11 per cent, from 8.2 tons to 7.3 tons. This was encouraging though nothing near as fast as the six per cent a year reduction scientists now say is necessary to avoid catastrophic global warming. But because of population growth our total carbon emissions only fell by 9 per cent (and it actually rose in 2010). We are told that by 2050, we'll need to reduce this overall figure by at least 80 per cent. For Cornwall that implies that, with a predicted population by then of around 700,000 our per capita carbon emissions will have to be down to just over one ton per person. On the present rate of reduction it's still likely to be over three tons.

Reducing current carbon emissions by 86 per cent in less than 40 years looks like a big ask. Especially as, after four years fall from 2005 to 2009, carbon emissions in the UK actually rose in 2010 by 4 per cent. And especially as carbon emissions from the Council-subsidised Newquay

Airport alone was forecast to rise from 15,300 tons in 2007 to 57,000 by 2030. At that rate by 2050 Newquay airport would have accounted for over a tenth of all carbon emissions if we hit the required targets. Except that aviation doesn't actually seem to be included in the Government's regional data!

So is Cornwall Council intending to leave the required reductions in greenhouse gases to somebody else? Perhaps, like the Eden Project, it supports relying on the morally dubious idea of carbon offset, whereby people in some poor African country reduce their carbon emissions to allow us to avoid the issue and carry on with our wasteful lifestyles (*This is Cornwall*, 15 Aug 2009). The fact is that achieving reductions in carbon emissions and resource extraction or improving key indicators of environmental quality such as waste generation or species loss is made a lot more difficult if not downright impossible if we carry on building over more and more of our land in order to welcome more and more in-migrants to join us in rushing around frenetically wondering where all those extra jobs went to. There is an impossibility theorem at the heart of the Council's Local Plan. On the one hand it contains a vision of changed behaviour, of saving natural resources, reducing waste and greenhouse gas emissions (*PA*, p.3). On the other it promptly contradicts this by not only cheerfully carrying on with the same old excessive population growth that we've seen for half a century but ratcheting it up even higher. This amounts to a dangerously complacent and irresponsible strategy that plays fast and loose with the environment that it claims to be protecting,

From contradiction to complacency

An example of Cornwall Council's brazenly complacent attitude came on page 2 of *Planning Future Cornwall: Our Preferred Approach* where it claimed that 95 per cent of Cornwall is 'undeveloped'. They meant not concreted over. In reality, most 'undeveloped' land has been developed and redeveloped for centuries by Cornish farmers and others. Actually ONS land use statistics for 2005 reveal that 8.3 per cent of Cornwall is 'developed', rather than the five per cent that the Council claims (http://www.statistics.gov.uk/hub/people-laces/planning/land-use).

Moreover, the amount of 'green space' in Cornwall had declined at a rate about 50 per cent faster than the loss of countryside in the English South West region over the previous five years. But never let some inconvenient facts get in the way of a good soundbite.

The implication of the Council's claim is that, as only five per cent is 'developed' there's plenty of space ripe for more building. Presumably when the population inevitably passes the million mark the Council will be informing us that 'only' ten per cent (or should that be 17 per cent) is 'developed'. So stop worrying and get on with building on the rest. But put this another way. The proportion of built-up land in Cornwall must have at least doubled since the 1950s. What took 1,500 years to achieve since the Romans left Britain has taken us just 60 years. On present trends it's likely to double again in little more than another 60 years. At what point does this doubling stop? At this rate it's only going to take about three more centuries for the whole of Cornwall to be 'developed'! Yet the Local Plan also states, in an amazing example of contradiction, that 'land is a valuable resource ... where appropriate we need to safeguard it' (*PA*, p.11). 'Where appropriate' clearly does not extend to the countryside around most of our main towns.

Indeed, the average man or woman in the street seems to be more aware of what's going on around them than the Council. The Cornwall Quality of Life survey of 2007 discovered that 63 per cent felt the biggest threat to Cornwall's natural environment was 'housing development'. Another 55 per cent felt 'growing population' was a major threat. When asked whether the Cornish environment was getting better or worse 42 per cent said worse while only 13 per cent thought it was improving The places where the number of people who thought things were worsening were highest in St Austell, Camborne-Redruth, Bodmin and Launceston, exactly those towns which have suffered some of the biggest population rises. The most frequently cited qualitative factors changing the Cornish environment were overdevelopment, too much traffic and in-migration and overpopulation.

Yet the Council chose to completely ignore the findings of that survey in its Local Plan even though it was based on a scientific sample of over 3,000 respondents. Instead, throughout the Local Plan they assert that communities up and down Cornwall have 'aspirations for growth' yet fail to indicate what evidence this is based on other than highly unscientific samples of responses at poorly attended consultation events. As a result we're going to get a lot more of what most of us have told them we don't want more of!

Being selective about the evidence is not confined to ignoring the Quality of Life survey. The Local Plan also adopts a most curious attitude to the social consequences of in-migration. In 2008 academics at Sheffield University investigated the strength of 'community resilience' across the UK. One of the measures they used was the recent rate of inward migration, arguing that the higher this migration rate was the higher the 'feeling of not belonging'. High levels of geographical mobility were associated with social fragmentation, with breakdown of trust and increasing levels of loneliness (http://sasi.group.shef.ac.uk/research/ changingUK.html). On absolutely no discernibly rational basis that I can discover, Cornwall Council turns this logic entirely on its head. Instead of reducing resilience it asserts that high levels of growth and mobility into Cornwall will 'enhance the viability and resilience of existing communities' (*CNA Vol 1*, pp 55 and 65). In the Orwellian world of County Hall/Lys Kernow white can indeed be described as black and black as white. Clinging economically to policies that have clearly failed in the past, unjustifiably making wild assertions about growth that fly in the face of academic consensus, turning a blind eye to the sustainability dilemma that its building proposals entail, the Local Plan becomes less of a plan for the future of Cornwall emerging from rational debate and more a justification for building plans that ride roughshod over local people's concerns.

The growth merry-go-round

What we seem to have is an incestuous circle. Cornwall Council, central government, the Convergence Office, the LEP, business organisations, consultants, the media are all locked together in a macabre dance of growth. 'Growth', hardly ever defined, is the mantra chanted daily to lull the participants into a semi-hypnotic trance. Once in this drugged condition, they become oblivious to the consequences of the growth they desire so much, a 'growth' that boils down in practice merely to more people, more houses and more infrastructure to facilitate it. Material gifts in the form of contracts and consultations are exchanged within the circle of devotees. When hard evidence threatens to intrude rudely on their state of unworldly euphoria then it's promptly banished by repeating the magic words 'growth', 'prosperity', assets' even more loudly. While doing so they congratulate each other on the wisdom of their collective analysis and admire the emperor's new clothes that they're all wearing.

Others may point out that their garments are moth-eaten, ragged and coming apart at the seams. But never reflecting, never doubting, faith in growth must not be allowed to falter. Even for an instant. Nothing is too sacred to stand in the way of the regeneration god who must be appeased. Regeneration should mean resuscitate, restore, repair, remedy but in this reality it only means redesign, reshape, replace. Cornwall and its people have to be reshaped to suit the requirements of the money-making machine. Our land becomes just a temporary or permanent bolthole for jaded refugees from the east, our countryside a playpen attached to a suburb. Cornwall's character is lost as its population grows steadily onwards to a million, never pausing, never stopping.

Cornwall Council's growth strategy is deeply flawed. In this chapter we have seen how it is flawed economically and socially. In the next, I shall examine the even more obvious environmental problems it brings in its wake. Moreover, it has one further consequence. Culturally, claims to 'safeguard and enhance Cornwall's special built and natural character' by 'managing' its 'distinctiveness and pace of change' so that we 'sustain a strong sense of place' is so much empty verbiage, incompatible with the central aim of accommodating rapid population growth and expanding the urban parts of Cornwall (*PA*, p.13). The uniqueness of Cornwall rests on the survival of a distinct people – the Cornish people. Implicitly, some argue that continuing the demographic policies of the past half-century threaten the very existence of that people by resulting in a population shift on a massive scale. Adopting a policy of continued in-migration means the Local Plan does not adopt due care and responsibility towards the Cornish people. By threatening to consign them to the dustbin of history it threatens the special character of Cornwall that it claims to safeguard. However, before discussing the fate of Cornwall's Cornishness in this blind commitment to population growth we need to examine in greater detail the environmental costs involved in the Council's million-people strategy.

Chapter 4

You don't know what you've got till it's gone: The environmental consequences of endless growth

Some of the facts we met in the previous chapter are worth repeating. In 2007 the vast majority of people in Cornwall, 98.6 per cent of them according to the Quality of Life Survey (pfa research, p.94), 'indicated that the natural environment was of some importance to them'. Almost two thirds identified housing development as one of the 'greatest threats to the natural environment' while over a half cited a growing population as another major threat. At the same time more than two thirds thought that the rising level of traffic was the third threat the environment faced. What therefore does it say about living in a democracy when those concerns are so completely dismissed in the Local Plan? This prefers to offer us a strategy resting on precisely those things that people recognise are the biggest threats to our environment – excessive house building, increased traffic and a growing population. Moreover, in the strange cross between a mad hatter's tea party and Orwellian dystopia in which Cornwall Council seems to dwell, these three aspects are miraculously transformed from threats to the environment into 'sustainable growth'.

More than that, rather amazingly one of the 'key principles' of the strategy that embeds the drive to a million-plus people is 'sustainable development'. In a sub-conscious echo of the Tory/Lib Dem Government's 'we're all in it together', the Council claimed in 2012 that 'we are a part of it, not apart from it' (*PA*, p.6). And just as 'we're all in it together' turns out in practice to mean being soft on bankers while demonising those on benefit, or cutting taxes for the rich while cutting services for the rest, the excruciating phrase 'we are a part of it, not apart from it' translates into 'we're determined to push on to a million people in Cornwall by 2100'. My distasteful task in this chapter is to outline some of the ways in which the

Council employs the rhetoric of sustainability. I'll look at various examples that point up the contrast between what it says and what it does before concluding that it is deliberately creating a very large smokescreen. Sustainability and talk of a 'green Cornwall' policy can only be seen as a deceitful and dishonest device designed to distract us from the actual policies of ultimate unsustainability which will inevitably produce a grey Cornwall. Like Cameron's Tory/Lib Dem Government what we get from Cornwall Council are green ambitions but depressingly grey actions (George Monbiot, *Guardian*, 29 May 2012*).*

Sustaining the sustainability myth

It was exactly 50 years ago – back in 1962 – that the first warnings appeared of the effect humans were having on this planet. Rachel Carson's *Silent Spring* focused on the detrimental effects of pesticides on wildlife. She accused the big chemical corporations of spreading disinformation. Ironic therefore that as I began writing this I read about research linking the catastrophic collapse of bee colonies to a type of pesticide known as neonicotinoid (*Guardian*, 29 Mar 2012). While some neonicotinoids were banned in Germany and Italy, in the UK the Department for Environment, Food and Rural Affairs blandly responded that the new findings did not change the Government's view, as 'the UK has a robust system for assessing risks'. A year later, despite the EU's safety regulators recommending a ban on neonicotinoids precisely because of their suspected role in decimating the bee population, the UK Government was still stubbornly insisting it was free to ignore their warning (*Independent*, 6 Mar 2013). It turns out that neonicotinoids are manufactured by chemical giant Bayer, who of course deny that their pesticides damage bee colonies.

Over those last 50 years concern about our effect on the environment has gone through several phases. In the latest and arguably most profound, the scientific consensus has been reached that human activity is causing irreversible global warming. On finishing his term as Government Chief Scientist, Professor John Beddington urged governments to start to take climate change seriously; 'The evidence that climate change is happening is completely unequivocal', he declared (BBC News, 25 Mar 2013). Not that governments have been listening. This dire warning came just a week after a budget that not only completely ignored the issue of climate change but blithely gave tax breaks to high carbon oil and energy companies. While politicians ignore the seriousness of impending climate change in their desperate search for the next growth fix, the existence of a scientific consensus has not stopped the big oil and gas companies and their paid mercenaries from vigorously contesting it. James Hansen, NASA climate scientist, says that 'the latest climate models have shown the planet is on the brink of an emergency' (*Guardian*, 7 Apr 2012). Proposing a global carbon tax, Hansen said that politicians were 'so clearly under the influence of the fossil fuel industry they're coming up with cockamamie solutions which aren't solutions'. However, Hansen's warnings were relegated to page 26 even in the *Guardian*. They were unlikely to have received much coverage in the climate change denying press.

As a species, we seem incapable of heeding the increasingly apocalyptic warnings about our addiction to fossil fuels. We know what the solution is – change our life styles, cut back on oil consumption, reduce our travel, invest more heavily in renewables, tax activities that create greenhouse gases – but we don't, can't or won't do anything about it. Politicians are paralysed. Either, as Hansen claims, they are in the pockets of the energy-squandering corporations, or they are too scared of the reaction of voters to sell the necessary change to them. We sleepwalk towards potential disaster. Lemming-like, our only reaction is to party on to the next supermarket or morosely join the end of that queue at the petrol station. Panicking ever so quietly, suppressing the screams, we wait for our next fix of fossil fuel. Unlike the bees we're incapable of acting in the interests of our species let alone the planet that sustains us. Some philosophers assure us we're capable of unselfish action for the common good but far too often we allow our individual fears and desires to override that ability to act in the broader common interest.

So it's actually not that surprising to find Cornwall Council indulging in the typical behaviour of our species and making organisational survival its top priority. Our planners might be dimly aware that things cannot go on in the same way for ever but, like rabbits transfixed in the headlights, they're unable to do anything about it. Or, worse than that, they run eagerly to embrace the oncoming vehicle. The vehicle in our case turns out to be the thundering great juggernaut of constantly growing population. By some time in the 2030s the number of people in Cornwall will have doubled compared with the 1960s. And it's well on schedule to double again before another century has passed. This is the central unavoidable core of the Local Plan which strangely neither the Council nor its councillors cares to talk about. Like the weather, it's something that apparently we can't do anything about. But in reality, again like changes in weather systems, population growth can be affected by political and economic decisions and actions, including the Council's own policies. If the Council's policies really have no effect then it's odd that Councillor Ridgers, a member of Cornwall Council's Cabinet, was telling people in east Cornwall that 'councillors are going to have to understand that one of their objectives is an increase in population' (*Cornish Guardian*, 3 Aug 2012)

Think globally, act locally

The Council smugly tells us 'we're a part of it, not apart from it'. But globally, we are consuming the earth's resources at a reckless rate. In a report published in April 2012 the Royal Society warned that 'rapid and widespread changes in the world's human population, coupled with unprecedented levels of consumption present profound challenges to human health and wellbeing, and the natural environment' (*People and the Planet*, 2012, p.12). It called for exploration of 'alternative models to the growth-based economy' (p.105). Two months later, the world's governments, meeting at another useless Earth Summit, agreed to ignore this. Instead, they decided to carry on 'stoking the destructive fires: sixteen times in their text they pledged to pursue "sustainable growth", the primary cause of the biosphere's losses' (George Monbiot, *Guardian* 25 Jun 2012). (For the depressing evidence for that ongoing loss see the UN's *GEO5 Global Environmental Outlook* at http://www.unep.org/geo/ pdfs/geo5/GEO5_report_full_en.pdf) This simple, inescapable fact and the impossibility of continuing that profligate level of consumption for ever appears to have passed our planners by. Instead, they concentrate on coming up with clever little crumbs of cant such as 'we're a part of it, not apart from it' as they merrily go on doubling up the numbers in Cornwall and plundering our resources. If we really want to be 'a part of it' then oughtn't we to be planning responsibly rather than doing our best to stoke up resource depletion in our own patch?

To understand this we have to grasp the two concepts of ecological footprint and biological capacity. Our ecological footprint or ecofootprint is the land and water area we require to produce the resources we consume and absorb the waste we generate. The biological capacity or biocapacity is the amount of useable resources that are available to us. 'If we use more resources than are available … so that the damage to the environment will increase, without recovery – this is non-sustainable living'. If on the other hand our ecological footprint is less than the biological capacity available to us then we are being sustainable (Peasgood and Goodwin, 2007, p.134).

The somewhat shocking problem we face on a global scale however is that our ecofootprint already greatly outruns our biocapacity. In Cornwall in 2004 each of us needed 5.4 hectares (our ecofootprint was slightly higher than the UK average of 5.3). But we only have 2.1 global hectares per person available to us. Put another way, to sustain our lifestyles we need more than two planets. As we don't have two planets our current way of life is diminishing the stock of resources available to us. In other words we're living off our capital. As we can't increase the size of the planet our present lifestyle is already unsustainable. Or look at it another way. Cornwall contains 354,628 hectares. But we need 2,862,000 hectares or eight Cornwalls if we were to rely on Cornish resources alone!

We are in serious resource debt and, on the global scale, we've been a very over-populated territory for some time now.

All this was clearly recognised in a report on the Cornish environment prepared in 2010. It concluded that 'the estimated ecological footprint of the area is well above a level of resource considered to be sustainable' (*Cornwall environment evidence report*, p.4). Action was needed to minimise resource use. The report went on to pinpoint the main problems. 'Population growth and the associated growth in housing and development are likely to increase pressure on the environment.' This was exacerbated by tourism, which was found to result in 'significant pressure placed on the environment [by] the additional use of natural resources such as water and energy, as well as potential environmental degradation and pollution, for example the impact of increased traffic on air quality and greenhouse gas emissions.' The report concluded that 'the environmental impacts of growth need to be minimised' (p.5). Later in the same report a rising sense of panic can be detected. 'The environmental impacts associated with economic growth must be minimised' (p.5). And who were the authors of this timely and extremely sensible report? None other than the Community Intelligence Unit at Cornwall Council!

Clearly, there's a clash of perspectives here. For example, the view from County Hall is a Cornwall where 95 per cent is 'undeveloped land'. The implication is that it's sitting around waiting patiently, just ripe for 'development'. I would prefer to see that land as a resource that, far from being 'undeveloped' has been shaped and farmed - developed in fact - by generations of Cornish farmers. It's provided us with food, fuel and space for leisure and relaxation for centuries. It's a resource that I would prefer to hand on essentially undamaged to future generations. Furthermore, for Cornwall Council doubling the population every 70 years or so amounts to 'sustainable development'; I see it as fundamentally *un*sustainable. For the Council, boosting our currently high population growth rate – as they admit 'one of the highest in the UK', becomes 'economic growth within environmental limits' (*PA*, p3). Meanwhile, 'delivery of new housing development in the quantity ... necessary [sic] is fundamental to achieving sustainable growth' (LPSP, p.23). From where I'm sitting that looks like sheer irresponsibility. Finally, the Council aims to 'make the most of our environment', a wonderfully ambiguous phrase that in the context of the preferred policy target of over 40,000 houses in just two decades would appear to boil down to 'by building all over it'.

In short, the key principle of the Local Plan – sustainable development (LPSP, pp.10-11) – is a hollow mockery. It actually just means development, a bit like the Government's new National Planning Framework, where all development is seen as 'sustainable'. 'Sustainable' has become a useful word, to be tacked on to things people might in normal circumstances be wary of in order to make them more palatable. It's the latest version of a series of inane and vague terms – a favourite in the 1990s being 'community' as in 'community by-passes' or 'community development'. Now so much has been termed sustainable that the word becomes utterly empty, stripped of meaning and signifying precisely nothing.

The grand 'overall aim' of sustainable development on closer examination becomes merely a 'sustainability checklist' for future building developments, a box to be ticked before planning permission is granted. Peering at the trees the council abysmally fails to spot the wood. Take its own 'sustainability appraisal' of the Local Plan. So what do the 596 pages of sustainability appraisal apprise us of? Even this in-house overview cannot avoid the bleeding obvious. Tucked away on pages 27 and 591 we find the conclusion that 'the [Local Plan] does not perform well in meeting the environmental objectives for Cornwall' and 'the housing policy will have a significant impact on the natural environment'. The appraisal also concludes that the Plan will have a negative long term impact on soil and food production, water, biodiversity, and the marine environment. Somewhat strangely however, it concludes that pursuing rapid population growth will have both positive and negative effects on climate change, air quality, landscape and the historic environment. Even more oddly, it asserts that rapid population growth will have a positive long-term impact on social inclusion!

But these conclusions are likely to have little effect on the growth juggernaut and will no doubt be ignored in the rush to provide planning permission to all and sundry. Indeed, by September 2012 permissions to build over 21,000 houses (over half of the minimum target proposed) had already been granted even in advance of the Local Plan being agreed. It seems clear that by ramping up the rate of granting permissions any opposition could be neatly pre-empted in advance. Despite the fact that Cornwall receives three times as many applications for residential development per head of population than does England, these applications in 2012 were 12 percentage points more likely to be agreed (see Our Cornwall website at http://ourcornwall.org/?p=224)

Green Cornwall or squalid Cornwall?

Last year I had cause to drive back into Cornwall from a trip upcountry. It had been a glorious early spring day up around Bristol. The sun was shining, people at the motorway service station were sitting outside, drinking their over-priced and over-sized coffees but in relaxed and smiling mood. But as Polson Bridge was passed things began to change. Progressing onto the higher ground past Tregadillet the clouds descended. By the time Jamaica Inn was in sight the temperature had dropped a full six degrees from the balmy Somerset Levels. Meanwhile, grey mist rolled across the road from the north, making it difficult to see the crows poking at the decaying roadkill which suddenly seemed to have multiplied. No other birds, indeed no animal life at all, was much in evidence, apart from a few sad-looking bedraggled sheep grazing morosely in water-soaked fields. A couple of daffodils tried to peek through the string of litter strewn along the verges.

As the scene of desolation deepened I had this weird feeling that I was entering Mordor. But the eye of Sauron had become the eye of Cornwall Council. And the eye of the Council alights on the A30 and doesn't see just a mundane strip of tarmac with noisy traffic, roadkill and litter. From the Council's viewpoint it's transformed, rebranded into

'Cornwall's Super Green Spine' (*PA*, p.13). Which just goes to show that that eye sees what it wants to see. Enthusiastically grasping post-modernism with both hands Cornwall Council takes the view that if you give something a different name then miraculously it becomes what it's named. In this respect what are we to make of the renaming of Penwith, Kerrier and the other districts as West 1 and 2, Central 1 and 2 and East 1 and 2 (*AMR 2010-11*)? A generation late perhaps, but 1984 has finally arrived. The perspective of Cornwall from the offices of County Hall and from where I sit is indeed very different. We might as well inhabit totally different planets. Instead of a squalid, uncared for environment of declining quality, the Council only sees a pristine, sparkling, shimmering 'Green Cornwall'.

Views of the environment can therefore plainly conflict. There is what we might call a green Cornwall view and a grey Cornwall view. The Council is inordinately fond of its Green Cornwall policy. It claims it's 'providing leadership in ...the transformation to a low carbon economy' (Cornwall Council website at http://www.cornwall.gov.uk/default.aspx?page=29305). Yet, this is promptly negated by ratcheting up the house building rate and relying on a population-led approach. It's impossible to reconcile these incompatibles. The grandiose discourse of 'leadership' for green communities and a green economy and the aim in the Council's Green Cornwall Strategy for 'Cornwall to become the most sustainable place in the UK and Europe' (p.3) completely contradict what the Local Plan delivers. The well meaning words of the Green Cornwall Strategy, all 'renewable sources', 'environmental technologies' and 'a low carbon economy' are fatally compromised by the commitment to business as usual and a high growth economy in the Local Plan. Indeed, the futility of all this rhetoric is sadly illustrated by a Green Cornwall vision that insists on including the naïve encouragement of 'sustainable economic growth'.

I'll return to the Council's definition of sustainable growth later but this glittering vision of a green Cornwall seen from the sterile bureaucratic bunkers of County Hall is surely at odds with what most of us see in our everyday lives. Take the matter of litter. Walk or cycle the highways and byways of our 'green' Cornwall and you can't fail to notice the rising tide of litter, a lot of it advertising a global fastfood outlet and various supermarkets. This is presumably deposited in the hedgerows by a post-Thatcher generation that treats the environment as just a convenient landfill site. If 'it is the aspiration of the Green Cornwall programme that Cornwall should not only match the national and European targets but should exceed them' (*Green Cornwall Strategy*, p.8) then why do we have such a litter problem when compared with our neighbours in Brittany? It's hardly rocket science, but we don't even seem to be able to manage a simple thing like controlling litter.

All the traffic lights are green for growth

Another way of unpacking the Council's definition of sustainability is to ask what level of growth it considers **not** sustainable. The original Core Strategy paperwork allowed us to answer this important question. For it included tables for each of Cornwall's 19 'community network areas' (CNAs) that summarised the various 'growth factors'. Policy objectives and environmental and socio-economic considerations were evaluated against the 'case for future growth'. The latter seemed to be taken for granted as a given, but let's ignore that for a moment. A helpful traffic light system was devised for those of us who couldn't read: green if the case for future growth was supported (an interesting choice of colour in itself carrying the subliminal message that growth is of course 'green'), orange for 'no conclusion' and red for 'suggests concerns over future growth'.

One of the factors being assessed against the case for growth was the environment. But the authors of the Core Strategy were reluctant to make a decision when it came to the environment. For all 19 CNAs they sat on the fence and concluded that there was 'no conclusion/further evidence required'. Apparently the evidence provided in the 500 plus pages of their own sustainability appraisal was insufficient. Let's remind ourselves again of this. It concluded that 'the housing policy will have a significant impact on the natural environment' (*SA*, p.28). But not significant enough to warrant any concerns. Even in areas like Bodmin, Hayle, Truro, Falmouth or Camborne-Redruth, where growth rates were set to rocket.

Before leaving the traffic lights we might ask how many times the Council concluded that there were actually concerns over future growth in any of the other categories.

Table 4.1: The planners' conclusions on the case for growth

Green: support the case for growth	138
Orange: no conclusion/further evidence required	71
Red: suggests concerns over future growth	0

Out of 209 possible cases where there might possibly be concerns, linked to environmental and socio-economic considerations, infrastructure and policy objectives, the Council concluded there were precisely …. none. No concerns at all. Nowhere. So even though proposed population growth rates at the time were 29 per cent in 20 years at Camborne-Redruth or Newquay, or 35 per cent at Launceston, or 40 per cent at Truro, or a possible 43 per cent at Saltash, or 50 per cent at Hayle, or even 70 per cent at Bodmin they could find absolutely no cause for concern. In fact at Camborne-Redruth ten of the eleven traffic lights were set at green, while at Bodmin, Hayle, Truro, Launceston and West Penwith we find nine green traffic lights. This stunning level of complacency sends an unmistakeable message that for Cornwall Council any level of growth, even 70 per cent in 20 years, is perfectly 'sustainable'. It's no matter whether a place has already doubled in size in little more than a generation (as has happened at Helston, Wadebridge, Bodmin, Launceston, Liskeard and Saltash) or were destined to double once more in less than a generation (as at Truro, Bodmin or Saltash). No concerns ruffled anyone's feathers in the growth corridors of County Hall.

In search of joined-up thinking: population growth and the private finance initiative

On page 12 of the Green Cornwall Strategy Cornwall Council states that their aim is to contribute 'towards cutting Cornwall's greenhouse gas emissions above national targets (34%) by 2020'. Yet on 29 March 2012 the Council released a press statement welcoming the decision of the Court of Appeal to grant permission for an incinerator at St Dennis. However, incinerators, while emitting less CO_2 than coal fired power stations, fare worse than gas-fired power stations and are 'dismal compared to other renewable sources' (Libby Peake, *Resource* 53, March 2012).

But incinerators also come with a fundamental paradox. They need a constant throughput in order to operate efficiently, so at St Dennis we'll have to provide 240,000 tons of waste a year for the next 30 years. The problem with this is that it then reduces the incentive to maximise recycling or go for a zero-waste policy. It actually ends up locking us into generating high levels of waste. Is this therefore where the joined-up thinking comes in? Providing such a level of waste becomes that much easier in the context of a 30 per cent population growth over the next 30 years. In other words the implied logic of the PFI incinerator contract is the exact opposite of Green Cornwall; it makes population growth a more rather than less 'rational' strategy.

Given these issues – its black mark for carbon emissions, the connection with population growth, not to mention the fierce opposition from the people of St Dennis – you wouldn't have thought an authority with pretensions to a Green Cornwall policy would have been so keen on a giant incinerator. To some extent the current Tory/Independent growth fanatics were backed into a corner on this one. The previous Liberal Democrat administration had saddled them with a disastrous Private Finance Initiative (PFI) deal with French-owned corporation SITA UK to build the incinerator back in 2006. Which goes some way to explain the otherwise inexplicable 360 degree policy u-turns since 2009.

The reason incinerators are so popular – in 2008 60 were in the pipeline across the UK – has little to do with green policies and a lot more to do with threats of fines from the EU, corporate power and the lure of PFI financing. An EU directive was passed way back around 1999 threatening to impose fines on local authorities for failing to reduce their landfill use. The perfectly laudable intention was to boost recycling and reduce greenhouse gas emissions. Even though recycling rates in the UK lagged far behind the European average unfortunately the Labour Government dragged its heels on encouraging local authorities to get their recycling acts together. So by the later 2000s a quick fix was needed to avoid mounting fines.

Step in the waste management companies. SITA UK dangled the solution in front of the Lib Dem council in 2006. It involved a 30 year £427 million contract to manage Cornwall's waste disposal and in the process build an incinerator. SITA control 12 per cent of the British waste market and leapt at the chance of a print-your-own-money PFI contract. PFI has been popular with credit-hungry central governments since the early 1990s as it defers the costs of investment to future generations and keeps infrastructure spending off the public accounts. It's also great for private businesses as it basically guarantees them a steady flow of profits for 25-30 years while removing most of the risk to the public sector. In a PFI deal, a consortium agrees a contract with central or local government or the NHS for example to build and manage a school, hospital, or a waste incinerator. PFI consortia usually involve a finance company, a company that does the construction and one that takes on the long-term management. The consortium borrows money from the banks and does the building. The government (in this case Cornwall Council) pays back the cost of the building, the interest repayments and more on top which becomes the profit for the private sector spread out over a period of around 30 years. It's basically a hire purchase scheme where infrastructure spending is deferred over an extended period of time. They are also ruinously expensive and poor value for money, which is why some NHS Trusts are now having their PFI repayments underwritten by the taxpayer. Meanwhile, with £301 billion being forked out to pay for assets worth £55 billion the corporations are laughing all the way to (and with) the banks (*Guardian*, 5 July 2012).

The PFI scheme with SITA was brokered by the Royal Bank of Scotland and AXA, the Paris based insurance giant - both these corporations incidentally being among the worst offenders for increases in their carbon footprint. And the RBS was a key player in the crisis of bankers' greed that led to millions of us having to pay the price of austerity packages.

Not that it's easy to discover the facts about the incinerator scandal as, because of the 'commercial confidentiality' involved in PFI contracts, decisions about the Integrated Waste Management Contract of which it is part have long been taken behind closed doors, with press and public regularly excluded. This is a convenient cloak behind which this issue – and any PFI scheme come to that, or the more recent privatisation proposals – is whisked away from public scrutiny and public money committed to private profits with ineffective democratic oversight. By the summer of 2012 the leadership core of Cornwall Council was frantically rushing to fulfil the Conservative/Lib Dem Government's agenda of outsourcing the public sector by contracting out another swathe of responsibilities so that private companies could make profits. This time it included libraries, the management and oversight of which were set to disappear from public scrutiny (*West Briton*, 2 Aug 2012). These plans were later rejected but, given the steady cuts in local government funding from a government determined to transfer local services from democratic accountability to an unaccountable private sector, a similar, smaller scheme inevitably reappeared on the agenda in February 2013.

The lessons of Cornwall Council's incinerator shambles are therefore twofold. First, financial rather than environmental considerations and the influence of large corporations are the real drivers behind policy decisions. Second, population growth makes decidedly questionable projects like incinerators more 'rational' and these in turn increase the pressure to continue along the unsustainable road of high population growth.

Sustainability or windbaggery? The example of Eden

Perhaps the main purpose of Green Cornwall strategies and sweet visions of 'sustainability' is ideological rather than practical. The Council must employ people with enough sense to realise that these are hardly practical policies in the financial and economic set-up within which it is forced to operate. The real agenda is not sustainability at all but, as we shall see in Chapter 7, growth. But a blunt, unadorned aim of 'growth at all costs' is likely to trigger a little opposition, even in Cornwall. How much better to disguise it in a nice, environmentally-friendly package, sparkling with sustainability and gleaming with greenness. Here, the Council has a perfect role model very close at hand - the Eden project. This, with its green rhetoric and its basis in tourism, nicely matches the romantic representations of a pale green Cornwall that underlie the Council's own thinking. It takes that traditional stereotype into new territory and provides a bridge to a 'New Cornwall' of designer lifestyles urban dreams and Cornish nightmares.

The Eden Project's domes are now icons of Cornwall. This tourist theme park snugly fits those enduring images of Cornwall as a purer, more natural sort of place, an antidote to metropolitan civilisation, a place to escape the hustle and bustle, stress and pollution of urban life. This of course is the same imagery that underlies mass tourism and, more indirectly, mass migration to Cornwall. The Eden Project is also heavily subsidised from public funds; it was one of the two main beneficiaries of Objective One/Convergence European grants along with the Combined Universities in Cornwall (two of the three universities of which are actually based in Devon).

By 2007 the Eden Project's former clay pit had swallowed £59 million of Heritage Lottery money (a tax on the poor according to Adam Smith), £26 million of European funding and £21 million from the former SW Regional Development Agency. Another £20 million had been provided by commercial loans, charities or reinvested income. As the Project itself puts it, 'dreams cost money' (Eden Project website at http://www.edenproject.com). In 2007 the operating surplus produced from its 1.2 million annual visitors was around £2.5-3 million. Yet, by 2012 the Eden Project was admitting that underneath all this hype about what a success it was things weren't quite so rosy. The surplus had turned into a loss of £2 million as visitor numbers shrank by 8-9 per cent in two years and the Eden Project management was looking to make 35 redundancies (*Western Morning News*, 29 Feb 2012). This was followed up a year later by announcement of another round of 70 redundancies (BBC News, 28 Jan 2013). The Eden Project had discovered the hard way that relying on never-ending growth might be unsustainable. This didn't however stop them looking for yet another handout in early 2013. In this they were supported by local business leaders who declared the Project a 'regional treasure' (although not specifying which region) and who called on the Government to hand over another loan of up to £7 million (*Western Morning News*, 7 Mar 2013). These are presumably the same 'leaders' who tell us there's no money left to fund the welfare system or pay for local government services any more. The Eden Project, like Newquay airport, has become too big to fail. Therefore, we have to go on feeding its voracious appetite for public subsidy, draining away money that might well have created a lot more jobs had it been invested in Cornwall's small and medium enterprises instead.

Don't get me wrong: the Eden Project has been involved in some good stuff. For example their Clear about Carbon project that aimed to boost carbon literacy in businesses or their 21st Century Living Project, which resulted in very intriguing suggestions for low cost and simple ways in which government action could lower families' carbon footprint (not that the Government listened). On the other hand the Eden Project has more than a touch of the Victorian schoolmarm about it, keen to tell us what to do but a little less forthcoming in telling the whole story about what it does itself. For example, nowhere on its otherwise informative website can I discover what its actual carbon footprint is or how it might have changed over the years. The biggest car park in Cornwall and a million visitors a year, the vast majority of whom arrive by car, might be thought to contribute a fair bit to the 27 per cent of Cornwall's greenhouse gas emissions from transport in 2009.

In similar fashion the Eden Project is surprisingly reticent about some of its other projects. For instance Sustainable Tourism in the Clay Country aims to 'increase the number of people visiting the Clays [sic]', a definition of sustainability that is remarkably close to Cornwall Council's simplistic 'sustainability is more' approach. Even more dubiously, it showcases its Clay Futures Community Engagement programme, aimed to 'encourage them [the clay communities] to consider the extent to which the plan could meet their aspirations'. The plan in question was the 'eco-town planned for mid-Cornwall'. This Clay Futures Community Engagement project was commissioned by none other than Cornwall Council in 2009 but it appears from the admittedly brief description on the Eden Project website that its purpose was to legitimate plans already made rather than put those plans themselves up for discussion. This echoes its Neighbourhood Planning Schemes which, just like Cameronian Big Society localism, gives the impression of allowing local people more say in planning their communities while strenuously steering them away from the big issues – such as the Local Plan for example.

The only detail about the eco-town project I could find on their website was a press release from Tim Smit dated 16 July 2009. This announced the Eden Project's involvement, along with Imerys Minerals and Cornwall Council, in the plan to build an eco-town in the clay country. For Smit this was 'an alliance beyond party politics and narrow sectoral interests ... that is truly representing a vision shared by all'. The hyperbole went stratospheric as Smit enthused about a 'legacy for the people of the Clay Country and Cornwall'. What a pity however that the people of Cornwall hadn't been asked in the first place whether they wanted an effective new town (well, actually new villages) and another 10,000 or so in-migrants. The Eden Project duly joined the other sectoral interests of French minerals and quarrying giant Imerys (profits for first quarter of 2012 €127 million) and developers of luxury bolt-holes for the rich, Egyptian-Swiss Orascom Development (net loss of 76 million Swiss francs in 2011 as a result of political unrest in Egypt), to form the quaintly named Eco-Bos to oversee the eco-town development.

In 2012 it was revealed that in 2008 the former SW Regional Development Agency paid off the outstanding £1.8 million from a loan of £3 million made by Cornwall County Council to the Eden Project back in 1999. The unelected RDA had insisted on a news blackout so this further subsidy for the Eden Project went entirely unreported until 2012. Tim Smit of the Eden Project was unconcerned. It hadn't been 'a bad investment' as the money was used to build a new road that 'opened up the whole of the former derelict Clay Country for an eco-town' (*West Briton* 31 May 2012). In other words, it wasn't such a bad investment as it enabled the population growth the Eden Project appears to be so keen on. Now that the 'eco-town' project has been moved to the back burner can we have our money back please?

Unsurprisingly, there's nothing on the Eden Project's website about their attitude to the Local Plan either. Yet what's this? We find that among those organisations in 2011 arguing for a growth rate of 57,000 more houses by 2030, thus boosting present building rates by a quarter, was none other than Eco-Bos. So when we strip away all the glib green pronouncements what do we find? It's the same story as with the Duchy of Cornwall: the same green flannel. The Eden Project turns out be merely a cover for property developers, irresponsibly ramping up population growth. Or is this another of its 'transformational social and environmental projects on our doorstep' (http://www.edenproject.com)?

Eco-towns and eco-communities: encouraging population growth

Eco-towns were the back-of-a-fag-packet wheeze of former Labour Prime Minister, Gordon Brown, desperate to ensure building houses in the countryside became more acceptable. Some of the more bizarre claims of wild-eyed supporters, insisting that the inhabitants of the proposed eco-town would all 'work from home, drive electric cars and use enhanced public transport' (*This is Cornwall*, 18 July 2009) were quickly ridiculed.

The other-worldliness of the whole mid-Cornwall project became even more apparent when it was revealed that it would include a 'luxury waterside marina' at Par. Presumably to cater for all those ecologically-friendly yacht owners who tread ever so lightly on the earth as they fly from city to marina, indulge in a bout of chillaxing and then fly back again to make another boat-load of cash.

Never mind that the clay country eco-community was pronounced to be 'unsustainable' by the Eco Towns Challenge Panel in June 2008 (BBC, 23 June 2008). Or that the Government's own Eco Towns Sustainability Appraisal of November 2008 spelt out 'the likelihood of high car dependency' and only graded the project 'might be sustainable'. The enthusiastic and witless support of the then Liberal Democrat-led Cornwall County Council and the former SW Regional Development Agency plus the possibility of EU funding ensured that it would go ahead. No matter that the Chief Executive of Orascom was quoted as saying the eco-town would aim to provide a range of housing 'from the guy on less than £50,000' to 'the guy that has £5 million' (a lot of those in Stenalees). Tim Smit still felt 'it's very exciting ... it is a real rip working with a guy who has a vision and who wants to do it as much for the legacy as for the money. People just need to believe because this is the best thing that will ever happen to St Austell' (*This is Cornwall*, 26 Mar 2010). There we have it. Just believe! Have faith in the half-truths of the press releases uncritically recycled by the media. Trust the claims of those sectoral interests who stand to make an awful lot of money out of this.

Some local politicians certainly had faith in this nonsense. From the safety of Redruth, Cabinet member Cllr Graeme Hicks was ecstatic. It was 'wonderful news for all the residents of the area. It reinforces our commitment to put the interests of local people first' (*This is Cornwall*, 10 Feb 2010). I must have missed something. Not the interests of Imerys or Orascom then? Or the Eden Project? But 'local people'. Even though only up to 40 per cent of the eco-town was planned even then to be 'affordable'. So how exactly does providing homes, 60 per cent or more of which were unaffordable, to attract and accommodate in-migrants, put the interests of local people first?

The detailed planning application (PA 11/01390) from Eco-Bos for their first tranche of 92 houses revealed the less than ecological truth about 'eco-communities' (for the term eco-town was long dumped in favour of the more cuddly 'eco-community'). The 92 houses come with the expected 60 bike spaces but, somewhat less expectedly, also 162 spaces for cars to accommodate the expected two-car households! The warning of the Eco Towns Sustainability Appraisal in 2008 turns out to have been spot on. So-called eco-communities in Cornwall encourage car dependence as a part of their wider, though less publicised, aim of assisting the Council's plans to boost inwards migration. Even the scaled down plans for the eco-villages were abandoned in late 2012 as, with considerably less publicity than the uncritical fanfare that greeted its unveiling, the eco-town project was quietly shelved as market conditions turned out to be less than propitious (*Western Morning News*, 5 Dec 2012). No profits so no eco-town. Which ought to tell us something.

Although, even as the writing on the wall for the eco-town was fast becoming plainer for everyone to read, it wasn't enough to stop Cornwall Council in 2011 from adopting eco-communities as one of its latest big ideas. Never slow to welcome any daft idea as long as it encourages more in-migration, it invited landlords across Cornwall to suggest more sites for eco-communities. 'Let a thousand eco-communities bloom' was the cry ringing through the corridors of County Hall. Eleven possible sites made their way into the original Core Strategy consultation document. The majority of these were actually existing urban extensions dressed up in new eco-community clothes but four were new proposals in rural areas outside towns. However, a brief glance at the location of these rural 'eco-communities' gave the game away. They were all within easy commuting distance of Truro, at Shortlanesend, Mitchell, St Allen and St Columb. Six of the others were right next to Truro, Camborne and Falmouth. The exception was Coldstyle Road at Liskeard. But that was a re-branded existing development project and anyway is within Plymouth commuter range. Take Maiden Green at Truro, next door to the stadium(-less) suburb at Langarth where 1,500 houses received planning permission in May 2012. This is being proposed by Walker Developments. Odd that their website doesn't actually call it an 'eco-community'. All I can find there is an 'eco-pilot' involving 27 houses, which will be built to Code for Sustainable Homes Levels 5/6 (only Level 6 is carbon neutral). In fact their website remained unchanged from pre-eco community days. Surely this couldn't just be another cynical act of re-definition in order to make planning permission even more likely, could it?

Absurdity descended into farce when, at the meeting of Cornwall Council on 27th March 2012 Cllr Kaczmarek was forced to respond to widespread criticism of the proposed standalone eco-communities on greenfield sites. He abjectly told councillors that 'these papers also included, in error, sites that had been submitted to the Council as potential 'eco settlements' which had not been considered by the authority. I understand these caused concern and as such I do not intend to take these forward further as part of the Core Strategy.' Some error! Strange also to be told that the eco-community at St Columb had 'been submitted to the Council', implying some outside agency offered the site. But the proposed location included 'Ruthvoes Farm and Quoit Farm ... both County Farms, owned by Cornwall Council' (Cllr Dick Cole's blog, 1 Mar 2012). Moreover, it seems that the portfolio holder responsible for housing wasn't told anything about the proposed eco-communities by his own officers. What does this tell us about the respective roles of officers and elected members at Cornwall Council? And did no-one at County Hall proof-read the Core Strategy? Perhaps the whole mad plan to increase population growth will turn out to be just an error too.

The LEP goes green? Hopes dashed

If the Eden Project isn't as green as it seems then can we look to other organisations? The Cornwall and Isles of Scilly Local Enterprise Partnership (LEP) unveiled its growth strategy in 2012. Its guiding principle is that 'the culture, communities and environment of Cornwall and the Isles of Scilly will remain special and unique'. It rightly accepts that 'if increasing the social and economic wellbeing of the people in Cornwall and the Isles of Scilly we destroy the environment – the landscape, its biodiversity, its communities, culture and heritage then we will have failed' (LEP, 2012, p.3). Well said.

However, these fine words are then fatally compromised by its worrying description of this precious environment as a 'great opportunity for economic growth' (p.7). The environment is valued 'as a business asset' and will be 'a natural magnet for the ambitious' (p.5). Having resurrected the moth-eaten and passé myth of the dynamic in-migrant (just like the authors?) the growth strategy later comes up with the interesting concept of 'environmental growth' (p.13). However, like 'sustainable growth' this is rapidly revealed as an oxymoron as it vainly strives to use 'economic prosperity' to 'enhance the environment' while refusing to admit that mindless growth is a part of the problem in the first place. Meanwhile, it turns a blind eye to population growth. Instead of seeking to manage and control the latter the strategy merely hopes that 'all new builds, including housing and other developments' will be 'leading edge environmentally'. And its fundamentally feeble commitment to the environment is betrayed by its hope that businesses will reduce their impact on the environment and lower carbon emissions 'where possible'.

So full marks for ambition but few marks for action. But at least more marks than Cornwall Council's Local Plan for honesty as the LEP admits that there 'may be little the LEP can do in this area'. The LEP is also proud that its strategy has an 'evidence base'. But this seems to be mostly a collection of statistics culled from Cornwall Council or other sources with an absence of context and the familiar lack of historical awareness. For instance, the LEP forecasts 'substantial net in-migration' but seems to have no problem with it. Indeed, it identifies 'fast growth sectors' as linked to population growth.

To sum up, there's little evidence here of any understanding of the consequences of current policies or hint of the new thinking that will be required both globally and locally to avoid those consequences. Brave new words looks very much like the same old business as usual. Away from the greenwashed policy documents, LEP chairman Chris Pomfret was quoted as saying at Newquay Airport that 'the central priority for Cornwall is economic growth. The existence of an airport ... is essential' (*Business Cornwall*, 28 May 2012). Sadly, 'environmental growth' had apparently not even survived the launch of the LEP's strategy.

Stop the greenwash: from irresponsible planning to genuine sustainability

It's clear that Cornwall Council and organisations like the Eden Project or the LEP are defining sustainability, if indeed they're defining it at all, in the sense of 'continuing to do something'. One suspects that for them it's a question of how to keep the population growth ball rolling. If we can it's sustainable. Only if, for some reason they find impossible to contemplate, we're not able to keep it on the road does growth become unsustainable. The original Core Strategy defined sustainability on page 6 of the Introduction to *Our Preferred Approach.* There it stated that it's 'about creating a better life for everyone, now and for generations to come'. This vague and anodyne concept ducks the issue of sustainability completely. In place of such flannel the Council should begin to look seriously and honestly at what sustainability means, taking into account the long term future. The Local Plan Strategic Policies document comes closer to a more sensible definition, 'a balance of decisions ... to meet our present day needs while not compromising the needs of future generations' (LPSP, p.10). Yet, it's clear the 'balance' has swung alarmingly from environmental maintenance to the need to make profits and this definition remains vacuous and essentially meaningless. Most people would tend to use the word sustainable in the sense of 'endure' or 'preserve'. Can we sustain life and the natural resources we all depend on in a relatively undamaged state?

By the end of the Council's own environmental evidence report of 2010 it becomes plain that we are living well beyond our means. Yet, because we're not allowed to think beyond the box of population growth the intrinsic dilemma of growth remains unaddressed. The evidence report rather hopefully calls for action to minimise the environmental impact of economic growth. But this idea that we can have our cake and eat it too avoids the stark reality that we have to confront. Growth itself is the problem. The Council's agenda, piling more and more people into Cornwall, makes the task of reducing our ecofootprint to fit the capacity of natural resources to support it steadily more difficult, if not downright impossible. We may, according to the Core Strategy, be 'a part of it' but the central policy contained in that strategy aimed to make us 'apart from it', if the 'it' is the environment we all ultimately depend on.

To do our bit to set an example we have to step up to the plate and take more responsibility for the consequences of our exploitation of our own small spot of the globe. This is surely what a real 'Green Cornwall' policy would imply. The rational response would be obvious: abandon a policy of infinite population growth. If the Council really wants a sustainable Cornwall it must replace its dead-end population-led growth policy with policies that work towards achieving a steady state population as a starting point for living within our means. If the natural environment is, as the Council asserts, 'unique and extraordinary' (*PA*, p.3) and an 'outstanding and distinctive' asset (p.13) and if 98.6 per cent of people in Cornwall think that the natural environment is of 'some importance to them', yet 41.8 per cent believe it is deteriorating as opposed to just 12.7 per cent who think it's improving (*Quality of Life Survey*, pp.94-97) isn't reducing the pressure of population growth the prudent thing to aim at? But instead of this logical response to our looming environmental crisis Cornwall Council's strategy is to pile on the pressure, crank up the building rate, plan for even higher levels of population, watch as the milestones to a million people and more in Cornwall tick relentlessly past.

Moreover, the Local Plan wriggles away from reality, desperately trying to hide the Council's core policy of encouraging in-migration, second home ownership and high population growth behind a rhetorical smokescreen of sustainability. It might win a lot more respect were it only to come clean and admit its growth agenda openly and honestly. Then we might begin a proper debate about it, a debate that the people of Cornwall have never been offered by a succession of political and economic elites. In its place, a torrent of greenwash is poured into Council documents. These ooze with fine-sounding phrases that turn out on closer inspection to be so much inane drivel, the weasel words about 'take a lead in the green agenda ... achieve a leading position in sustainable living ... be a green peninsula ... reduce greenhouse gas emissions ... make the most of our environment' all boiling down to suburbanising our countryside. This embarrassing greenwash and the conclusions of Cornwall Council's own evidence report are then promptly binned as the Local Plan assures us that in some curious but unexplained way we will 'prosper through housing', even though we haven't particularly prospered by the past 50 years from some of the fastest housing growth in the UK. Only in the topsy turvy world of Cornwall Council can building at least 42,250 houses and planning for a population growth of near 20 per cent in 20 years be defined as a 'careful use of natural resources'.

The level of greenwash correlates with the planned rate of growth. As the latter rises so does the former. But instead of spending time and energy designing an environmentally friendly discourse in order to mystify and confuse those of us gullible enough to swallow this fatuous flim-flam, why doesn't the Council treat us like adults, drop this threadbare cover and admit its real agenda? When will it abandon its cruel deception and come clean about what its policy actually is? When will we see it honestly and openly admitting something along the following lines?

We want to increase the high population growth rate we have endured in Cornwall for the past half-century by another few percentage points over the next 20 years. This is in line with our population-led growth strategy. We believe that nearly doubling the current population to almost a million by the end of the century will be the best strategy for Cornwall, its people and all those who will become its people over the next three generations. Our own research shows that this will have a profoundly negative impact on our environment but we are confident this is a price we must pay in order to accommodate another 350,000 in-migrants and several thousand more second-home owners and make them and the existing population prosperous.

If the present unsustainable million-people population strategy is taking us down the path of environmental degradation and irresponsibly piling up problems for future generations to solve it is also having a serious cultural impact. Unlike the environment, where the Council is forced to invest time and resources producing a smokescreen of rhetoric to divert our attention from the consequences of its own policies, it appears supremely indifferent to their cultural impact. There's another, wider point here. Henri Lefebvre predicted in the 1970s that if places are treated merely as products to sell to consumers all that will be created will be units of identical places (Lefebvre, 1991). And while the environmental and aesthetic effects of the million-people strategy are producing a ticking time-bomb the cultural effects have already changed Cornwall almost beyond recognition. The next chapter turns to this cultural revolution.

Chapter 5

Ssh, don't mention the Cornish: The cultural consequences of endless growth

If the latest population projections are anywhere near accurate the UK can look forward to an increase in population equivalent to building *twelve* new Birminghams in the next 25 years. The mounting pressure on local environments, loss of countryside and open spaces is something everyone everywhere will have to confront in coming years. But here in Cornwall we have an additional dimension. In Chapter 3 I identified some unique aspects of housing and population change in Cornwall, the combination of high population growth, peripheral economy and low wages for example. As I shall argue in later chapters we also have particular political problems related to our yawning democratic deficit and the lack of a forum for public debate of these issues. But on top of those we also have the cultural impact of population growth. For those of us who are Cornish the relentless house building programme can be a constant nagging ache, a slow burning fuse that threatens to blow up the bridges connecting us to our land and our past. No wonder that some are convinced this is a deliberate exercise of colonialism. 'Space-changing' and 'transformative regeneration' from where we sit look depressingly familiar. Is it merely the latest version of a project to engineer a fundamental shift in the ethnic composition of Cornwall, in the process ending the very existence of the Cornish people as a recognisable group? In exploring this question, we need to be a lot clearer in distinguishing between the native Cornish, those who were born and/or brought up in Cornwall and the subjectively Cornish, those who regard themselves as Cornish. As we shall see, estimates of the numbers of the latter are often a lot lower than the former but could potentially become a lot higher.

Who are the Cornish?

But first, before assessing what impact the Local Plan might have on us we need to know who we are. The Cornish can trace their origins as a people back to pre-Roman times. Then, before the lifetime of Christ, Cornwall, along with the rest of Britain, was inhabited by people speaking a language later defined as Celtic. As the Romans left, others arrived from what is now Germany, Denmark and the Netherlands to settle in eastern Britain. Over the next 400 years or so these peoples, gradually coalescing to form the English, spread their influence westwards. In a process that is still very unclear the Celtic language of the Britons (or maybe Latin in south-eastern Britain) was replaced by the English language of the newcomers, added to later by Scandinavian influences in northern parts. Whether this was as a result of extermination and ethnocide or through cultural assimilation is still an open question. Linguists tend to favour the former while archaeologists now plump for the latter. Placenames tell us that by the tenth century from Kent to Devon the Celtic language was no longer used, replaced everywhere by English. Everywhere that is but in Wales, Cornwall and for a time Cumbria and south west Scotland. Wales retained its own ruling classes and princes to the end of the thirteenth century. The territory of Cornwall had been conquered politically by the eleventh century - at least in theory - but the people of Cornwall continued to speak their Celtic language with the exception of those in the district north of Launceston. There, beyond the River Ottery, Cornish placenames were replaced before the tenth century. This is evidence for a possible ethnic cleansing of this area in the 800s.

All this may seem like ancient history. Actually it is ancient history. But the survival of a non-English language west of the Tamar, its presence etched into the very landscape which the Cornish had named, was a constant reminder for later generations of their non-English origins. Politically, the Cornish may have been drawn into the English state. But, surviving into the age of literacy, their distinct language ensured that culturally they remained something else – something apart, something not English. In addition, the presence of a Celtic-speaking society across the

Channel in Brittany (the result of an exodus of Britons from south-western Britain in the fifth/sixth centuries) and the return of some of them to Cornwall itself as economic migrants in the fifteenth and early sixteenth centuries, plus the Celtic-speaking Welsh across the water from the opposite coast, provided permanent examples of what might have been. Cornish may have given way to the English tongue in east Cornwall by the time of the Black Death of the mid-fourteenth century, in mid-Cornwall by the civil wars of the seventeenth century, and even in the far west by the time the industrial revolution was gearing up. But a Celtic past and the presence of pan-Celtic links could not be so easily eradicated.

In Cornwall, even in its most English or British moments the cultural resource of those sparks of a non-English identity waited to be re-ignited. And all the time a less specific pride in being Cornish burned brightly. Its flame became especially fierce in the early nineteenth century as mining and Methodism created a unique rural industrial society. For a time this even blazed on the global stage as the emigration of thousands of Cornishmen and women, mainly to Australia and North America, created an all too brief flowering of international connections. 'Cousin Jack' communities were linked back home by letters, flows of money and the constant coming and going of migrants. After all that, the twentieth century could seem like an anti-climax.

As the Cornish overseas lost touch and concentrated on becoming Americans or Australians, the Cornish at home took solace in their families and communities and licked their wounds. With their mining economy slowly crumbling around them they were gripped by a profound sense of defeatism and powerlessness. The temptation was to resort to nostalgia, fondly remembering the 'good old days' but abandoning the quest for a new Cornwall. But not everyone succumbed. A small group of revivalists ceaselessly strived from the later nineteenth century onwards to reconstruct Cornwall's Celtic roots and to use them to restore confidence. Yet even (or perhaps especially) this band of dreamers too often fell foul of romanticism. Their distaste for Cornwall's arrested industrialisation caused them to turn for inspiration to a medieval Cornwall and a pure high

Cornishness based on its written medieval language. This was too impossibly remote ever to strike an easy chord with the average Cornish person trying to earn a crust scrabbling around among the wreckage of a de-industrialising Cornwall.

The depths appeared to have been plumbed by the late 1950s. Cornwall's Celtic roots were a matter for antiquarians but of no practical significance. The pioneers who founded MK in 1951 had either given up in despair or embarked on a decade of twee cultural nationalism that few others were aware of. Out-migration had re-established itself after a wartime interlude and the majority of Cornish people seemed resigned to a future as a labour reserve for the new mass tourism dependent on the vagaries of urban disposable income and Keynesian budget management. Those that weren't looked east, leaving as soon as they could to join the conveyor belt of social mobility provided courtesy of the welfare-bureaucratic state.

Unnoticed at first, in the 1960s things began to change. Already, net out-migration had been replaced by net in-migration even before the newly established Greater London Council unveiled plans in the mid-1960s to build estates for Londoners at Camborne-Redruth, Bodmin and Liskeard. These triggered a major campaign of resistance. At the end of the day this seemed to have resulted in victory as these 'overspill' plans were soundly defeated at Camborne-Redruth and Liskeard. Only Bodmin town councillors voted to accept overspill. The arguments in favour of this population transfer were eerily similar to the ones now put forward by those who were and are so keen to impose up to a 35 per cent a decade growth rate on Bodmin and another dose of in-migration. More people would create more jobs and lead to prosperity. It didn't in the 1960s and 70s and it won't in the 2010s and 20s. However, the planned working class migration from Greater London had distracted people from the stealthier unplanned middle class migration from the Home Counties that had already started. Within a few years of seeing off overspill outside Bodmin, campaigners began to realise that was a hollow victory.

It became obvious during the 1970s that more and more people were drifting westwards in search of dreams of the 'good life'. But their dreams were others' nightmares. Would Cornwall and Cornishness survive the influx? Or would it be washed away by a tide of more articulate middle class incomers, bringing with them a London-oriented Home Counties culture? In 1986 a study of this counter-urbanisation painted a grim picture 'of a Cornwall swamped by a flood of middle-class, middle-aged, middle-browed city-dwellers who effectively imposed their standards upon local society. Integration and assimilation was a one-way process – of "urbanisation" rather than "ruralisation"' (Perry et al, p.129).

For those living through this period of cultural change it was indeed an unsettling time. We weren't moving but our world seemed to be moving around us. The familiar everyday accents of our youth were fast disappearing, replaced by strange tones from upcountry places. It was, and is, all too easy to assume that the thousands of newcomers thronging our towns had little knowledge of and even less sympathy for our heritage. For them Cornwall was surely just a place to escape to, somewhere that held fond memories of past holidays, a place of leisure, where suburban dreams could be lived out. For some Cornish, this looked like merely the modern manifestation of that remorseless and instinctive drive on the part of the Anglo-Saxons to move ever westwards, inexorably sweeping away any inconvenient native cultures that happened to lie in their path. For the majority it was something grumbled about in private but a process that we were powerless to stop. Decades of docility and defeatism had prepared us quite nicely for this new onslaught from the English heartland.

The end of Cornwall or the renaissance of Cornishness?
But this reaction was too pessimistic. While the intelligentsia agonised but did very little, ordinary Cornish folk reacted by resorting to their family roots. In the face of mass migration an existential need resurfaced to reconnect with their land, to prove to themselves that they were indeed rooted in that land and had prior rights to it. Having Cornish surnames in

your family tree took on more importance. Tracing your ancestry back to the glory days of the early nineteenth century somehow legitimated your right to be Cornish. The doomsayers of the 1970s were proved wrong. The end days of Cornishness had not arrived. Or at least not yet. Rapid population growth created its own reaction. A new pride and assertiveness began to be evident by the 1990s. The Cornish, or at least some of them, were, to their and others' amazement, not prepared to go quietly.

The black and white flag of St Piran, dismissed by the powers that be as the despised flag of MK in the 1960s, has now become ubiquitous, proudly fluttering across Cornwall. People turned to those artefacts of revived Cornishness that a small minority had been flogging with little apparent success for half a century. Now their years of effort finally bore fruit. It was immaterial how bizarre the exact content of their re-inventions was – whether a revived language or a Cornish tartan. Their role, like the actual surviving evidence of the Cornish language in placenames or surnames, or landscape features from standing stones to engine houses, was symbolic. They acted as reminders that Cornwall is different, that the Cornish exist, that we're still here and we're intending to stay. They became totems of a revived sense of who we are, poles of potential resistance, hints of what might be.

The truth is that despite the mass inwards migration since the 1960s, or perhaps because of it, we are not only still here but uncannily our numbers appear to be growing. Cornwall's history had produced a split consciousness. Or possibly something better described as a hybrid consciousness. At some times we could be fiercely Cornish, at other times meekly English. This chameleon identity was most frustrating to Cornish nationalists who preferred a simpler 'Cornish not English' identity and viewed the messier lived identity of Cornishness as a form of false consciousness. But in the twentieth century to display your Cornish patriotism on those infrequent occasions when the Cornish rugby team were winning, yet a few weekends later cheer on England against Wales wasn't false; it was taken for granted. What's been noticeable however since the onset of the Great (Inwards) Migration of the 1960s is that a steadily growing proportion of people in Cornwall are now prepared to define themselves as Cornish *rather than* English. This tendency is not something quaint and traditional. Far from it. It's a new phenomenon. Its occurrence at a time when the proportion of people actually born or brought up in Cornwall is gradually shrinking is no coincidence.

Of course, identities are in fact quite fluid and usually defined in relation to others. In Redruth, where I've lived for 35 years now, I might still identify myself as an east Cornwall man as I grew up in Liskeard. However, when in Camborne I might prefer to don my adopted Redruth man status. If I'm forced to go to England I'll certainly state my identity as Cornish. But if I'm in France I might call myself British. A small scale survey in 2008 tried to measure this relational aspect of identity. It found that 41 per cent of those questioned felt either 'Cornish and not English' or 'more Cornish than English'. Another 14 per cent felt 'equally Cornish and English' while the other 43 per cent were more English than Cornish (Willett 2008). This illustrates the polarisation of identities that has taken place. More of us are now more likely to define ourselves as Cornish as opposed to English and only a small minority as both. Given the mass in-migration of the past half-century these data also imply that at least some in-migrants must be choosing to define themselves as Cornish in addition to, or rather than, English.

This is a welcome sign. Any ethnic group constantly renews itself through people choosing to adopt it. Fundamentally, ethnicity is not a biological given; to some extent it involves a cultural choice. Not a completely free choice as choosing to belong to a group is one thing, being accepted as a member by those who already identify with it quite another. But any ethnic group has to be able to assimilate people in order to survive. This is especially the case with the Cornish, given the context of steady population growth and the relative shrinkage in the number of those people who can claim Cornish descent.

From exclusivity to inclusivity: native Cornish and adopted Cornish

I'll return to the issue of how many of us are left later in this chapter. But for now I'd like to turn to a related issue – one of two problems from which Cornish ethnicity suffers. The old saying that 'a cat can be born in an oven, but that doesn't make it a pasty' still operates in Cornwall. In order to establish their ethnic credentials too many prefer to reserve those credentials only to those whose family roots lie in Cornwall. Professor Charles Thomas in 1973 defined someone as Cornish if they were born in Cornwall with both parents also born in Cornwall. Overly tight definitions, or the commonly stated notion that someone has to live in Cornwall for at least two or three decades before being 'accepted', are signs of a lack of confidence. While symptoms of a siege mentality are perfectly understandable in the context of uncontrollable social change, they are dangerously incompatible with the survival of a self-confident, outward-looking people. The growth in the numbers defining themselves as Cornish rather than English hints at a more confident sense of cultural identity. But it now needs building on so that the 'adopted Cornish' can be assimilated and begin to identify with the place they live in rather than the place they come from.

Over-exclusive Cornishness is one hurdle we have to overcome. An excessively nostalgic Cornishness is another. A letter in the Guardian about the Tory/Lib Dem Government's pasty tax sagely informed the chattering metropolitan classes that 'a true Cornishman or Cornishwoman eats an oggie cold' (*Guardian*, 26 Mar 2012). Really? The implication of this debatable assertion is that nothing must ever change from the days when our great grandfathers took their pasties down the mines with them for their crowst. Comforting perhaps in the face of unstoppable change but a slight overstatement when we note the number of pasty shops in our towns doing a roaring trade in hot (or even tepidly warm) VAT-rated pasties. Remembering the past with pride and affection has its place but nostalgia for a world that has gone can be counter-productive. If we can only do things in the way that we've always belonged to do them how will we ever find the new ways necessary to build a Cornwall not answerable solely to external agendas but one that primarily accommodates **us** instead of in-migrants and is controlled by **our** agendas.

We have to move beyond the self-imposed shackles of a native exclusivity, embrace a more flexible Cornishness and be open to change that we control rather than continue to be victims - quaint or not - of change that we don't control. Despite the predictions of the doom-mongers of the 1970s we find that Cornwall and the Cornish have survived and in many ways are stronger than before. Different certainly. More confident in some ways, more explicit, more in your face. But still this isn't enough. While we've survived the first shock of mass migration we remain vulnerable. As we educate one generation of incomers another generation arrives to take its place and we have to start all over again. This is an enervating process and there's no guarantee we can keep this up for ever. As the proportion of native Cornish inevitably shrinks are we certain there will always be another generation that perceives themselves as Cornish? Or, like several native American tribes, are we ultimately doomed to extinction, melting away unnoticed and unmourned?

As sanitised and hi-tech reminders of our heritage are provided courtesy of heritage lottery and European money, as the Cornish language makes a miraculous comeback (albeit in an overly purist and proto-medieval form), as the St Piran flags are whipped by the westerly gales, a paradox creeps upon us. Cornishness (perhaps in a new guise) seems more secure and explicit just as the Cornish themselves teeter on the brink of extinction. The ways of our parents and grandparents are no more, soon to be as curious and foreign as the ways of those medieval peasants who spoke our former language. We may be more culturally confident but we are still granted little or no political respect, or even awareness of our right to exist. We are still casually ignored, blatantly patronised and persistently misunderstood. We're still being asked to look on helplessly as the landscapes that were the playgrounds of our youth disappear under the houses and roads of a new population. The gut-wrenching ache as familiar fields and lanes are sacrificed cannot easily be shared by those who have just discovered Cornwall. There is an indefinable extra commitment, a special sense of loss and grieving as we watch our land being torn up in front of us. Somehow that pain has to be united with the pride we feel in being Cornish. We have to demand our right to have a say in the future of our land. And more. Our history provides us with the resources of difference that could be welded into a powerful political demand for recognition as more than a mere English county. These resources might enable us to wrest back control over our own planning powers, to build the space to ensure that we can welcome new arrivals and together build a Cornwall that we can all be proud of. The Cornishness of Cornwall provides us with the resources for change. A change from endless, pointless population and housing growth that's producing a suburban replica of anywhere else.

Back in 1988 in *Cornwall at the Crossroads* we called for a breathing space in order to start to discuss, debate and build that new Cornwall. There was a small flurry of interest and then it became business as usual as our pleas were quickly forgotten. Now in 2013 the need for a breathing space has become that more urgent, especially as our own Council has thrown in its hat with the developers and wants to take us even faster towards a million people. Parish councillors, particularly in the clay country but elsewhere too, have begun to call for a breathing space. This is the time to start to funnel those hesitant concerns, channel the small voices of dissent, and join them to our anger at discovering what is happening to our land and raise our voices loudly again for different policies and a better way forwards.

The Local Plan and the Cornish

Recently, I've been suffering this recurrent nightmare. The Cornish nation is stuck on a runaway train. The train hurtles along, sparks flying, a symphony of impending doom from its horn echoing back from the enveloping darkness outside. Stations flash past. They have numbers, not names. 400,000, 500,000, the next one 610,000. But we never stop. Just career through. Litter blows around forlornly in our wake as the only evidence of our passing.

Some of the passengers, most of them packed like sardines in standard class (the first class carriages are almost empty) wonder vaguely why we don't stop. The tannoy infuriatingly announces the next station stop will always be the one after the next one. A few are getting alarmed at the ominous clangs from the rails and the way the train's beginning to make little jumps as we race across the points. But the strange thing is most people don't seem to notice. Or care. They're lost in their in-train entertainment screens or locked away inside laptops and smartphones, oblivious to the outside world or the destination. Others carry on partying. Or eating.

Up in the cab the driver is hunched over the controls. His hand rests on the power lever, but this one has a big sign on it saying 'growth'. It's like a deadman's handle. If he lets go of the growth lever he's been told the whole train will grind to a halt in the middle of nowhere. The passengers will have to disembark into a searing hot desert – no water, no shade. To prevent that disaster the driver has to keep the train going. Faster, ever faster.

By his side is his assistant. This guy used to operate the brakes and saw his role as protecting the passengers and preventing the train running out of control. No longer. Now, he urges the driver on. Give it some welly my son, more speed. Keep pressing that lever. Was that a red signal we just passed? No matter. Both driver and assistant have been rendered colour-blind and all signals are at green. Even if they're red.

There's going to be a helluva scat up if we go on like this. Panicking, I look for the communication cord.

But there isn't one.

So what exactly does the Local Plan have to say about the Cornish or about the responsibility of the Council to protect and sustain this ethnic group? The short answer is nothing at all. The Core Strategy made no mention of the Cornish people as such in any of its 366 pages of consultation documents. In fact it seemed a bit embarrassed altogether about using the word 'Cornish'. It only resorted to 'Cornish' four times as an adjective – 'the Cornish context', 'Cornish language', 'Cornish World Heritage Site' and 'Cornish average'. This echoes a curious predilection among bureaucrats to use Cornwall as an adjective rather than the word Cornish. As in the odd phrase 'Cornwall towns' rather than Cornish towns which found its way into a previous structure plan. To some extent this just reflects a wider tendency – Cornwall cottages, Cornwall media for example, although almost never Cornwall pasties. In the latter case the media seem to be able to use the word Cornish willy nilly even to the extent of describing pasties made in places such as London and Leeds as 'Cornish' (BBC Newsnight, 28 Mar 2012). For all Jeremy Paxman's Oxbridge trained superciliousness he doesn't seem to realise that the Cornish pasty has had Protected Geographical Status since August 2011. This means that only pasties baked in Cornwall should be described as 'Cornish' pasties. Or maybe the patronising Paxman does know this, but like the rest of his insufferable metropolitan class, prefers sneeringly to ignore it.

But I digress. Unlike Paxman and his pasties, Cornwall Council prefers to avoid the word 'Cornish' entirely. Despite lobbying by Cornish organisations the *Local Plan Strategic Policies* document still fails to mention the Cornish people. And the single reference to 'Cornish culture' appears in the section devoted to Bude (LPSP, p.116). This is strange as they have policies in place that are supposed to protect the Cornish. For example the Council's Equality and Diversity Framework of April 2010 states that it seeks to 'protect and promote our Cornish heritage and culture ... the Council is sensitive to the unique heritage and culture of Cornwall and to those people in our community who describe their origin as Cornish'. Leaving aside the slight unease about encountering the phrase 'those people' and the nagging question of who is meant here by 'our', in practice this is supposed to mean the Council assesses the impact of 'policies and services we develop and implement'. Fine words indeed but essentially they turn out to be yet another example where a bureaucracy believes that having a statement on paper is sufficient and absolves them from all responsibility for actually doing anything about it.

As part of their 'Equality and Diversity' framework the Council commits itself to 'equality impact assessments'. Sure enough, they wrote one assessing the Core Strategy. And what does this rather skimpy 12 page document say about the impact on the Cornish of continuing to accommodate a high level of in-migration – the policy at the heart of the Local Plan? The Cornish got two mentions. The Council, no doubt after exhaustive research, concluded that 'the Core Strategy should provide positive impacts for the following groups' and towards the bottom of a long list that includes virtually everyone possible we find 'ethnic groups (including Cornish)' (*Equality Impact Assessment*, pp 2/3). Apparently this miracle will occur through the 'positive impact of the provision of community facilities'. Reading this, I don't know whether to laugh or cry. Is it a deliberate snub? Or is this pathetic nod towards their policy just the result of appalling ignorance? Or are they having a joke at our expense?

This insulting conclusion turns a blind eye to the inevitable consequences of a population growth that stems entirely from in-migration. The percentage of people who are born and/or brought up in Cornwall – what we might term the native Cornish – is steadily falling and the Council's leadership wanted it to fall at an even faster rate. Were they not aware that this would appear to be breach the Framework Charter for the Protection of National Minorities? This Council of Europe treaty was ratified by the UK in 1998 and endorsed by Cornwall County Council's leadership in 2007. Cornwall Council's official support for this was reaffirmed in 2011 when the leaders of all the political groups on the Council signed up to the Cornish National Minority Report 2. But the Framework Charter includes Article 16. And Article 16 states the following.

All parties shall refrain from measures which alter the proportions of the population in areas inhabited by persons belonging to national minorities

So the Local Plan (and all previous strategic plans) plus instructions from the Department of Communities and Local Government to plan to accommodate projected population growth caused by in-migration would seem to contradict this article. But not one word appears in the Council's Equality and Diversity Assessment in relation to this rather important matter. Does this mean that no-one at the Council reads the small print of what they're signing up to? Or are they aware of Article 16 but hope that if they quietly overlook its potentially revolutionary effect on their plans to go on altering the proportions of the population in Cornwall no-one will notice?

Altering the proportions of the population

There is considerable confusion, none more so than in policy circles, over the word Cornish and who or what qualifies as Cornish. Two uses of the term are possible. The first rests on an objective reference to things that are Cornish because they happen to be located in or associated with Cornwall. This can apply to artefacts such as the pasty, geographical features such as beaches, cliffs or settlements, or people, such as the native Cornish. The second use invests the term with more subjective meaning. In this case a pasty is not Cornish just because it's baked in Cornwall. Instead, the concept of a Cornish pasty invokes other things such as memories of home, family meals, or even a proud mining history. When it comes to people this second, more subjective meaning encompasses those who would claim a Cornish ethnicity, which might include some but not all of the native Cornish plus others. Uncertainty about this prefix and its more subjective, ethnic associations go a long way towards explaining the reluctance of policy-makers to employ the term.

Back in the 1950s according to the Census the proportion of Cornish-born in the population was around 75 per cent. That indicates the minimum percentage of native Cornish in Cornwall, as some people living in Cornwall of Cornish descent would have been born elsewhere and others would have been living in Cornwall since childhood and been effectively assimilated. Since 1951 there has been no comprehensive survey of the proportion of native Cornish in Cornwall. When in the 1960s hospitalisation of births in east Cornwall was moved to Plymouth, birthplace statistics became fairly meaningless. In any case the Census stopped reporting them. The former Cornwall County Council was not keen on collecting such data, reluctant to give any importance to Cornish ethnicity.

As mass in-migration set in during the 1960s the proportion of native Cornish in the population began slowly and inexorably to shrink. The last relevant, properly conducted survey – of seven electoral wards in mid and west Cornwall – was carried out in 1982/83 (Perry et al., 1984). This discovered that across all seven wards 57 per cent were Cornish born and 43 per cent in-migrants, although these included some who had moved to Cornwall as infants. Around one in five of those people born in Cornwall were actually return migrants, having left Cornwall at some point but then returned (Perry et al 1986, p.84). The proportion of non-Cornish, what this study described as 'new settlers', ranged from a high of 67 per cent in Carbis Bay/Lelant to just 18 per cent in St Stephen in Brannel. While the Lizard and Feock also had Cornish minorities, the Cornish remained in a majority in the other areas of Truro Tregolls (64 per cent), St Just in Penwith (64 per cent) and Redruth South (72 per cent). But almost 30 years of further in-migration will have eroded the proportion of Cornish born to under 50 per cent, unless out-migration has become greatly skewed towards the non-Cornish. Despite Cornwall Council's 'equality and diversity framework' which 'robustly' commits them to collect data for ethnic monitoring purposes no scientifically acceptable surveys of the proportions of non-movers, return migrants and 'new settlers' has been conducted during the last quarter of a century.

The 1983 survey implies a fall from around 70-75 per cent at the time of the 1951 Census to 55-60 per cent. As net in-migration did not begin until the early 1960s this had occurred in little more than 20 years, a drop of around 15 percentage points at a time when the population rose by 22 per cent. This in turn might suggest that for every one per cent rise in the population the proportion of native Cornish falls by around 0.7 per cent. Using this as our base we could calculate the proportion of native Cornish in the population in 2012 to have fallen by maybe another 17 per cent, to be as low as 40 per cent. Numerically however, this method is nonsense as it implies that the proportion of those born in Cornwall will hit zero per cent sometime later this century. As children of in-migrants are born in Cornwall, then the proportion of Cornish-born is bound at some point to stabilise. It's also possible that the proportion of non-Cornish among out-migrants has increased considerably since the 1960s and 1970s, as higher education opportunities in our tertiary colleges and universities expanded, and as the number of transient residents, arriving on a whim and leaving in desperation, goes up. Given current rates of in-migration, lower than in the 1960s and 70s, it's likely that the stabilisation point has now been reached. But whichever way you cut the numbers, it's pretty clear that the proportion of native Cornish in Cornwall is now somewhere between 40 and 50 per cent, not as low as some Cassandras claim, but nonetheless a clear minority.

This has two consequences. First, it means that not only are the Cornish a national minority within the state in which they are governed but, unlike the Scots or Welsh, are a national minority in their own homeland. One might think this unenviable position would make those who represent us that much more determined to ensure their policies work to promote and protect this group, beginning by ensuring that their minority status is not eroded even further. But lamentably, this does not appear to be the case. Quite the opposite in fact as the Council eagerly sought to drive up the rate of population growth in Cornwall by building at least 49,000 and preferably more like 60,000 houses with no apparent thought for the consequences for the ethnic composition of the population.

Second, it produces a situation where whose who wish to see more protection for the remaining Cornish adopt a minority rights approach. Their argument is that as the Cornish become a minority the danger of marginalization increases. The possibility of the Cornish exerting their will on the democratic process disappears. Instead, a non-Cornish majority with no real connection to the place in which they live is able to impose their views on the population and shape the land to suit their own convenience. More generally, the slow erosion of Cornwall's native population has resulted in community fragmentation as, contrary to the Council's complacent claims, continuing along the path of rapid population growth undermines community resilience and cohesion.

A report submitted to the Local Plan 'consultation' in 2012 by *Bewnans Kernow*, representing 65 Cornish cultural organisations, concluded that 'Cornwall has a unique demographic environment which entails a special care and responsibility for maintaining the homeland of this ethnic group in a sustainable fashion' (p.15). Needless to say, no Cornish organisation seems to have been actively consulted on the Local Plan by Cornwall Council in advance of its production. This contrasts with ongoing discussions with pro-housing growth lobbyists.

From fading minority to re-emerging majority: retaining the Cornishness of Cornwall

Nonetheless, I remain sceptical about an across the board minority rights approach in defence of the Cornish. And for the following reasons. As I have argued above, as the scale of in-migration became clear back in the 1970s a rising sense of panic gripped the Cornish intelligentsia. Professor Charles Thomas wrote in 1973 that there were 'not many real Cornish left, and not all that much left of real Cornwall' (1973, p.21). As we have seen, quantitatively the proportion of Cornish-born in Cornwall has been driven down. But as I have also pointed out, qualitatively the characteristics of the Cornish within that surviving proportion have changed. The Cornish are now more confident in their Cornishness.

The rather confused attempts at ethnic monitoring that have taken place – confusing race and ethnicity as a result of the English obsession with the former and failure to understand the latter – have asked people more subjectively to state whether or not they were Cornish. In the large scale Quality of Life survey of 2009 26 per cent opted for 'Cornish' as their ethnic origin. (This implies that a good proportion –

maybe as many as a third - of native Cornish chose not to define themselves as Cornish.) The figure of 26 per cent was slightly lower than the 30 per cent across a range of smaller scale parish surveys in the 1990s and 2000s where people subjectively defined their ethnicity. A recent doctoral study of the extent of Cornish ethnicity concluded that the proportion of ethnically Cornish people, using statistical techniques to establish the proportion of those 'who self-identify as Cornish', is around 25 per cent (Husk 2012). This figure is in close agreement with the 2007 Quality of Life Survey and reinforces earlier evidence from parish surveys. However, despite the sophisticated techniques employed, the basis of this conclusion – the seven per cent who self-declared as Cornish on the 2001 Census form – is hardly robust. Nonetheless, 25 per cent must be assumed to be the minimum proportion of self-consciously Cornish Cornish; it is not of course the same as the proportion of native Cornish.

But something strange and unexpected has been happening. Since 2006 the Cornwall Pupil Level Annual Schools Census (PLASC) has collected information about the subjective ethnicity of schoolchildren, those of primary age being supplied by parents. Every year the percentage of Cornish children increases, even as the proportion of native Cornish goes on declining. In the first survey of 2006 the proportion of self-identified Cornish children in our schools was 24 per cent. By 2008 this had risen to 30 per cent. Last year (2011) as many as 41 per cent said they were Cornish. At this rate the Cornish will soon be in a majority again. The PLASC surveys are evidence of a greater willingness of children and their parents to choose to define themselves as Cornish. The numbers of the rising generation prepared to self-identify as Cornish must give rise to the strong possibility that the proportion of self-consciously Cornish, as opposed to native born and bred Cornish in the population, is increasing and could soon comprise a majority again if only population growth was slowed down.

Moreover, in 2001 it was possible via a complicated procedure to define oneself as Cornish in the Census. This involved the counter-intuitive act of stating you were not British. Nonetheless, a total of seven per cent in Cornwall still took the considerable trouble to write in their ethnic group as Cornish. Calls for the ONS to include a Cornish tick box for the 2011 Census were predictably disregarded, despite a campaign backed by 4,000 people with over 40 MPs supporting that campaign in the Commons. Yet, the proportion self-defining as Cornish in the 2011 Census grew. A new question on 'national identity', for which the Cornish option was similarly denied a direct tick box, resulted in 14 per cent of people in Cornwall taking the trouble to go through the complicated business of asserting Cornish as their 'national' identity. In Wales, where a tick box for 'Welsh' was available, 66 per cent declared a Welsh national identity. But in 2001 without a tick box the numbers in Wales declaring a Welsh ethnicity was very comparable to the figure for Cornish national identity in 2011 at just over 14 per cent, or double the proportion declaring a Cornish ethnicity in 2001. On a pro rata basis this might suggest the proportion of people in Cornwall who would regard their Cornish identity as their national identity should be somewhere above 33 per cent. The important point here is that even while the proportion of objectively Cornish people (those born and/or brought up in Cornwall) is steadily diminishing as the result of demographic change, the proportion of subjectively Cornish people (those prepared to identify themselves as Cornish) is equally rising (maybe as a result of the same demographic changes).

Here's the thing. We may be a national minority within the British state but why settle for minority status in Cornwall itself when here we still retain the possibility of claiming majority status? With 40 per cent native Cornish, a growing proportion of whom are now asserting their Cornishness, plus an unknown but presumably growing number of incomers who are prepared to identify themselves as Cornish, we still have a window of opportunity – a window to build on the cultural resurgence of the past twenty years and demand our right to retain Cornwall as the homeland of a distinct people. If we allow the Cornish to become an interesting historical relic, a minority group consigned to the museum shelves and the local histories, then we wittingly or unwittingly throw away our link to two thousand years of the past and give up a critical weapon in the struggle to obtain the right to make our own decisions about how we live and what sort of Cornwall we want here – in Cornwall.

If, in contrast, Cornwall remains the homeland of a majority group of Cornish people and that majority becomes more self-aware then we can more easily demand recognition and respect from central and local government as well as from European levels of governance, which appear to be more sympathetic to our case. However, this is a window of opportunity that is in danger of being closed as population growth proceeds and if the political/bureaucratic plan to increase it further succeeds. The difficulties of inducting a new population into awareness and respect for the unique heritage of the place they have chosen to reside in will become ever more difficult if Cornwall becomes less distinctively 'Cornish'. Both less Cornish in terms of the environment around us; supermarkets, housing estates and industrial units tend to look the same whether they're in Cornwall, Canterbury or Caithness. And less 'Cornish' in terms of its society. The decline in the proportion of native Cornish has to be halted and reversed – and within the next generation if we are to have any chance of retaining a Cornwall that is still in some way recognisably Cornish.

Chapter 6

The drive to a million: Who gains from growth?

We have seen how the Council had become determined not just to continue the stale, failed policy of population-led growth but keen to step it up. We have also seen how the much vaunted economic and social advantages of pursuing this policy have been a lot more ambiguous in practice than in policy documents. This isn't a question of anticipating the future effects of a brand-new policy; the rapid population growth rates in Cornwall over the past half century furnish us with all the evidence we need. We have also seen how encouraging high population growth gradually reduces the proportion of native Cornish. Although people can still be assimilated and Cornishness has proved to be far harder to eradicate than many would have expected and some might have hoped, we are fast approaching a tipping point. That point arrives when the proportion of native Cornish in the population becomes so small that Cornwall is no longer Cornish. After that no matter how many iconic memorials to our culture are built they will stand as glitzy reminders of a dead culture, sterile mausoleums honouring the burial of a culture that could once trace its lineage back for a couple of millennia.

And while a cultural tipping point looms, we are also rushing recklessly towards an environmental tipping point. Or maybe we've already raced right past it. We've seen how we're living beyond our means. Environmentally, even the current population in Cornwall consumes a lot more resources than Cornwall itself can provide. Claims to be building a 'green Cornwall' turn out to be empty words spun in a context of unremitting population growth. This irresponsible policy – coupled with uncritical acceptance of policies aimed at over-generalised growth at all costs and more material consumption – makes attaining a sustainable balance increasingly unlikely if not downright impossible. Although the Council itself produced the evidence showing the negative impact of its plans for high population growth in its Environmental Impact Assessment of the Local Plan, it chose to ignore that evidence. Instead it gleefully pours more fuel on the fire, seemingly revelling in the prospect of increasing the population towards a million by the end of the century.

Clearly, despite all the evidence that the population growth strategy will have a damaging economic, social, cultural and environmental impact, Cornwall Council has deliberately locked us into it with few apparent qualms about the future. So we need to ask this rather important question. Why, given all the evidence of its negative long-term impact, is the Council so intent on continuing, even speeding up population growth? This is not an easy question to answer. There are a number of factors that combine to produce this policy folly – a policy resulting in the exacerbation of problems rather than their solution. Some of them exist at an individual level; some at a structural level. Some are peculiar to Cornwall; many flow from the general assumptions that drive planners and politicians everywhere towards growth. But a range of factors combine in different ways in different individuals to produce the desperate drive to a million and, one might be forgiven for thinking, well beyond. In this chapter I begin by asking who benefits from population growth on this scale. We shall follow the money and identify those interests set to gain from the great sale of Cornwall. In Chapter 7 I'll move on to follow the ideas behind the million-people strategy and ask why the idea that high population growth is good for us has become so entrenched. Chapter 8 then completes this trilogy of chapters devoted to the reasons why housing and population growth have become the largely unquestioned policy panacea. It focuses on the way the tourist industry and the associated imagery of Cornwall works to produce a high level of in-migration.

Money, money, money: the source of all evil

Ask the man or woman in the street and they may well have a simple answer for our councillors' failure to control development pressures – they stand to gain from it. Sadly, the greed and dishonesty of MPs back in

2008, as they devised ever more ingenious ways of boosting their expenses, served to give all politicians a very bad name. Local councillors are widely assumed to be in it for what they can get out of it, a populist consensus fanned by superficial local press reporting that concentrates on the expenses of local councillors and high visibility financial irregularities, such as the failure of four Liberal Democrat councillors to pay their council tax on time (*Western Morning News*, 2 Feb 2012). Or the alleged dubious practice of one of those same councillors, which is supposed to have helped secure permission for 1,500 houses at Threemilestone right next to land that he owned where a similar building application for another suburban extension just happened to be in the pipeline (*West Briton*, 10 May 2012).

Yet this is unfair. A few high profile cases serve to distract us from the majority of councillors who make no unearned personal gain from their role. Most entered politics with a genuine desire to serve the community. The problem is not *too much* pay for councillors; it's *too little*. The payment that backbench councillors get is hardly extravagant and in fact tends to restrict the pool of those who can afford to be councillors to the self-employed, those with a decent pension, or the well-off. The problem is also not too many councillors, but too few. As we shall find in chapter 8 we have fewer elected representatives per head of population in Cornwall than virtually anywhere else in western Europe. To do their job properly - to be social workers or parish priests and represent pavement politics issues and in addition to be expected to think strategically about the future of Cornwall - demands full time councillors. That way we might get a council more representative of the population. That would have to be an improvement on the present situation, where we suffer a majority of part-time, unrepresentative, amateur politicians who are all too often vulnerable to capture by a cynical developers' lobby

For the background of our councillors is hardly designed to produce a critical or sceptical approach to housebuilding or to population-led growth. A full 42 per cent of councillors either own more than one house, or own land, or have interests in tourism or property speculation.

This has to be regarded as a minimum figure as the comprehensiveness of the answers in the councillors' register of interests varies considerably. For example, one councillor used to describe himself as a holiday cottage proprietor but did not declare any ownership of property in Cornwall. Maybe his properties were all upcountry. Or maybe he rented his holiday cottages from someone else and then sub-let them. Such a background is unlikely to make them over-critical of claims that more and more houses could solve all our problems. The likelihood of having such interests is even higher among the ten strong Cabinet, where at the time of writing four own more than one house, another has land in addition to their own home and a sixth runs a building company.

While anyone who rents out land or property stands to gain from a rising population, those involved in tourism or with a background in the small business retail sector would also expect to make personal gains – either directly or indirectly – from a growing population and the growth in demand that it brings. Let's not be mistaken however. There's not necessarily a direct relationship between ownership of property or land and attitudes to development. In fact, some of the more consistent opponents of excessive population growth have been owners of multiple properties. Nonetheless, the socio-economic make-up of Cornwall Council is one possible factor explaining the less than vigorous opposition to the growth clique's plans for Cornwall even if it may not be the most important factor.

Just meeting the aspirations of the people

While our gurus of growth offer their panacea with a considerable dollop of greenwash, the fact that others stand to gain financially from the chosen policy remains firmly in the shadows. Unwilling to identify exactly who might gain the most, instead they insist that population growth on this scale is required because 'the people demand it'. This is possibly the most dishonest packaging of the lot. The growth gang like to give the impression that 'it's not us, guv, we're just meeting community aspirations'.

For example, in the tables that accompanied each of the 19 'community network area' discussion papers in the original Core Strategy one of the policy objectives evaluated against 'growth' was 'community aspiration', presumably meaning what communities want. Starting down in West Penwith we read that 'growth can help deliver many of the aspirations of local communities'. It appears that the people of Hayle and St Ives were also keen on growth for 'the area has aspirations to grow both in terms of housing and employment'. Meanwhile, at Helston 'growth will help deliver many of the aspirations communities have'. Moving on to Camborne-Redruth we could discover that of course the area 'has aspirations to grow in terms of both housing and employment, and growth can help maintain the existing retail centres and community facilities and enable new community facilities to come forward'. It was the same story at Falmouth and Penryn, where, amazingly, 'growth can enable many of the local community's [sic] aspirations to be delivered'. In Truro we also discovered that 'growth can help deliver many of the aspirations of local communities'. To cut a lengthening story short, precisely the same wording was used at St Agnes, St Austell, St Blazey, Newquay and Launceston

In the china clay area 'can' became 'will' as the planners adopted a more muscular 'can-do' mission – 'growth will help support the regeneration of villages and the local economy and enable the delivery of affordable homes', although precisely why clay villages still stood in need of more 'regeneration' when they've seen growth rates of up to 70 per cent in the last decade was left unexplained. At Bodmin, there was no doubt at all about it. The town 'has aspirations to grow in terms of both housing and employment'. Even up at Camelford it seemed 'the area has aspirations to grow to some degree so long as it is planned and is sensible'(?) They may not have been so keen in Bude but the planners reminded them sternly that 'growth will help maintain Bude's role as the local service centre for the area', while at Liskeard/Looe they were much more enthusiastic as 'growth will help to deliver many of the aspirations of local communities'. Over at Saltash/Torpoint the Council's in-depth research into local views was lacking, replaced with 'growth can help support the regeneration of

Saltash and Torpoint town centres and new housing development will mean more people will fall within their respective catchment areas'. Only at Caradon (Callington and Calstock) was there some hesitation, with no explicit mention of growth and no uncovering of the universally massive local aspirations for growth. Viewed from the cosy confines of the County Hall growth bunker, the Council is therefore merely innocently meeting the wishes of communities that are all aglow with aspirations to grow.

What is less clear is where the evidence for these aspirations can be found and when these communities were actually asked. As we've seen, there was no evidence at all of any aspiration for increased population growth in the 2007 Quality of Life Survey, the last scientifically conducted attempt to garner residents' views. Quite the opposite in fact, as the people then seemed a little more sensible than their leaders and concluded that population growth was one of the biggest threats to the Cornish environment.

Or meeting the aspirations of the developers

In 2011 the Core Strategy underwent one of its rounds of consultation. People were offered three options for a housing target – 38,000, 48,000 or 57,000. (And to remind ourselves – the actual number of houses built in the previous 20 year period was 41,320.) Given what we are told are the overwhelming 'aspirations to grow' out there, it seems a mite perplexing that 64 per cent of the individuals who submitted their views in this consultation plumped for 38,000 or fewer. Meanwhile, most of the town and parish councils that responded also preferred 38,000 and none of them wanted more than 48,000.

Yet several other organisations were keen on *more than* 57,000. Here's a list of them.

- Bell Cornwell, town planning consultants based in Exeter

- Catesby Property Group, residential and commercial developers from Stratford on Avon

- Cranford Developments Ltd, a land and development company from Staffordshire

- Drivers Jonas Deloitte, commercial property consultants with offices in London, Slough, Birmingham, Manchester, Leeds and Scotland

- Hawkstone SW Ltd, property developers with their registered office at Coalville in Leicestershire

- Linden Homes SW, offices in Saltash but part of the UK-wide Galliford Try building group, which includes Midas Homes, Stanford Homes, Rosemullion Homes and Gerald Wood Homes

- Persimmons Homes SW, a UK-wide building firm with its HQ in York

- Strongvox Homes, a regional housebuilding company based in Taunton

- Taylor Wimpey, the UK's largest housebuilder with its head office in High Wycombe

- Tetlow King Planning, a planning and development consultancy from Bristol which on its website boasts of overturning a rejection of 67 houses at Padstow on appeal

- WainHomes, based in Okehampton

- Willow Green Farm Ltd and Newham Farm Ltd – local developers who want to build lots of houses on a greenfield site on the edges of Truro

And the following all plumped for 57,000 houses, still 16,000 more than the actual building rate for the past two decades.

- Ainscough Strategic Land, a development company from Wigan

- Barratt Homes, a housing developer whose registered office is in the same small Leicestershire town as Hawkstone (see above)

- Boyer Planning, town planning consultancy with offices in Cardiff, Twickenham, Colchester, Wokingham and London but not Cornwall

- Chaddlewood Investments Ltd, based in Devon?

- Coastline Housing, a not-for profit housing association in West Cornwall

- Eco-Bos, a partnership of Orescom, Imerys and the Eden Project that was building 'eco-villages' in mid-Cornwall

- First Devon and Cornwall, a bus company

- Garden Centre Group, which operates 119 garden centres across the UK but just two in Cornwall – Wyevale at Lelant and Par Garden Centre. Interestingly, its chairman is Andrew Sells who was also chair of Linden Homes (see above) from 1991-2007

- Imerys Minerals, French

- Indigo Planning, a London company that specialises in securing planning permission

- Lowena Homes, property developers from Threemilestone

- Ludgvan Leaze Developments, Crowlas property developers

- Mccarthy and Stone (Developments) Ltd, property developers from Bournemouth

- Mark Buddle planning consultants of Cambridge

- MBL Developments Ltd, a construction company based in Derby

- Porthia, property developers from St Ives

- Savills, a global real estate services provider which is London based

- Trago Mills, Ukip funders and merchants at Trago near Liskeard and Falmouth

- Turley Associates, a planning and urban design company from Manchester

Notice anything? An awful lot of the companies that called so loudly for us to increase our rate of housing growth were based well outside Cornwall. And most had a direct vested interest in a higher housing target. In reality, asking property developers and their friends in the housing industry whether we should build more houses is a bit like asking them if they'd like a lot more money.

Overall, a full 87 per cent of the businesses that responded to the consultation – the majority of them with a vested interest in the outcome - wanted to increase the build rate to 57,000 or higher. No parish and town councils wanted more than 48,000. No voluntary organisation in Cornwall wanted more than 38,000. Most of the businesses who would gain financially from a higher housing target were in favour of faster population growth; most local organisations and individuals wanted to slow it down a little. Needless to say, having carefully considered all these representations Cornwall Council's planners at the time plumped for 54,000. The inescapable conclusion must be that the Council's bureaucrats have been captured lock, stock and barrel by the development lobby.

The developers' lobby

The developers' lobby in Cornwall pushes at an open door. Like the pigs and the farmers in Orwell's *Animal Farm,* it's become very difficult to distinguish between property developers and Cornwall Council's leadership these days. The Council's real agenda was bluntly revealed in January 2012. Its Leader Alec Robertson positively preened himself when reporting on a trip to London hosted by the Local Government Association and the British Property Federation (BPF). According to its website the British Property Federation is a well-heeled lobbying body that includes 'some of the biggest companies in the property industry – property developers and owners … investment banks'. Its 'lobbying successes' include injecting 'realism' into the Government's carbon reduction policies in the interests of landlords. It also strongly supports the Government's new National Planning Policy Framework which in the eyes of the BPF is not intended to produce a developers' paradise at all. Of course not; it merely 'streamlines' the planning system. Interestingly, GVA Grimley, Cornwall Council's favourite consultants, pop up as members of the BPF as does its favourite supermarket Sainsburys.

In 2012 Chief Executive of the BPF Liz Peace felt she had to respond to a letter from MK councillors in Camborne that accused the BPF of 'pushing for even higher levels of housing' in Cornwall (*West Briton* 20 May 2012). She denied that the BPF has a view on how many homes should be built in Cornwall. Yet BPF members include Drivers Jonas Deloitte, Indigo Planning, Savills, and Turley Associates, all of whom urged Cornwall Council to build 57,000 or even more houses in the 2011 round of consultations on its Core Strategy.

She claimed that the BPF 'do not represent volume housebuilders'. Yet its website says it 'aim[s] to create the conditions in which the property industry can grow and thrive'. She assured *West Briton* readers that her members would not build on green fields. So where does she think the 57,000 houses they called for (or the 42,250 in the Local Plan come to that) would be built? And in any case she thinks councillors should 'welcome any moves' by 'their [sic] council' to overcome 'barriers to growth'. Which of course in Cornwall includes building more houses to encourage a higher population.

Incidentally, one of the BPF's other 'main priorities' is to 'campaign against policies' that might 'wipe millions off the value of the assets' of wealthy overseas investors now bidding up property prices in London (Liz Peace, *RPS Update*, 16 Sep 2011).

In any case, Cornwall Council's Leader showed not a jot of shame at being associated with this bunch. Quite the contrary; Cornwall Council was 'one of just six councils to join this group which demonstrates our growing reputation on the national stage'. Instead of that delusion of grandeur we should perhaps have read 'growing reputation as a soft touch for property developers'. Further down the message came the ominous news that 'Cornwall has been selected as a place-based study area. This means we will be working with senior British Property Federation representatives, developers and local private sector partners to carry out a detailed analysis of potential barriers to growth in Cornwall and identify *appropriate solutions*' [my emphasis]. The central element of 'growth' for the hapless Robertson was the Council's 'ambitious housing programme' which is why the BPF, developers and private sector partners were all slavering at the prospect of more profits from Cornwall's out-of-control property boom. Not content with the current helter-skelter journey towards a million people in Cornwall, Robertson, Cornwall Council's Cabinet and its senior officer cadre were brazenly working with the developers' lobby to speed it up.

François Hollande was reported as saying during the French Presidential election of 2012 that 'my real adversary has no name, no face, no party; it will never be a candidate, even though it governs. It is the world of finance' (*Guardian* 21 Apr 2012). Similarly, we won't find the developers' lobby standing for election in Cornwall or putting forward their million-people plus manifesto for public approval.

Government: corporate capitalism's salesperson

If the lure of personal gain isn't sufficient and constant pressure from the developers' lobby doesn't do the trick then we have another source exerting pressure on Cornwall Council to build for a million people. And we find that source in London in the offices of central government. While Scotland and Wales now have devolved powers, Cornwall's perceived status as a mere English county ensures it continues to enjoy a colonial relationship with an over-centralised government in London. In Chapter 2 I pointed out how government set planning rules such as predetermination, which gagged opposition to development from councillors and reduced the possibilities of them actually representing their communities. We also have the new National Planning Policy Framework which, despite cosmetic tinkering, still contains a presumption in favour of 'development' as long as it's 'sustainable'. As we saw in Chapter 4 the extremely loose definition of 'sustainability' adopted by Cornwall Council should not give us too much confidence that 'sustainability' will carry any meaning. Indeed, in the *Local Plan Strategic Policies* document of 2013 (p.11) it seems to mean working 'with applicants to find solutions which mean that proposals will be approved wherever possible'!

But there are other mechanisms through which central government severely constrains the ability of local government to plan strategically. The most critical is the necessity imposed by the Department for Communities and Local Government for local authorities to have a five-year supply of land available for housing. The importance of this lies in the fact that if they don't then they have 'to consider applications for housing more favourably' (*AMR* 2010/11, p.8). And Cornwall doesn't. Or at least not according to the Secretary of State's decision on an appeal at Bude when Eric Pickles overruled Cornwall Council's rejection of a planning application from Midlands property developers Catesby to build 400 houses, a supermarket, shops and a retirement village on 50 acres near the town (*Cornish Guardian,* 3 Aug 2011). Pickles concluded that Cornwall did not have a five year supply of land.

But this is a fine example of the circular logic employed to justify continuous growth. The conclusion stemmed from a projected growth that in turn was based on the ONS projections – projections that I've already demonstrated (see Chapter 1) greatly overestimated Cornwall's population growth. Those projections were themselves in any case based on past trends. So because we've had high growth in the past we must have high growth in the future. This is like saying to an alcoholic because you've drunk too much in the past you need to drink a lot in the future. How are we ever supposed to get ourselves off the wagon and escape this Catch-22 like addiction to population growth that central government locks us into?

Cornwall Council dutifully concluded that it didn't have a five year supply of land in ten of its 19 Community Network Areas (*AMR* 2011/11). But have I got this right? It only fails to meet government requirements because central government was assuming, on the basis of dodgy ONS projections, that population would grow by 93,000 over the next 20 years and we had to have a supply of land sufficient to meet that growth. If population were to grow by a slightly lower amount we would have enough. But as the ONS in 2012 shaved 13,000 off their 2030 population projection for Cornwall then don't we have enough now anyway? Of course, if we only had to meet the needs of our own people we'd have about five times as much land available as we need. And of course this conveniently assumes that building follows demand for housing and has nothing at all to do with producing that demand. And in a classic example of moving the goal posts to favour developers the National Planning Policy Framework now proposes to increase the requirement from a five-year supply of land to a six-year supply!

It's difficult to know who's most culpable here. Is it a bullying government that forces us to appease developers by building to accommodate in-migration and unsustainable population growth? Or is it Cornwall Council, which persists in portraying the totally inaccurate impression that somehow it sets 'our own agenda which responds to the needs of Cornwall' (*PA*, p.1). Either the Council is deluding itself or deliberately deluding its people. That *should* read 'central government sets our agenda which responds to the needs of those who wish to move to Cornwall or buy second homes in Cornwall'. All the fine Tory/Lib Dem chatter about localism boils down to localism as long as you want to add even more houses to the minimum that we tell you are 'needed'. And if you don't like it we'll force you to take it by overruling local planning decisions. Instead of colluding with this charade why doesn't Cornwall Council inform its people openly that it has very little choice when it comes to planning policy, that its hands are tied and that it is therefore unable to come up with a properly sustainable plan for our future. By not doing so it is playing a very cruel joke indeed on those to whom it's supposedly answerable.

More than a cruel joke however, as I suspect Cornwall Council planners and its Cabinet agree wholeheartedly with the thrust of central government policy. There is for example some evidence that the rate of granting planning permissions increased after 2009. It's difficult to be certain about this as the planners' Annual Monitoring Review contains no data on the annual number of permissions granted as opposed to houses completed. Nonetheless, a huge number of permissions to build have already been given even in advance of the Local Plan being agreed. This means that the Council has in large measure pre-empted the housing target, which makes all the 'consultation' about it something of a mockery.

Table 6.1: Housing permissions granted in advance of the decision on a strategic plan

CNA	Built, being built or permitted at September 2012	Percentage of final proposed target for each CNA
West Penwith	950	38
Hayle and St Ives	2004	84
Helston and the Lizard	962	53
Camborne, Pool and Redruth	3088	69
Falmouth and Penryn	1077	27
Truro and Roseland	2529	84
St Agnes and Perranporth	329	30
Newquay and St Columb	2206	61
China Clay/St Austell/St Blazey, Fowey and Lostwithiel	3110	57
Wadebridge and Padstow	775	46
Bodmin	580	18
Camelford	390	43
Bude	720	58
Launceston	982	65
Liskeard and Looe	987	49
Callington and Calstock	466	47
Saltash and Torpoint	274	21
Total	**21,429**	**51**

As early as April 2011, well before the final consultations on the Local Plan, almost 16,000 permissions had already been handed out. Just 17 months later this had risen to 21,400. It seems that the Council had already committed us to building well over a third of their original target or over a half of the business-as-usual 42,250 target, before we'd even decided what the target should be and just two years into a 20 year plan! Here's the total number of permissions already granted in the various Community Network Areas before any decision on the Local Plan's housing target was actually reached.

It's a pity that such data is not easy to come by. Or maybe not. Maybe it suits the Council who can then come up with all sorts of assertions that are almost impossible to check. Take for instance the claim that 'past completion rates show that approximately 260-300 dwellings per year have been constructed in the CPIR area' (*CNA* Vol 1, p.66). CPIR refers to Camborne, Pool, Illogan and Redruth although the Council's Planning Annual Monitoring Review of 2010-11 manages to spell Pool as Poole, thus transferring the area to Dorset (p.84). A Freudian slip perhaps? But wherever does the figure of 260-300 completions come from? As a table on the next page of the same report shows, completions in the 'CPIR area' in 2010-11 were just 91. Add that to the 3,597 growth in dwellings in the previous 19 years in this CNA and we have 3,688 additional dwellings, an annual rate of 184, well below the 260-300 cited. Have 2,000 houses been knocked down, burnt down or otherwise disappeared in Camborne-Redruth over the past 20 years? Or was the Council deliberately inflating the completion rate to disguise the massive increase in the rate of growth that they wanted to impose on this district?

The Council's orgy of granting planning permissions at twice the building rate has surely guaranteed that five or six years of housing land supply that Pickles is so keen on. In fact, it equates to eight years supply with the 42,250 houses target, and that's assuming that only 80 per cent of permissions result in a new house. Or perhaps not, as some of the larger schemes will be phased and, as the prospect of profits are curtailed at present, housebuilders prefer to sit on their permissions but not build on them. Which means that Cornwall may still not have a five or six year supply of land! This imposed central demand to maintain an excessive stock of land for housing therefore ensures the continuation of the Alice in Wonderland merry go round of mass permanent and temporary migration that we have to live with.

Bribes to build

Central government sticks come with central government carrots. Current government policies reflect an even more 'business friendly' attitude than did New Labour. Which is hardly surprising from a Tory party 40 per cent of whose MPs are businessmen and women. It translates into all sorts of inducements to allow housebuilders to build and make money – such as the Government's New Homes Bonus. This rewards local authorities that build houses with a bribe of a payment equal to the council tax for each new property built. In 2011 Cornwall Council heard they would get over £5 million from building 2,237 new houses (*St Austell Voice*, 8 Dec 2011), yet another reason why building more houses to sell to more people from upcountry might seem to be such a good idea in the short-term world of local councillors.

And then there's the Community Infrastructure Levy, originally introduced by the former Labour Government in early 2010. This encourages local authorities to opt in to a more formalised version of section 106 agreements – see Chapter 2 (although it's in addition to S106 rather than in place of it). Local authorities will charge a levy on developers which is then used to 'fund new infrastructure to unlock land for growth' (DCLG, *Community Infrastructure Levy, an overview*, 2011, p.5). Under this, developers will pay for things like roads, schools, hospitals, social care facilities, parks, leisure facilities and green spaces in the neighbourhood of the development. This is supposed to be fairer and faster than the previous system of 'planning obligations' or section 106 agreements. But because it results from 'consultation' with developers and communities (not much evidence of the latter) it results in spending 'that developers will feel worthwhile'. In other words, while supposedly delivering 'the outcomes that local communities want', it is in fact still developer-led. Infrastructure gets built in places where profits can be made not necessarily where it's needed by local communities. This then acts as another useful carrot to dangle in front of councillors. The more houses are built then the more substantial is the Community Infrastructure Levy, and, given the demand to build in Cornwall, the Council might be expected to be able to charge a relatively high levy rate. Of course, councillors don't look further than the new roads, schools and hospitals that are promised. But as the Government makes plain these are all about 'unlocking future growth' – that means more infrastructure to allow more houses for more in-migrants who will then need more roads, more schools and more hospitals. And so the sorry saga sweeps on.

Developers weren't happy about the original Community Infrastructure Levy and managed to get it revised. They also lobbied very successfully for the Government's new National Planning Policy Framework which gives the green light to building by containing a presumption in favour of development. The central state therefore emerges as the final guarantor of the million-people plan for Cornwall. Its power guards the arrangements required to push the plan forward; meanwhile the local state (in the shape of the elected Cornwall Council and unelected local quangos) collaborates closely with developer interests. Furthermore, if elected representatives are minded to resist this process then, drawing on what sometimes appears to be a bottomless pit of financial resources, developers can afford to fight every stage of the planning process. Threats of going to appeal work wonders to concentrate the minds of councillors worried about losing thousands of pounds in lost court cases. As we have seen the £millions casually offered in planning gains and S106 agreements are a tantalising inducement for councillors who might be hesitating. No wonder that opponents feel they're fighting with one hand, if not both, tied behind their backs. And, as I shall argue in Chapter 9 even their sole weapon - democratic pressure on elected representatives – has in recent years been steadily whittled down.

Our land must be sold

In this chapter I've concentrated on two potential beneficiaries of the million people strategy, local politicians with interests in the housing and tourism sectors and the developers' lobby. Of these the latter is by far the most important. It works to keep Cornwall Council focussed on its task, which is to boost population growth by 'accommodating' untold thousands of new permanent and temporary residents over the next few generations. To ensure the Council doesn't falter in its allotted role central government stands ready to change the planning rules whenever necessary in order to guarantee the continuing accumulation of the built environment.

Cornwall Council therefore has to pretend that communities across Cornwall are drooling at the mouth at the prospect of even faster population growth, all feverishly aspiring to 'grow'. Meanwhile, the community that is keenest on growth operates on a much wider stage. This less visible, but nonetheless vociferous and powerful, community is wedded to the endless compound rate of growth that guarantees it a steady flow of profits. Its core lies well beyond Cornwall and it spreads its net widely. It's a community of land and resource owners that has little time for the deeper meanings of community, for history, culture, memory or landscape. It's a community driven by entirely different values. If profit and capital accumulation demand it then landscapes have to be destroyed and built anew. This is the stark reality of regeneration and place-shaping. The task of the busy mercenaries of the project class that now infest our institutions is to make it happen, to change local communities so that this other community continues to prosper.

Large construction and development companies from upcountry stand to gain most from the council's policy of concentrating housebuilding around the towns in large, new, suburban developments. But let's not forget the host of other fleas that live on their backs. Rapid population growth is also excellent news for local landlords if they have land near towns (or even distant from towns if the Council's eco-community projects had become reality). Not to mention the big supermarket chains that are attracted by a potential market steadily growing by up to ten per cent a decade. And then there's the estate agents, surveyors, solicitors and others who take their share from the marketing and selling of all the new houses.

Finally, we mustn't lose sight of the local press. They rely for a large chunk of their advertising revenue on the pages of housing advertised for sale in their property pages. It would be very foolhardy indeed to imagine that it would be easy for newspapers to take a principled stand against the million-people strategy and thus kill the goose that lays this particular golden egg. However, while there are plenty of material factors that help us understand the rush to a million, the search for explanations can't stop there. The underlying prospect of financial gain is overlain and obscured by a web of ideas that justify growth and it is to these that the next chapter must turn.

Chapter 7

The drive to a million: Who believes in growth?

'Human history', said H.G.Wells, 'is, in essence, a history of ideas'. Ideas can indeed sometimes change the world. But not all ideas. Ideas that are backed by powerful material interests and help to reproduce their power seem to do a lot better than those that question and unmask powerful interests and institutions. Another ultimately unhelpful idea is that we live in a society where we're entirely free to make our own choices. This affectation leads to the view that things only change because we want them to and our choices make the world around us. To an extent there's something in this. Our consumption choices can and do affect markets and prices. Our political choices, if we can be bothered to make them, can and do affect policy regimes, within limits. Our (or more likely someone else's) investment choices can and do affect jobs and communities. But to assume from this that the world is created entirely through the exercise of free will misses a large part of the picture. One glance at the millions of pounds devoted to advertising serves to remind us that our choices can be, and are, influenced by the ads and the mass media, by what we read and hear around us, and by ideas about what is practicable, realistic, reasonable or desirable. And the exercise of free will is ultimately constrained by factors such as the distribution of income. We're all free to buy second homes but some can exercise that freedom a lot more easily than others.

Nonetheless, despite the existence of obvious constraints on our choice some, particularly those signed up to Cornwall's growth agenda, continue to assert the importance of the individual's power to shape their environment. For example, one of the members of Cornwall Council's Strategic Planning Committee in 2011 claimed that 'it is not the supermarket that kills a town. It is the people of that town who kill it by being lured to the new and shiny supermarket. If we just resisted that lure maybe, just maybe our town centres would be in a better state … real power is people power' (Cllr Andrews Wallis's blog, 20 Dec 2011). This is all very well as far as it goes but turns a convenient blind eye to the role of corporate power in deciding to build a supermarket in the first place and that of politicians and government in agreeing its location. It's blind to the structural context within which we as consumers make our choice of where to shop while simplistically playing down the rules that maintain and reproduce the structures within which we live.

We clearly have some choice but not under conditions of our own choosing. There are several powerful influences that work to exert pressure on our thinking so that we choose the path of growth rather than the path of sustainability. In this chapter I will continue the search for possible reasons why we are stuck on this dangerous and unsustainable road. But here I move from the material and the monetary to the whims of councillors and the ideas about growth that make avoiding a million-plus population in Cornwall so difficult.

Can-do Cornwall: the growth groupies

Some at the heart of the growth project presumably believe in what they're saying. These are the people that assure us that adding more houses and more people to what we already have in Cornwall, topping up the 57 per cent growth we've already had since the 1960s, will lead to 'transformational regeneration'. The planned population growth of our towns on an unprecedented scale will inspire 'resilient communities'. Meanwhile, we will all 'prosper through housing' (*PA*, p.5). Presumably such pro-growth sentiments were general among the Council's Cabinet and the strategic planning team. These were the same people who were extremely reluctant to scale down their original plans for 53,000 houses over the next 20 years to their final target of 45,400 and even less prepared to settle for the business-as-usual 42,250 target. This key group did not view increasing the housebuilding rate by 19 per cent over that of the period 1990-2010 as any problem at all.

But let's be charitable. No doubt a few of them had fallen for the argument that in order to build more affordable homes, we must build more unaffordable homes. They may genuinely think that we can build our way to a position where all our people are decently housed. As I pointed out in Chapter 3 high building rates accompanied by a high level of in-migration did not work in the past. But this time, coupled with a strong affordable homes policy, they convince themselves that it will. Even though the number of second homes and holiday homes rose sharply to account for a large proportion of the extra houses added in the 2000s. Their aim is at least understandable though sadly over-optimistic and misconceived. Others in this group possess a more generic belief in population-led growth, believing rather vaguely that it will produce jobs and prosperity for all of us, in-migrants and locals alike. Such simple faith, despite the absence of evidence for its likely success, is entrenched in the core of Local Plan enthusiasts. This group hardly gave a second thought to the projected extra 93,000 people that they were originally told we had to accommodate over the next 20 years. Finding more than four Truros for them to live in wasn't an issue at all. A population total of over 630,000 by 2030 didn't worry them in the slightest. They were quite willing to sacrifice the countryside to the god of population growth. They lost no sleep worrying about the long-term consequences of their policies. They must be aware that continuing on this path would have produced a population of over a million by the end of the century. Either they realise this and welcome it, believing that a crowded urban environment is preferable to our present small-town society, or they have a serious lack of imagination. Or they're unable to do the sums.

In recent years, a markedly more aggressive argument for growth emerged among the upper echelons of Cornwall Council. This growth machismo culture was spearheaded by senior officers and the Council's Cabinet. Alec Robertson, the Council's former Conservative Leader and Kevin Lavery, its previous Chief Executive, proudly signed off a document entitled *Can Do Cornwall: Helping to Build a Better Future* in November 2011. Some of us may naively have believed that Cornwall Council was a democratically representative body answerable to its electorate. Apparently not. According to the Council's leadership it was now a private company with *Can Do Cornwall* rebranding it as 'Cornwall plc'. Even councillors otherwise uncritical of the growth agenda pilloried it as a 'ghastly collection of jargon and spin-speak' and 'puffed-up nonsense' (Hey Jude's blog, 19 Nov 2011). This appallingly written document waxed lyrical about 'our natural environment [which] is flowing with potential to underpin sustainable growth'. This latter was going to 'bolster our economy at twice the national rate of growth', led by 'an exciting and sustainable housing programme'. In the growth bunker of County Hall there was an 'acclaimed Cornwall Conversations dialogue with local people', although local people might have been forgiven for failing to notice it as communications with the council periodically went into meltdown – as in 'Council gets 8,000 calls per day over refuse issues' (*Cornish Guardian*, 18 Apr 2012).

The can-do twins – Robertson and Lavery – gave the game away in their can-do document when they revealed 'an ambitious ten year programme to deliver 30,000 ... new homes ... including 10,000 affordable homes' (*Can do Cornwall*, p.4). But that was equivalent to a 60,000 population growth in just ten years, or 11.3 per cent, the fastest growth rate since the 1970s. And 30,000 houses in just ten years was a 20 year rate of 60,000 rather than 49,000. The inner core of the Council had inadvertently revealed the real scale of its growth agenda. All the dreary management-speak about 'engine house for change', 'functional economic areas', 'collective community visions' or 'transformational change' (in the world of the growth bunker we have to be constantly reminded that change is 'transformational' despite the difficulty of imagining change that doesn't transform things) was to be given meaning by a can-do council leadership. 'We are raring to go ... gaining a reputation for designing the future'. The document stated the growth philosophy bluntly. It very precisely predicted that 'by 2022, by implementing the transformational [sic] changes set out in this bid, we expect that living, working and studying in Cornwall will be substantially improved'. Thirty thousand new houses would have created 15,000 new jobs by 2022 (p.10). Hold on a second though. Whatever happened to the estimates bandied around elsewhere that each new house creates one new job (*PA*, p.9)? Given that our natural population is stable then doesn't 30,000 new houses imply 30,000 new job-seekers. Thirty thousand more job-seekers chasing those 15,000 jobs will do wonders to drive down wages further while tightening labour discipline. Not to mention increasing unemployment.

This over-excitable and aggressive flummery ended with a pledge to 'drive further growth' and was promptly endorsed by four of Cornwall's MPs (Tories Eustice and Newton and Lib Dems Gilbert and Rogerson), along with the four NHS chief executives, the chairman of the Cornwall and Isles of Scilly Local Enterprise Partnership, the director of the Combined Universities in Cornwall and the principals of Cornwall College and Truro College, the district manager of Jobcentre Plus, the chief executive of Coastline Housing and the area manager of the Devon and Cornwall Environmental Agency. While this growth clique, most of whom are well paid from the public purse, happily committed us and our environment to a massive population growth over the next ten years, the leaders of the non-Conservative political groups on Cornwall Council declined to endorse the document.

Plainly, the leadership of Cornwall Council had decided to abdicate its responsibility to protect the people of Cornwall from the ravages of over-development which have been mounting now for the past half century. The top-down agenda of Cornwall Council's leadership backed by the managers of Cornwall's quango-state was willing to pay any conceivable environmental price in order to placate the god of growth. This swaggering, machismo can-do culture was a new development, pitchforking Cornwall Council into a leading role in pursuit of population-led growth. 'Bring it on', brag our reborn growth apologists as, cock-a-hoop, they strut their stuff. You want a million: we'll give you a million. Even if you don't want a million we'll give you a million.

But isn't all this bombast and bluster just a tiny bit over the top? For all the big talk about growth, the high population pleaders still hesitated to translate their vision unashamedly into the Local Plan. If a million people is the shock therapy we need then why hide it behind a veil of environment-friendly rhetoric? If growth is so good for us then what's the point of the smokescreen about sustainability? Why do Cornwall Council spokespersons bother hotfooting it to the media with disinformation about reducing the rate of housebuilding when they clearly want to do the opposite? If growth is the answer - and this is the unmistakeable message of the arrogant *Can Do Cornwall* - then why are they so reluctant to admit it publicly?

The honest thing would surely be to argue openly that a million or more people and the suburbanisation of our land is the solution to all our woes. But they don't do that. Instead they hide behind greenwash, gibberish and dodgy data. *Can Do Cornwall* turned out to be all sound and fury but little substance, the prancing of a small elite who had convinced themselves if not the men and women they were supposed to represent. The proponents of this top down agenda lived in a vacuum. They heard what they wanted to hear; they got told what they wanted to get told, sealed off from reality. Let's say goodbye to them as they swagger off into the sunset (or in some cases to the other side of the world), slapping themselves on their backs and talking loudly about transformational change, as we turn to the more intriguing question of why so many others buy into the growth agenda.

Doh! Dumbed down and dozy?

A more important factor could be just plain ignorance. I've already mentioned that there is a taken-for-granted assumption among planners that population growth precedes housing growth. Somehow, population will rise irrespective of the number of houses being built. The 'logical' outcome of this is that as growth in the number of people is fixed and will happen anyway then if insufficient houses are built some people will be without houses and the price of houses will rise because supply does not meet demand. This model of how the housing market works assumes that the demand is the active, externally produced independent variable but one that is somehow unconnected to supply. However, a moment's reflection is enough to realise that, like all markets, this one results from the interaction between buyers and sellers (and critically of mortgage providers).

Imagine that a thousand people would like to move to Porthemmet. We could therefore predict that the population of Porthemmet will rise by a thousand. A thousand extra people would require around 500 houses. But what if Porthemmet Council decides to allow the construction of not 500 but only 250 houses? Would 1,000 people still arrive? If they persisted in doing so they'd have to double up, half of them sharing houses. Or some of them would have to camp on the beach. But would the desire to move be so strong that they still moved even though there were insufficient houses for them? Or would they not look around and decide that perhaps, however nice Porthemmet was, they'd either look elsewhere or stay put? In this example it seems obvious that decisions on the supply of housing affect the behaviour of potential migrants.

Aha, that may be so, our doubting Thomas responds. But prices would go up thus pricing the local fishermen, craft artists and Celtic jewellery sellers out of the market. Unable to buy a house, they or more likely their children would have to move and the available property would go to the better-off incomers. Like all myths, there's certainly a grain of truth in this. If supply lags behind demand there's going to be upward pressure on house prices. But, switching from Porthemmet back to Cornwall, the unanswered question then becomes how many houses do we have to build to bring down house prices in Cornwall? Back in the 1960s house prices here were much lower than in south east England, a fact that triggered mass movement from that region, origin of two thirds of in-migrants. Since the 1960s the housing stock in Cornwall has doubled, allowing a population rise higher than all but seven English counties. But even this growth in supply has not prevented house prices rocketing. Prices in Cornwall have gone from being among the lowest in the UK to among the highest outside the south east. We're now told that Truro is one of the most expensive, or most unaffordable, places to live in Britain, up there with Oxford, Bath, Winchester and Cambridge, and is 'fast becoming a non-Cornish zone' (*Western Morning News*, 3 Apr 2012). But the number of houses in Truro rose by around three quarters during this same period. So what possible number of houses would have been needed in order to stop this happening? Twice as many, three times, five times, ten times? And do we really want to pay the environmental and cultural price? The truth is that we could build many times the current number of houses in Cornwall and buyers outside Cornwall could still be found to live in them, either permanently or temporarily.

And the reason for that is that the effective demand to move to Cornwall is virtually infinite when compared with the finite housing stock in Cornwall. Let's take another predicted result of market mechanisms. Back in the late 1980s I remember a discussion with a regeneration 'expert' who assured me that if things were 'left to the market' demand would soon begin to fall as congestion and environmental degradation made Cornwall less attractive. Within a generation, she argued, the rate of population growth would automatically decline and then stabilise. The market would return things to equilibrium. So stop worrying and start to love the market. Twenty-five years on and she's long gone back over the Tamar. And I'm still waiting for those market mechanisms to work. Although the growth rate has begun to fall, it's falling painfully slowly. And too slow to save Cornwall from suburbanisation. Moreover, the Council is working hard to make it rise again. The market 'solution' isn't working. It's given us economically unaffordable housing and culturally and environmentally unaffordable population growth. And that's putting aside the way the market treats 'undeveloped' land as worthless unless built on.

This is why looking to the market to solve problems of homelessness is flawed. On the contrary, the market produces homelessness. At the same time, as we saw in Chapter 1, the equivalent of over a third of new houses built in the 2000s ended up as second homes or holiday lets. We already have a housing crisis despite a chronically high rate of house building. Building even more houses will not solve it as it hasn't solved it in the past. In fact those who argue this most strongly often have a vested interest in increasing the supply of unaffordable houses. It's merely a convenient fig-leaf behind which the population growth/demographic transformation can hide. The depressing thing is how many people are taken in by the glib talk about building our way out of the housing problems we have.

TINA: There Is No Alternative

Some of our 'opinion-formers' are zealous go-for-growth-fanatics, others might be predisposed to population growth because of their background in property speculation or tourism, some may even sincerely believe that they are giving people what they want, showering jobs and houses around from their crazy cornucopia. Others may just be confused about the way the housing market works. Some just can't work out the long-term consequences of present growth policies or imagine the Cornwall that it's destined to create. But perhaps the largest category includes the dedicated followers of TINA. These include those who have no great faith that we can build our way out of our dilemma but reluctantly conclude that continuing along our unsustainable growth path is required because they're unable to think of an alternative. One can sympathise with this resigned attitude. After all, there's a whole host of structural factors which ensure that we sign up to business as usual. Which in this case amounts to protecting the right of some people to buy up our heritage and then sell it off to others.

An inability to consider alternatives to a planning policy system that is both unfit for purpose and thoroughly captured by the developers' lobby may also stem from cultural antecedents. Decades of being overlooked and neglected by an over-centralised government in London have produced a culture of defeatism in Cornwall and a shocking lack of ambition. Decades of failing to make a noticeable impact have led to a mindset that hesitates to demand change because of the inevitable prospect of yet another rebuff. Those same decades also produced an overly-uncritical stance towards the 'wise men from the east', those who arrive touting 'new' and 'dynamic' solutions which on being unwrapped turn out to be the same old stale policies well past their sell-by date. There is nevertheless a readiness to adopt these out of sheer desperation. What a relief at last! Someone has all the answers. So we'll leave it to them. A defeatist mindset is a vulnerable mindset, particularly attracted to the currently fashionable emperor's new clothes and latest big idea.

I'll return to the latest big idea in a moment but TINA is closely related to another factor that helps explain why our 'leaders' sign up so easily to the growth strategy, despite all its drawbacks. This is a lack of Cornishness. By this I don't mean that policy is led by the non-Cornish, although it is. Or that not enough native Cornish are involved in decision-making, which they aren't. But even if they were I doubt whether the policy presumptions would be that much different. Indeed, given the fatalism deeply ingrained in our psyche after a century and a half of de-industrialization things could be just as bad. (I can't imagine them being much worse.)

No, by lack of Cornishness I mean the unaccountable refusal to use the Cornish card in policy-making or in negotiations with other levels of government. As we saw in Chapter 5 Cornwall is a land with non-English origins and home to one of the native peoples of these islands. This has three obvious consequences. First, it makes it significantly different from English counties. Second, it gives those responsible for charting its future a special duty of care and responsibility. But third, it provides us with an argument for special treatment. A different place obviously requires different solutions. Yet instead we get thoughtless, short-sighted and one-size-fits-all solutions – new imported 'answers' that recreate the same old problems, only in a repackaged guise. More houses, more people, more growth. The aim seems to be to make Cornwall increasingly like the south east of England and then all our problems will magically disappear. Maybe they're right – they'll all disappear because there'll be no such thing as a distinctly Cornish Cornwall left to conserve or worry about.

Our trump card stares us in the face – Cornwall's right to special and different consideration – but we stubbornly refuse to use it. Or it's used inconsistently. It was wheeled out from a sense of panic in the early 2000s when the former County Council was threatened by the prospect of unitary local government at the more rational district council level. But it plays no part – not a jot – in the Local Plan. Remove the formulaic references to 'Cornwall's special built and natural character' and the key principles of the Local Plan could be applied to any place anywhere. Like unthinking robots, we do things because everyone else does them. But by injecting ourselves with the magic ingredient of Cornishness we just might give ourselves both the confidence and the arguments for the special recognition - for example regional planning powers and a planning inspectorate for Cornwall - that will ultimately be required to escape the dead end of population-led growth.

The Latest Big (Daft) Idea

Local councillors in Cornwall have always been easy meat for the big idea – the simple policy that promises to provide all the answers. Big ideas have another advantage. They usually involve highly visible iconic outcomes. Here's the existential opportunity to imprint oneself on the landscape. Whatever else I might have done, that regeneration project, this supermarket, that airport, those houses, that road was my legacy. Look on my works, future generations, and tremble in awe. Or at least look at what my vote helped to build. Understandable perhaps but a costly exercise in personal hubris and self-aggrandisement in the long run.

Newquay airport is a prime example. This big idea revolved around the notion that any region worth its salt has to have its regional airport. This is then backed up by assiduously repeating the unproven claim that aviation boosts economies and is absolutely essential for businesses to grow and prosper. In that excruciating phrase being touted around these days by the neo-liberal zombies it signals that we're 'open for business'. The Liberal Democrat leadership on the previous County Council fell for this line of argument and began to spend public money on Newquay airport in 2007. No matter that half of the airport's business involved holiday trips and only a quarter business trips (*Newquay Cornwall Airport Draft Masterplan*, 2008, p.3.8). No matter that most of its flights were to destinations that could be reached with far less environmental cost and not that much more slowly by rail. No matter that the project blithely planned to increase carbon emissions from air travel in Cornwall by a phenomenal 356 per cent in just 25 years (see CoSERG, 2009, p.3). No matter that the airport acted to boost the market for second home sales (for example *Daily Telegraph*, 'Consider Property in Cornwall', 16 Mar 2012). No matter that effectively what the Council was doing was using public money to subsidise the better-off who are far more likely to use air travel. (For every one flight a person from social classes D/E (the poorest) make, someone in social class A makes ten (Bishop and Grayling, 2003, p.64)).

By the time the Lib Dems who had bought into this white elephant departed, £45 million of capital spending - taxpayers' money - had been poured into the County Council-owned airport. Cornwall County Council's medium term financial strategy at the time estimated its total cost as £56 million, while another £20 or £30 million of grants from the Regional Development Agency and the EU topped up the project. Since then the Council has gone on subsidising the airport by up to £4 million a year. Increasingly hysterical claims that it's 'crucial to the prosperity of Cornwall' (*West Briton*, 5 Nov 2009) began to wear a bit thin when the bankers' crisis hit. Passenger numbers plummeted faster than a gannet choking on a chip as the 431,000 passengers of 2008 turned into just 209,000 by 2011, dropping by 26 per cent in 2011 alone (*Western Morning News*, 23 May 2012). In 2010 Newquay airport, which we had been informed in all apparent seriousness in 2009 by the chairman of the Newquay Airport Board was essential for 'success in your economy', came 297th out of 300 European airports in terms of passenger growth. As we were also told it needed 950,000 passengers to break even things did not look that good.

However, as Newquay Airport got stuck on the runway before take-off, the surrounding rhetoric spiralled out of control. Its reliance on the generosity of the public purse wasn't enough to stop 'business and tourism leaders' comprehensively burying their collective heads in the sand by claiming that the economic benefits were 'massively encouraging'. Nor did it make Tim Jones, the lugubrious spokesperson for the Devonwall Business Council, think twice before concluding that 'the airport is Cornwall's greatest asset for income generation in the long run. It will be one of the biggest economic drivers in Cornwall' (*This is Cornwall*, 9 Feb 2011). (This was 'long run' as in the very long run presumably). Unfortunately for Tim, this turned out to be the typical hogwash as even the former South West RDA concluded that 'the relationship between high growth sectors in the region and air travel appears to be weak' (SWRDA, 2007).

After some initial hesitation when doubts within senior ranks of the Council temporarily surfaced (*This is Cornwall*, 5 Aug 2010), the Tory/Independent controlled Cornwall Council turned out to be just as attracted to the iconic big idea as was the Lib Dem County Council. Although increasing panic about the dismal prospects for the airport led to its rebranding as Newquay Aerospace Hub. Despite the probably more deserving claims of other areas the Cornwall and Isles of Scilly Local Enterprise Partnership was dragooned into supporting a bid to make the Newquay 'aerohub' an Enterprise Zone in 2011. The plan was to use the £2.5 million of extra funding this draws in from central government together with the laxer planning controls that accompany it to kick-start associated businesses which might just keep the airport afloat. In a typical example of the hyperbole that accompanies this project it was claimed the aerohub would bring 2,500 jobs (*West Briton*, 12 July 2012). And within three months Chris Ridgers, the then Cabinet portfolio holder for economy and regeneration, had magically inflated this figure to 5,000 jobs (*Western Morning News*, 3 Oct 2012). Growth in wages or household incomes may be hard to achieve but the growth industry of preposterous claims of job creation based on no discernable evidence was booming.

This last desperate throw of the dice illustrates perfectly how iconic big ideas get out of control. The logic of their momentum leads to good money following bad until they reach the point – as in the case of Newquay airport – where failed projects are allowed to distort strategic planning, let alone possess any visible relation to other policy aims. I'll give the last word on this to Betty Levene of Friends of the Earth – 'Planning to vastly expand air travel to and from Cornwall while claiming that we're aiming at a low carbon economy is a particularly absurd example of this sort of refusal to deal with reality'. Quite so.

Park and rides: redistributing car traffic

We see precisely the same reluctance to address reality in Cornwall Council's infatuation with its latest big idea – park and rides. In March 2012 Cornwall Council's strategic planning committee gave the green light to a project on the eastern edge of Truro at the junction of the A39 from Newquay and the A390 from St Austell. This involved the Duchy as landowner, the upmarket supermarket chain Waitrose (part of the John Lewis Partnership), and a consortium of local businesses and landowners, which included Cornwall's biggest old money landowner, the Tregothnan estate. Over 19 hectares of attractive grade 2 and 3 agricultural land sloping down towards Tresillian were to go. Hedgerows, a woodland copse, grass and gazing cows were overjoyed at the prospect of being regenerated into an up-market supermarket, a hundred or so houses in a twee retro-development (a mini-version of the Duchy's Poundbury urban extension at Dorchester) and a large car park described as a park and ride. It may of course be of no relevance at all that the planners describe the topography as 'both interesting and challenging, located at the head of a valley ... from within the site fantastic views of the valley and beyond to the clay country hills are to be found' (Strategic Planning Committee agenda 8 Mar 2012, item SP/274). The whole has been rather oddly christened the Truro Eastern District Centre. Odd because it's not the centre of anything but an eastwards extension of Truro. Or perhaps it's intended to be the centre of an as yet unannounced new district eventually joining Truro to Tresillian?

Granting of planning permission for this was not entirely unexpected. After all, the third key player in the application along with Waitrose and the Duchy was none other than Cornwall Council itself. More than a key player as it turned out that the Council had approached the Duchy asking to build on its land. And despite the Duke of Cornwall's concerns about 'fashionable obsessions' the Duchy promptly agreed. Far from providing a hands-off disinterested evaluation of building proposals Cornwall Council is now a key player in pushing forward such proposals, encouraging and cajoling developers and landowners to bring forward schemes to build on Cornwall's green fields. In this case the Council was the lead applicant in a planning application to be determined by ... itself!!

Maybe I'm old-fashioned but surely if this were to happen in a less 'developed' country it would rightly be deemed a potentially deeply corrupt arrangement that makes a mockery of democratic procedures, behaviour typical of a banana republic. But no. In a society where we're supposed to gape open-mouthed at the antics of feudal institutions such as the monarchy such strange proceedings are viewed as perfectly acceptable rather than a ludicrous charade. In the unlikely event of Cornwall Council's own committee turning down the application I assume Cornwall Council would have lodged an appeal against itself.

The centrepiece of the Truro eastern urban extension is the park and ride, carefully planned to complement the existing western Truro park and ride at Langarth. At first, the planners made great play about the promise that the eastern park and ride would 'ease traffic congestion', claiming it could remove 15 per cent of peak traffic in the morning. Even if we accept this somewhat miraculous outcome the real purpose of the park and ride is clear. The planners were beginning to harbour 'serious concerns' about the considerable traffic delays which they could see coming in a few years time on the eastern approaches to Truro (report to SP Committee SP/274 8 Mar 2012). The park and ride is a stopgap designed to increase Truro's capacity and keep the whole insane growth show on the road for a few more years.

We're back to the growth dilemma identified by Tim Jackson. Our economic system has to grow constantly (economists reckon that a capitalist society is 'healthy' with a three per cent annual growth rate) or it's in crisis. Similarly, in Cornwall population has to go on growing or we'll be in crisis, at least according to the planners. You might think the more obvious solution to traffic congestion would be to do everything possible to reduce traffic movements while seeking ways to stabilise and reverse the unsustainable growth of population that generates that traffic in the first place. But no. This logical answer is ruled out of contention by the rules of the game. In contrast, even more people have to be shoehorned into Truro to keep its shopping centre from collapsing into rack and ruin. So the only solution the former Carrick District Council could see, the one which Cornwall Council then enthusiastically adopted, was another park and ride.

There was just one small problem with this particular park and ride. While the traffic modellers were busily computing how much traffic the park and ride would remove from Truro's streets they seem to have overlooked the effect of placing a park and ride right next to a tempting new supermarket (not to mention a household waste recycling centre and another 100 houses). In their revised traffic estimates they were forced to concede that 'there is an increase in traffic due to the development'. But don't worry. 'Mitigation measures' would reduce their impact and in rather contradictory and confusing fashion the planners could still assert that 'increased traffic flows' were 'unlikely'.

Cornwall Council's innovative approach to park and rides might be to plonk housing and supermarkets right next to them, but this isn't the usual way urban planners have used park and rides to try to reduce traffic levels in cities across Britain. Research on eight such early park and rides published in 2000 found that in all eight cases the reduction in the number of vehicles travelling into the urban areas was more than offset by an increase in traffic outside the towns. According to the author, Graham Parkhurst, it turns out that park and rides hadn't reduced traffic flows overall at all. In fact, their effect was to increase them by about five per cent on average. He concluded that park and rides were 'better described as a policy of car traffic redistribution than a policy of car traffic reduction'. Cornwall Council's park and ride enthusiasts were either ignorant of this academic research or chose not to inform the councillors on their Strategic Planning committee of it, preferring to rely on reiterating the myth that this particular park and ride could not increase traffic.

Maybe the radical innovation of placing a supermarket right next to a 1,400 space car park (which we're told will 'have the appearance of a green field when not in use') will indeed make this park and ride different from all the others. Perhaps, unlike all the others, this one will magically reduce traffic. However, most people outside the Council's growth bunker might be prepared to bet the opposite will occur. If people were dozy enough to accept the advice of Tory Cabinet Ministers and queue at petrol stations to panic buy petrol thus producing the very shortage they wanted to avoid in the spring of 2012 then I'm sure they won't hesitate to drive miles to visit the only Waitrose supermarket west of Saltash (for the moment).

Even a cursory glance at the relatively sparse data provided in the Council's planning application to itself ought to make us a little bit more sceptical about its claims. For a start the planners boast that the western park and ride's success is proved by the 600,000 fewer car journeys into Truro since August 2008. That sounds a mighty impressive number. But their own Traffic Statistics tell us that average daily traffic flows into Truro from the west in 2009 were 27,600. Bear with me. The 600,000 claimed saved car journeys into Truro over two years equates to around 820 journeys each day. Eight hundred and twenty cars a day as a proportion of 27,600 means that traffic flows were reduced by three per cent. Meanwhile, the general growth of traffic on Cornwall's primary routes in 2009 had risen again after a hiccup in 2008 caused by the recession and regained its historic trend rate of 3 per cent growth a year. Thus, even if we accept these numbers then the savings from the western park and ride equalled just a year's traffic growth. So even on the Council's own figures the eastern park and ride might provide a mere 12 months respite from rising congestion levels in and around Truro given the growth agenda we're locked into. Which doesn't look like much of a reason for destroying a high value landscape. Not only for a year but for ever.

Yet the unlikely outcome of a reduction in congestion is probably not the real reason for Truro's eastern urban extension at all. For there's a growing trend to use other things – a park and ride to the east of Truro, a stadium to the west – to legitimate the accompanying housing and supermarket plans. Is it just coincidence that having a park and ride (or some other supposedly more desirable development) included nearby might make the suburban extension more acceptable to all and sundry? Are park and rides (or sports stadia come to that) an intrinsic, indeed necessary, part of the million-people plus project?

For whatever reason, park and rides are the flavour of the month at Cornwall plc. At the same Strategic Planning Committee meeting where the members voted eleven to eight to sacrifice the rather pleasant rural landscape east of Truro to the great god of consumerism they also voted for a park and ride at St Erth station. This will also have 'grass surfacing' which, with the retention of existing hedges would 'help retain a rural character'. But however much the 'rural character' is 'retained' there's no getting away from the fact that this is basically another big car park. Moreover, it's not exactly clear who will use this particular car park. Although that didn't stop the rather improbable claims that it would relieve pressure on the A30 and reduce congestion not only in St Ives but in Penzance, Camborne, Redruth and even Truro and St Austell! (*Cornishman*, 15 Mar 2012). Ominously, Graeme Hicks, Transport portfolio holder, hoped that the 'new transport interchange will be a trigger for future local investment'. 'Future local investment' in Cornwall almost inevitably translates into investment in housebuilding. Which reinforces the point that these developments play a critical role in the wider million-people plus agenda.

Despite widespread local opposition, councillors voted sixteen to five for the St Erth park and ride. Interestingly, a mere three of the 21 councillors who voted on both park and ride applications voted against both of them. In addition to these park and rides another is going ahead at

Fowey and there are plans in the pipeline for a third park and ride south of Truro, no doubt to be associated with another large scale housing project. Meanwhile, the Council has already given permission for a park and ride to be associated with the Sainsburys supermarket to be built on the site of Penzance heliport. Within half a mile of two existing supermarkets, Sainsburys forked out £2 million of Section 106 'community benefits' in order to obtain this permission (*Western Morning News*, 20 Oct 2011).

In their response to the public enquiry on the east-west distributor road at Camborne Cornwall Council claimed in June 2012 that 'the St Erth park and ride site ... will enable people from west Cornwall to access [Camborne-Redruth] by rail more easily'. So, rather than catching a train at Penzance, we're being asked to believe in all seriousness that people from Penzance and points west will drive to St Erth. Once there, they'll park their car, travel by train the rest of the way to Camborne (or Redruth) and then catch a bus to Pool, thus exchanging a fifteen minute car journey for one of up to an hour on public transport! The sheer idiocy of this claim can only be explained by the fact that Cornwall Council's 'rebuttal' at the enquiry seems to have been supplied courtesy of Parsons Brinckerhoff, a global consulting firm (turnover in 2010 £213 million, with profits of £12.6 million) who may not be fully cognizant of local geography.

The bigger picture: the dilemma of growth

In all this we mustn't lose sight of that bigger picture alluded to in Chapter 4. For the biggest big idea is that growth is good for us. Unfortunately, this then segues into the idea that it can be sustained indefinitely, at which point it becomes a big, daft idea. This big idea is itself sustained by various structural factors that work to convince us of the common sense of growth, just the medicine we need in fact. We all survive within an economic system which demands that we grow in order to attain stability. This presents us with a very stark choice indeed and one that decision-makers and opinion-formers are hardly immune from, although they tend to take it for granted. On the one hand we have growth. But on the other if we don't have growth we have collapse. There seems to be no middle way. If, in our frantic search for ever-growing material prosperity, we resemble mice running in never-ending circles in treadmills then so be it.

The alternative - collapse - is too ghastly to contemplate. This is why even the neo-liberal policies of deregulation and a redistribution of wealth away from the majority to a tiny minority of super-rich that paved the way for the economic crisis of 2008 are still with us. The world's policy makers quickly drifted back to the failed but familiar business-as-usual policies with austerity packages that effectively make the majority pay for the sins of the small minority. Our economy is truly too big to fail. If global policy-makers are unable or unwilling to contemplate an alternative to a system that feeds off incessant and endless growth then little wonder that our local elites are incapable of seeing beyond an ever-growing Cornwall.

In that sense they're hardly likely to listen to warnings of environmental or cultural disaster or worry about a million-people plus Cornwall, or give much heed to the arguments in this book or the campaigns of local objectors against plans to carve up the countryside for more suburban housing. The very idea of limits to growth is anathema to them. Those that put that argument forward must expect vitriolic attacks, often along the predictable 'nimby', 'naysayer' or 'standing in the way of progress' line. Or we'll be told, apparently in all seriousness, that 'if we don't build these houses/that supermarket/ this iconic transformative regeneration project we'll be taking Cornwall back to medieval times/the dark ages/the stone age'.

For the disciples of growth there can be no limits. The very idea is unthinkable. The only sustainability that really matters is the ability to sustain current levels of growth, indefinitely. Never asking what the end product of all this growth is, the means have become the end. Warnings about consequences such as the inevitable global warming have to be ignored in the process. Turn a blind eye to news that the Arctic ice shrank last year by a record amount (*Daily Mail*, 20 Sep 2012). Forget the warnings of mass species extinction on a scale not seen since the age of the dinosaurs (*Independent*, 11 Sep 2012). Such things can't be allowed to interrupt the accumulation that produces the over-heating. Indeed, we're told that they can only be solved by reinvigorated application of the very mechanism that's causing the problems in the first place – growth.

Which is why, even though half a century of population growth has hardly led us in Cornwall to an elysian paradise of plenty, we're informed that more of the same is just the tonic we need. Deaf to evidence of the past, blind to the limits of the future, the growth machine must roll on, crushing whatever might be in its path. To help it do so energy corporations pour millions of dollars into (highly successful) campaigns to undermine and confuse the scientific consensus on climate change. More indirectly, a massive media, marketing and PR industry marshals its resources to ensure that we continue to look at the world in a way that makes growth the only possible game in town. And if we aren't convinced by disinformation we can be distracted by the trivial, the shallow and the superficial. The promised land of growth economics has to be accompanied by the media circus of a celebrity culture. As long as we don't start to question the central contradictory insanity of our economic system then any cost is worth it.

But it doesn't end there. In Cornwall we are left with one final long-term factor locking us into never-ending population growth. This one is important enough to warrant its own chapter.

Chapter 8

Meet the new Cornwall: Same as the old Cornwall

If the state and the development lobby's pressure on local elites and the ideological power of the growth myth weren't enough we have a final factor unique to Cornwall. This operates to fuel the growth culture and twist it into a particular shape.

In 2011 an eight part TV series was produced extolling Cornwall and fronted by Caroline Quentin. This was aired in 2012 and triggered a rush of enquiries to estate agents and accommodation providers. According to the *West Briton* (15 Mar 2012), the holiday lettings company Unique Cornwall saw a thirty-fold jump in visits to its website while the phonelines to Miller Commercial didn't stop ringing. These programmes, where Quentin 'discovered' Cornwall (as have so many others over the past century), selected a particular image to project. According to the paper they concentrated on 'high end tourist destinations portraying the county [sic] as some sort of Knightsbridge on Sea'. It was a 'more middle class portrayal, promoting the county [sic] as a land of sun, sea and a rather nice glass of sparkling rosé'. Malcolm Bell, head of VisitCornwall, blandly stated 'that's not necessarily a bad thing ... Viewers watched people being happy, loving where they live, in a spectacularly beautiful place, living a highly environmental, high quality life'.

Strangely, despite all the management waffle about 'can-do cultures', 'robust financial strategies' and 'transformational change' in *Can Do Cornwall*, neither that text nor the Local Plan documentation make much of the decade-long project to move Cornwall up-market. Our coast is no longer ringed just by rocks and fat gulls but by restaurants and fat gourmets. Rock is now the destination of choice for every drunken public-school party-going dude. Property prices boom as luxury housing is marketed to the super rich and they bid up prices through asset speculation. Cornwall is now wired into the heart of London's financial services sector in a way that was unimaginable a few decades ago. It's rapidly becoming a bolthole for the rich. Cornwall Council, while not explicitly mentioning this, betrays no visible intention of resisting it. There appears to be a tacit acceptance that creating reservations for the rich along our coasts generally improves the tone of the place and is a welcome development, bringing lots of money to Cornwall which might just trickle down to the grateful peasants.

Despite its name, once we scratch the glitzy surface of this 'new Cornwall' project we find it's just new make-up slapped on the tired old floozy of tourism. We were breathlessly told that all those businesses in London who were frantically ringing Cornish estate agents after being duped by Caroline Quentin's 'lifestyle programmes' were eagerly seeking 'aspirational businesses' (as opposed presumably to unpromising or hopeless businesses). But the 'aspirational businesses' they were desperately seeking turn out to be those offering a 'lifestyle opportunity, typically galleries, small boutique hotels and niche environmentally friendly holiday parks' (*West Briton*, 15 Mar 2012). So, step away from the meaningless post-modernist verbiage and we have the same old tourism, red in tooth and claw although in reality looking a bit grey and grizzled these days. It's still feeding off hackneyed and trite representations of Cornwall as a more natural, slightly green lifestyle retreat and the antithesis of metropolitan angst. The 'new Cornwall' may try to sell sophisticated exclusivity but at its core this is no new Cornwall at all. It's one we've been very familiar with ever since the Newlyn School of painters imposed their vision of Cornwall on us way back in the 1880s.

What's tourism ever done for us?

So what exactly is the problem with tourism? Readers of a sensitive disposition may like to skip the next bit as it contains disturbing material.

In his blog in October 2010 Independent Councillor Andrew Wallis enthusiastically reported a meeting of the Council's Tourism Panel. Those present were apparently regaled by facts and figures showing how important tourism was. The only slight problem however was that the facts and figures didn't actually add up. It was claimed that tourism provided Cornwall with £1.5 billion a year and made up just over 20 per cent of Cornwall's economic product. Councillors were also told that tourism employed 21 per cent of the Cornish workforce. Suspicions should have been aroused by the rather amazing coincidence that these two figures – the proportion of GDP and the proportion of the workforce - were roughly identical. Because that would imply that tourism, with its higher proportion of low-paid, part-time jobs, nonetheless manages to be just as productive as the rest of the economy.

One area where achieving growth appears to be dead easy is that tourism statistics. For the purported importance of tourism to the Cornish economy is subject to dizzying levels of inflation. The '20%' reported by Cllr Wallis was within a week inflated to '25% of our GDP coming from tourism' by Simon Tregoning, managing director of Classic Cottages (*West Briton* 7 Oct 2010). By July 2012 Kim Conchie, CEO of the Cornwall Chamber of Commerce was heard on Radio Cornwall in a silly season piece on how rain is bad for tourism. Mr Conchie said 'as we know, 34% of Cornwall's GDP is tourist-related' (BBC Radio Cornwall 3 July 2012). Needless to say, the Radio Cornwall presenter let this pass without requesting the source for these interesting statistics. In fact, 'tourist-related' could mean anything. If I owned a bakery and one tourist came in to buy a pasty but my other thousand customers were all locals then I suppose the business might be 'tourist-related'. So why stop at 34%? Why not 50%. Or 80%? Or even 100%?

Something wasn't quite ringing true here. In fact, according to official labour market statistics, tourism-related jobs in Cornwall in 2008 made up 14.4 per cent of all employee jobs, not 21 per cent (Nomis official labour market statistics, at https://www.nomisweb.co.uk/). Even if those jobs were as productive as the rest (which stretches credibility well beyond its limits) this suggests a tourist sector income of somewhere around £1 billion rather than £1.5 billion. But what's gratuitous inflation by at least a half among friends? Furthermore, tourism is becoming less rather than more important to the Cornish economy. Back in 1995 14.8 per cent of paid jobs were found in tourism. True, the absolute number of tourism-related jobs has jumped by 32 per cent since then. But non-tourism jobs grew even faster – by 35 per cent. This stands in stark contrast to the rest of Britain, where tourist jobs grew by 28 per cent and all jobs by just 17 per cent.

There are alternatives to credulously swallowing the usual hype designed to assure us how tourism is vital to our very existence. We now have a more reliable calculation by the Office of National Statistics (2011) which measured the importance of tourism expenditure in regional economies. So how important is tourism to Cornwall? By the amount of attention it receives it must be at least 50 per cent surely. After all, everyone tells us that there's nothing else going on in Cornwall but tourism and without the tourist pound we'd all starve. But what a surprise! The ONS discovered that in fact spending by tourists contributes a mere 11 per cent to spending in Cornwall. Furthermore, the level of GVA attributable to tourism in Cornwall is 7 per cent, which is actually lower than its contribution in northern Scotland, North Yorkshire, outer London and Surrey & Sussex. So the next time some know-it-all tells you that we're dependent on tourism in Cornwall, remind them that the catering trade contributes around a tenth to the Cornish economy, and is less important here than in London and the Home Counties. Having said this obviously tourism remains an important part of the Cornish economy. But first let's get its role in proper perspective and second, let's then also consider the considerable short and long-term negative consequences of tourism.

Face the facts rather than believe the spin. Fortunately, the share of tourism in our economy is declining. I say 'fortunately' because of the disastrous knock-on effects of an economy over-dependent on tourism. In an all too brief flash of lucidity immediately following the award of EU Objective One funding to Cornwall a decade backalong, some of Cornwall's ruling clique belatedly recognised that tourism compromised their grand plans to boost the Cornish economy. They wanted to diversify. While not exactly spelt out, the corollary of this was plain. The role of tourism had to be reined back. This was a welcome although desperately delayed realisation.

Since the 1890s anyone who has cared to think about such matters has recognised that tourism is a blight. For instance, it condemns Cornwall to a low-wage economy. But tourism brings with it much, much worse consequences than poverty wages and seasonal unemployment. Not only does it tie us to an ailing economy vulnerable to changes in income and fashion in the centre and politico-economic events on the Continent but more crucially it reinforces external representations of Cornwall as just a place to holiday in, not somewhere to be taken at all seriously. In the longer run it encourages past holidaymakers to become present residents (either permanent or temporary) and plays a – perhaps *the* – key role in encouraging and maintaining high levels of in-migration. Tourism locks us into a dire demographic regime of excessive and unsustainable population growth which is fundamentally reshaping Cornwall's culture and thoughtlessly tearing up our familiar landscapes.

Facts about the precise role of tourism in our economy are ultimately irrelevant as tourism thrives on myth and mystery. Unfortunately, the tourist lobby survived the scare it got when that flash of rationality momentarily illuminated decision-makers at the end of the 1990s. It had burrowed too deeply into the fabric of local governance to be so easily exorcised. Lobbyists such as VisitCornwall survived. And indeed prospered. Cornwall Council pays VisitCornwall via its Cornwall Development Company up to £4.5 million a year (the exact amount is for some reason difficult to find in the Council's budget), to hype up Cornwall's tourist sector. What happens is that VisitCornwall or its big brother Visit Britain pays some consultant to come up with back of the fag packet conclusions about the importance of tourism based on wishful thinking and guesswork. This is then churned out to the public by an uncritical local media. Meanwhile VisitCornwall and the Council have been busy rebranding tourism to appeal to a more up-market 'quality' clientele, which explains their enthusiastic endorsement of life-style media blitzing.

But tourism is an insidious serpent slithering into the Cornish body politic. Or, if you prefer another metaphor, a leech fastened onto our institutions, sucking the life blood from them, corrupting and distorting policies and encouraging colossally wasteful policy follies.

For example, questions might have been asked about the make-up of the new Local Enterprise Partnership (LEP), established in 2011. Given its share of the economy, one would have expected the tourism lobby to have had one seat on the eleven member LEP board. Instead two are directly involved with tourism and another couple have close links. Several of the rest clearly share traditional tourism-generated myths about Cornwall. Gaynor Coley is the Managing Director of the Eden Project tourist theme park and Tim Smit's partner (*Western Morning News*, 7 Mar 2013), while Simon Tregoning runs Classic Cottages, marketing 700 holiday cottages. He also chairs the Partnership Board to VisitCornwall and various lobbying groups such as the Cornwall Commercial Tourism Federation and the Cornwall Association of Holiday House Agencies. Then we have the Leader of Cornwall Council, which funds VisitCornwall. This was formerly Alec Robertson, with a background in the 'hospitality' trade. Not to mention Robin Teverson. This Liberal Democrat peer and Cornwall Councillor was chairman of Wessex Investors and Hotel Operators, a Plymouth based group of property developers which is involved in housebuilding projects at Launceston and Liskeard. He was also previously adviser to the group with a substantial interest in 'The Beach', the massive second home development at Carlyon Bay.

Caving in to the tourist lobby: the case of Crinnis beach

London-based property developers the Commercial Estates group plan to build 511 second homes on Crinnis and neighbouring beaches. Well, they've been planning it for yonks now but still not actually building yet as the project remains on hold 'until markets improve'. Meanwhile, the site remains a desolate place of decrepit buildings, high security fencing and rusting hulks of metal (*Western Morning News*, 11 Mar 2013). Commercial

Estates had its outline planning permission finally confirmed in the summer of 2011 after many years of hot disputation going back to 1990. At that time, the former Restormel Borough Council, renowned for granting planning permission at the drop of a hat to the first developer who happened along with a wad of cash, gave permission for 511 luxury tourist apartments to be built on two of the three beaches at Carlyon Bay. Nothing much then happened for several years. Until a bunch called Ampersand, trading as 'The Beach', bought the derelict Coliseum, Cornwall's rock music venue of choice in the 1970s and 1980s, along with 50 acres of land behind the beaches.

They then stuck in a planning application for apartments costing from £400,000 to over £800,000 each. These were going to rear up behind the beach and came with leisure and retail space. All this was to be fronted by a sea wall to protect it from rising sea levels. This rise is of course exacerbated by people doing things such as driving their four by fours to their luxury apartments in places like this or nipping onto the next convenient plane from London to Newquay for a weekend break. According to the *Independent* (22 June 2007), this interest coincided with the 'tourist tide' created by the Eden project, another example of the insidious knock-on effect of that particular theme park. The same newspaper reported that Ampersand had spent a reputed £100,000 buying window and sales space in Selfridges in Oxford Street to publicise their plans for expensive boltholes in Cornwall to their likely market.

The company began the beach works at Carlyon Bay preparatory to building in 2002/03. But there was one small problem. They hadn't actually got detailed planning permission first. Developer Johny Sandelson was unperturbed. 'I don't think it is likely or credible that consent will be rejected', he confidently stated, while dismissing growing local opposition as 'a minor irritant' (*Evening Standard*, 13 May 2008). His arrogance was well founded as Ampersand was working hand in glove with Restormel Council planners. Unfortunately for Sandelson, who left Ampersand at the end of 2003, the plans were called in and Ampersand withdrew its application in 2004. The Government, in the face of a well organised local protest campaign, called a Public Inquiry which dragged on until 2006 when permission for the beach works was refused on grounds of sustainability, transport and coastal planning. Ampersand was given a generous four years in which to restore the damage they had caused to the beach and reopen public access. In the meantime even the toothless Advertising Standards Authority found Ampersand in breach of its advertising code. In May 2004 they upheld two of the five complaints made by the Cornwall Wildlife Trust about Ampersand's ludicrous claims that no natural habitats would be lost.

Having stalled for three years and refused to put right the havoc they'd wreaked on the local environment, it transpired in 2009 that Ampersand had quietly re-opened negotiations with Cornwall Council planners, perhaps even with the same ex-Restormel planners who had loyally supported them throughout the Public Inquiry. A planning agreement was reached on 2nd June 2009, conveniently a few days before the unitary elections. This put forward another proposal. It was, they trumpeted, a 'new approach'. This must have been a previously unknown way of defining 'new' as the scheme still involved building 511 luxury units though this time some of them could be residential rather than holiday homes. Ampersand made much of the brownfield site of the old Coliseum but up to 30 per cent of the building was to be on land outside this area, including Polgaver Beach, which was not part of the original application.

Ampersand was in fact a front body for Commercial Estates Group, a privately owned property investment company with offices in Harrogate, London and Cornwall. This company, founded in 1989, in 2010 had a portfolio of 89 properties, including 'The Beach', with a total capital value of £547 million. Its chairman was Gerard Versteegh, a Swedish property magnate worth around £200 million and ranking 377th in the *Times* Rich List of 2008. In 2007 Versteegh owned a small £20 million home in Kensington.

Local campaigners viewed the company's strategy as one of wrecking the beach and leaving the site a complete shambles. That done, local voices would start squealing about the need to clean it all up, for example by a nice, tidy luxury housing development. Voices such as those of Malcolm Bell, at the time head of South West Tourism. Bell was 'bemused by the objections' in 2007, asserting that 'a new development must be better than the brownfield site currently blotting the landscape'. He was not alone. The *Western Morning News* threw its weight behind the development in 2007. 'Cornwall needs a classy plan like this' they bleated, unfazed by the utter lack of evidence for their statement.

Given its record of deliberately encouraging the sale of Cornish assets and support for unsustainable population growth, Cornwall Council's decision in 2011 to allow this 'development' came as little surprise. It justified it by its 'economic benefits' and by the fact that outline planning permission had originally been given 20 years earlier, albeit by the deeply compromised former planning authority at Restormel. Predictably, if rather tiresomely, building 511 residential units entirely aimed at an upcountry and upmarket demographic was defined in the brave new old world of Cornwall Council as 'forward thinking and sustainable'. Even more predictably, its developers describe it as 'bold and transformational'. They 'want to be part of Cornwall's bright future' but, rather more ominously, also want 'Cornwall to be part of us' (at www.carlyonbeach.com). As we tremble at the thought of that, note that the planning application was accompanied by the rather startling claim that these 511 units plus the associated works will have a 'human scale'. This is the latest buzz-phrase building proposals now include. (What were they before? Inhuman?) Moreover, in a familiar sleight of hand worthy of the inner sanctum of the Magic Circle, the parking for 840 more cars will actually generate a 15 per cent reduction in carbon emissions. The planners in 2011 claimed this tourist-focused venture would also have a moderate or major 'beneficial effect' on local tourism. Hold on though. Wasn't this the 'strategic' planning committee? And didn't the strategy that accompanied Objective One funding recognise Cornwall's over-dependence on tourism as one of its fundamental problems. So is it no longer a problem?

A chorus of local businesses had been tempted by the idea that catering for the luxury tourist and second-home market by effectively urbanising a beach would help 'regenerate' St Austell. St Austell Brewery boss and chair of St Austell Business Economic Forum James Staughton was one. Local Lib Dem MP Steve Gilbert, who had sat on the fence on the scheme during the 2010 general election, was another and wrote to the Council in support of the vested interests favouring 'The Beach' (*Cornish Guardian*, 29 Jun 2011). At least local businesses have the excuse of a vested interest. And Lib Dem politicians are hardly the most consistent folk in the world. The problem the Council's Strategic Planning Committee faced was that their officers informed them that legally planning permission for 'The Beach' already existed so they had little choice but to nod it through in 2011. Some were more enthusiastic than others however.

One councillor warned at the time that opponents to plans like this can 'lead to an in [sic] balance of the true public feeling' (Cllr Wallis's blog, at http://www.cllrandrewwallis.co.uk/2011/07/carlyon-bay-has-future.html). So they should be ignored? What a quaintly old-fashioned view of the planning process. Rational and disinterested councillors make decisions in the public good, clinically determining the 'truth' of public feeling after listening to the cut and thrust of reasoned argument from developers and the public. The problem with this rosy vision is what's left out. Where are the cynical developers with their financial resources, the mercenary consultants, the Council's own planning department? These agents work assiduously behind the scenes to promote the degeneration of Cornwall and protect their own jobs and profits. But they're lost to sight, hidden from the public gaze, conveniently airbrushed out of the picture, innocent and invisible as the juggernaut of hyper-development rolls on over our land.

The Olympic spirit: captured and canned by the tourist lobby
If we want to pursue the inescapable influence of the ever-present tourist lobby further we might turn to the route of the Olympic torch relay that was not actually a relay in 2012. This quasi-militarised exercise in

corporate sponsorship and mass distraction was designed, so we were assured, to bring the torch to 95 per cent of a breathlessly expectant population. Strange then that in Cornwall it took the utmost care to avoid our largest urban conglomeration completely, steering well to the south of Camborne-Redruth. George Eustice, Tory MP for that benighted area and down-to-earth farmer or wily PR operator depending on the phases of the moon, was not at all pleased. Personally, I'd have thought that this was an occasion for wild rejoicing on the part of the inhabitants of Camborne-Redruth, spared the awful embarrassment of being herded out to gawp at a flaming torch. But for George it was a 'cock-up'. He asked 'what on earth were the organisers thinking'? (*West Briton*, 24 May 2012).

Well, what were they thinking? The London 2012 Organising Committee (LOCOG) claimed in the local press (*West Briton*, 10 Nov 2011) that the route was decided 'using local expertise'. But who were those anonymous experts who told them to bypass Camborne-Redruth and veer instead through as many touristy places as possible? Visit the Committee's website and we discover that the route was decided after a series of workshops involving 'local authorities … plus representatives from tourism, heritage, sustainability, culture, education and sport.' These workshops were organised on the basis of the 'regions and nations' of the UK. So, as the Cornish nation has to be ignored on the orders of Nick Clegg, did 'local expertise' reside at a regional level?

It appears not, as we find out that there were County [sic] Working Groups and a 'Team Cornwall' that was focused on 'engaging the county [sic] in the world's greatest sporting and cultural festival'. We're told Team Cornwall was a 'multi-skilled' partnership involving:

- Cornwall Sports Partnership (which includes agencies of Cornwall Council)
- School Sports Partnerships (with a heavy involvement to the education authority which is of course Cornwall Council)
- Cornwall Museums
- VisitCornwall (funded by Cornwall Council)
- Cornwall Council Leisure (part of Cornwall Council)

- Cornwall Council Economic Development (also part of Cornwall Council)

This body was therefore heavily connected with Cornwall Council, which directly runs three of the six partners and indirectly has a major say in two of the others. Sure enough, the County [sic] Working Group was chaired by Adam Paynter, Lib Dem Cornwall Councillor for Launceston North. And it was serviced by Cornwall Council, which provided its secretary. However, despite being funded by public money, there were no publicly accessible minutes of its proceedings. In the absence of transparency or evidence to the contrary, we can only assume therefore that the 'local expertise' involved in advising on the choice of route lay not a million miles from Truro. Which is presumably why Council Leader Alec Robertson was distinctly unsympathetic to the whinges from Camborne-Redruth's MP. He said

> While we appreciate that some communities may be disappointed that LOCOG has not chosen their particular town or village as part of the official route, this does not mean they won't be able to join in the party, as the aim is for those areas to host the Olympic Torch Relay on behalf of their surrounding communities (*West Briton*, 10 Nov 2011).

To find the identity of those who ignored Camborne-Redruth, once Cornwall's 'central' district but now apparently just a community 'surrounding' Helston, Falmouth or Truro, George Eustice might therefore have profitably looked no further than Lys Kernow. For the 'local experts' turned out to be Cornwall Council, heavily involved in advising and supporting a route designed solely to boost Cornwall's ailing tourist industry.

Of toilets and taxes

In southern Europe humiliated politicians are prised from office. In Cornwall politicians squabble over who pays for public toilets. In 2011 Cornwall Council first proposed cutting half of them. Toilets that is rather than politicians (although see next chapter). They then partly backtracked in the face of public concerns. At first glance it looks as if the two issues – panic in the eurozone and closing toilets in Cornwall – are unconnected. But they are connected. They're both facets of the same phenomenon – the attack on the living standards and civilised conditions of the many to protect the wealth of the few.

Whether from millionaire Tories or Lib Dems in the UK, well-heeled 'social democrats' in Greece, or sophisticated French figureheads at the IMF, the message for the rest of us is identical. Work harder. And longer. For less pay. And we'll make sure you do by slicing your pensions to poverty levels. And while we're at it we'll slash the infrastructure of the welfare state. It's full speed to barbarism so the toilets – not much chance of an honest profit there – have to go. Whatever you do don't mention the fact that the so-called debt crisis could be solved almost overnight by taxing the rich. We mustn't touch the ***£4.5 trillion*** the top 10 per cent own. For they're our wealth creators – the geese who lay the golden eggs. And in any case we – the political class – are all in it together with them. So let's divert your attention with large helpings of nationalism, Olympics and the royals, and squabbles over toilets.

But where are the ringing denunciations from our local politicians of the threadbare 'austerity programme' or the attack on the poor designed to stiffen up labour discipline? Where are the innovative local solutions that might pay for the toilets? For example, now is surely the time to revisit the excellent proposal for a locally set tourist tax. In June 2011 it was left to Cornwall Council's corporate director for planning Tom Flanagan to raise the possibility of a £1 a night tourist tax. (In an amazing coincidence Flanagan surprisingly took voluntary redundancy from his £135,000 post just months afterwards (*West Briton*, 23 Dec 2011)). Yet this eminently sensible idea was soundly pilloried in the local press. It was hardly a surprise that the tourist lobby hysterically condemned it. But so did Tory and Lib Dem councillors. Yet in Brittany tourist taxes - levied by communes (equivalent to our parish level) – are commonplace and vary from €0.50 to €2 a night per person. According to VisitCornwall tourists spent 23 million nights in Cornwall in 2008. So a modest 50p a night tourist tax could generate at least £10 million.

This would be enough to pay for the shortfall in Cornwall Council's toilets budget six or seven times over. Or pay five years of the bus subsidy that council leaders are cutting. Or, to put it into terms they're more likely to understand, it's equal to three years of money thrown down the toilet at Newquay airport. It only seems fair that tourists should pay towards the facilities that they use. This would have the added advantage in the medium term of reducing our dependence on tourism and in the long term contribute in small measure towards helping to reduce in-migration. It looks like a no-brainer. So why was no councillor brave enough to champion it?

Land of myth and misinformation

Tourism thrives on contrasts as well as myths. The lazy, leisurely periphery in contrast to the workaday, busy core. Work time is replaced by 'free' time. The world is turned upside-down for a fortnight or a long weekend. A carnivalesque atmosphere of unrestrained libido takes over from suburban man and woman. The mundane morphs into the mysterious. And what do the hordes of happy holidaymakers find when they arrive? Traffic jams. Just like home. Which gets tourism bosses indulging in an annual silly season of whining and whinging.

Tim Jones, Devonwall business spokesperson, lamented in the summer of 2010 how 'the delays are affecting how tourists, in particular, perceive the Westcountry. It is a poor way to greet people arriving in the peninsula. There were reports at the weekend that it took some people eight hours to get from London to Devon'. Head of *VisitCornwall*, Malcolm Bell, chipped in: 'Because of the lack of resources, we are not going to be able to build our way out of the problem although we might be able to improve key pinch points. As the adage says, necessity is the mother of invention and innovation' (*This is Cornwall*, 19 Aug 2010) And what innovation did they call for? For the government to set up an 'emergency committee' to 'tackle gridlock'.

Pardon me, gents, but isn't the underlying problem crystal clear to all but business and tourism leaders? A combination of rapid population growth and the fantasy of ever-increasing tourist numbers in a finite space inevitably leads to …. well, congestion.

The possible answers to this dilemma are not that puzzling. The first is to build a lot more roads. This isn't on the agenda, outside relatively short stretches of new road at Camborne, Newquay and Bodmin and dualling short bits of the A30, the aim of which is to enable even more houses to be built and a lot more in-migrants and second home owners to be accommodated. But major new dual carriageways are not the current policy answer. Not because they only encourage our suicidal rush to species extinction. Nor because it will speed up the process of transforming Cornwall into a replica of everywhere else and therefore fundamentally undermine the basis for the whole tourist industry. It's because the government doesn't have the spare cash at present. That leaves us with the other option which must surely be to limit tourist or in-migrant numbers. Or both. But as any hint of policies that might work towards reducing tourism or in-migration causes the brain cells of the business and tourism class to start shorting out, that answer is not allowed to be defined as 'practical' politics.

It's tricky therefore to see exactly what an 'emergency committee' could achieve, apart from tinkering with those 'pinch points'. So tourist policy is doomed to match the requirements of the economy for an ever-expanding market, even if this ultimately destroys what's being sold. So cram them all in. Add to the overcrowded hell that Cornwall has become. Meanwhile, we residents will remain out of sight and out of mind, cowering indoors. There's no worry that our moaning away at the chaos of modernity will disturb the peace of the sparkling necklaces of aluminium, rubber and steel draped across our landscape. Come on in and join the fun. Enjoy the jams. The place is lovely. Or was once.

This is not the only time when some of our opinion-formers give the distinct impression of having lost their marbles. When disinformation fails, the tourist lobby is disturbingly prone to resort to hysteria. A good example took place in 2012 when government-induced petrol panic buying threatened to ruin the Easter tripper trade. Tourism bosses in Cornwall called for 'the Government to send in troops to quell widespread fuel panic' (*Western Morning News*, 31 Mar 2012). Curiously, the panic buying was described as 'hysteria' but the over the top call for the army to step in was seen as perfectly reasonable.

Loving Cornwall to death: the prison of external stereotypes

We have to look beyond Cornwall for the reason the slightly off-the-wall nuttiness of our tourism lobby is taken with all due seriousness by the media and other 'opinion-formers' in Cornwall. Local myths are fed by wider stereotypes that are deeply ingrained in English society. These are the stereotypes I identified in Chapter 4 – of Cornwall as a 'purer, more natural and faintly green sort of place, an antidote to metropolitan civilisation, a place to escape the hustle and bustle, stress and pollution of urban life'. The high in-migration rates of the past half century have now inevitably given those stereotypes wide currency even in Cornwall itself, especially among a mobile and transient 'project class' that is keen on imposing suburbanisation on us disguised as regeneration.

For an example of the stereotypes in action let's take the Mor Cliff development near Chapel Porth at St Agnes. This is by no means the worst sort of building in Cornwall, involving seven 'eco-friendly' holiday homes built to high specifications. But note the colour supplement lifestyle magazine language used to market them to prospective buyers (http://morcliff.co.uk/). Pictures of deserted beaches and countryside are accompanied by the headings 'fantastic views', or 'inspired by the elements'. We are reminded (several times) of the 'deep blue ocean, rugged coastline and wild green countryside' which 'perfectly combine to create a setting of tranquillity and relaxation'.

The message is come to Cornwall to relax in 'an inspirational setting', in an area of outstanding natural beauty (which makes one wonder how the development ever got planning permission in the first place). Although this area of outstanding natural beauty will soon have an additional seven parking spaces and related number of vehicle trips up and down the narrow local lanes. Here, you'll 'find your space' amidst 'ever changing scenery' in a 'traditional Cornish location'. The holiday homes are located next to St Agnes, 'a charming little town full of Cornish character, lively, welcoming and community-spirited', although increasingly blighted by up-market second homes. Further afield are the 'Cathedral City of Truro' and of course the conveniently situated Newquay/Cornwall Airport. Also mentioned are Tate St Ives and the Eden Project, those other quintessential elements of 'new Cornwall' marketing. And if you get jaded by all that then Cornwall is 'a food lovers' paradise'. Finally, under the tag 'Cornwall [sic] activities', just in case we've forgotten we're again reminded of the 'magnificent sandy beaches, wild green countryside, huge craggy cliffs'. All in all, Cornwall is 'one big, beautiful playground' for anyone who can afford the £265,000 to £450,000 needed to buy one of these holiday homes.

The company behind this - Bromley Estates Ltd - is rather coy about itself. Could it be the same Bromley Estates who are property developers based in Shropshire? Their agents are Pure Cornwall, a company marketing luxury holiday cottages and self-proclaimed 'experts in Cornwall [sic] property sales throughout the county [sic] of Cornwall'. Unfortunately, Pure Cornwall, based at Truro, was unable to use its expertise to advise Bromley Estates to revise the odd choice of name for its development - Mor Cliff - half Cornish, half English. What's wrong with Als an Mor (or Sea Cliff come to that)? But this is hardly surprising from developers who either warp Cornish placenames into meaningless gibberish, get the grammar bizarrely wrong (for example the toe-curling

Lowen Bre at Truro) or replace them with foreign names such as Acorn View or Meadow Lakes.

Purveyors of the 'new Cornwall' also seem constitutionally unable to escape the assumption that Cornwall's future lies in accommodating a never-ending flow of in-migrants. An example cropped up in journalist Robert McCrum's sneering piece rubbishing the 'separatists' of MK (*Observer*, 24 Jun 2012). McCrum wrote about the 'golden triangle of Padstow, Rock and Polzeath which is linked to the global economy, drips with superfast broadband and positively gleams as it enthusiastically throws itself into the growth of English domestic tourism'. Resorting to the typical device of doubling the importance of the latter in the Cornish economy – never let a few facts disturb some comfortable stereotypes – McCrum interviewed a hotelier who stated 'we should be selling the idea that, down here [sic], you can do a day's work and still have an hour's surfing before it gets dark, the quality of life we have to offer is extraordinary'. Offer to those yet to live 'down here', that is. Thank heavens for this dynamic new thinking.

However, the same stereotypes cast their shadow much further than the holiday cottage trade. For an example of how far they dominate the cultural space take the BBC's Election 2010 site. This website contained a series of constituency profiles. But when it came to Cornwall it soon became very plain that the BBC couldn't cope with empirical facts and had to replace them with crude stereotypes.

Two myths in particular permeated the six Cornish constituency profiles. The first was the myth of tourism. In five of the six constituencies tourism was picked out for special mention. In St Ives, the short 250 word profile still found space to swoon over the 'cultural history,' mild climate', 'wide sandy beaches' and 'beautiful landscape' which 'generates millions of pounds for the tourist industry'. The artistic community and Tate St Ives 'draw in thousands more visitors per year'. But what are the facts? In Penwith, according to the NOMIS website, tourist-related employment amounts to 21 per cent. But the biggest employment sector is not tourism at all but public administration, education and health, with 28 per cent. But this was rendered invisible. The only non-tourist occupation that got a mention was the 'thriving construction industry'. Which is suitably mysterious as it's not particularly thriving in Penwith and employs fewer people there than in the rest of Cornwall.

This unhealthy fixation on tourism was then churned out across the other constituencies. In Truro and Falmouth, where the main points of interest for the blinkered BBC were the 'cathedral city of Truro, idyllic Roseland peninsula and the historic packet ship port of Falmouth', we were sagely informed that the 'main industry is now tourism' and that distribution, hotels and restaurants account for 40 per cent of employment. This was wrong on both counts. First, distribution includes a lot more than tourism and to suggest that the latter equates to the former was disingenuous in the extreme. In fact in Carrick the total employed in tourist-related jobs is just 10.5 per cent, not that much higher than the British average of 8.2 per cent. Second, the proportion employed in distribution, hotels and restaurants is actually 27 per cent, rather than the BBC-inflated 40 per cent. Again the main employer by far in this constituency is the public sector. But the BBC preferred made-up statistics to informing us of real facts such as the higher than average number of part-time jobs in Cornwall or the proportion of second homes, neither of which were deemed worthy of mention.

In the St Austell and Newquay constituency the residents of St Austell were bemused to read that it is dominated by the 'big tourist towns of St Austell *and* Newquay'. Here again, the BBC falsely asserted that 'tourism is the biggest industry', noting the Eden Project and surfing. Factually extremely challenged, it then made a rare foray out of tourism to tell us that the clay industry was booming and employing 3,000 people at St Austell, 'Cornwall's largest town'. Sorry, wrong again. On all points.

North Cornwall was of course 'particularly famous for tourism' while South East Cornwall had a 'thriving tourist industry'. Yes, tourism is more important as an employer in east Cornwall. But the BBC's tedious obsession with tourism didn't allow them to tell us that it actually accounts for 14.2 per cent and 13.4 per cent of employees in North and South East

Cornwall respectively, about one in seven. Even here, public sector jobs are far more important.

We all know – well, at least the BBC does – that where there's tourism there's retired folk. South East Cornwall, we read, has a 'high proportion of retired people'. Furthermore, in Cornwall generally there's a 'quarter more retired people than the national average'. Sounds huge. But don't worry about pavements thronged with mobility scooters. The actual contrast is less striking. In England and Wales the proportion of people over 65 amounts to 16 per cent of the population. In Cornwall, it's 20 per cent. In Caradon it's actually a little lower – at 19 per cent.

The second hoary myth the BBC wheeled out in its constituency profiles was rurality. This blinded it completely to one of the fastest population growth and loss of countryside in the UK. It goes without saying that these failed to get a mention. Instead, we read that in Camborne and Redruth of all places 'there is a great deal of rural land ... much of it uninhabited'. Planned housing growth of more than a third over less than 20 years? Don't worry citizens; you're living in an uninhabited desert. The bizarre absurdity of this was then later demonstrated in the same profile which unblushingly went on to say that the constituency has 'one of the highest [population density rates] in the South West'! This constituency profile staggered on to tell us that much of Cornwall's poverty is concentrated here. Which I guess explains why Camborne and Redruth is exceptional by being spared the lazy reference to the importance of tourism. In reality, the most deprived wards in Cornwall are found at Penzance. But silly me; I forget. That's slap bang in the middle of a tourist arcadia of cultural history and beautiful landscape so poverty mustn't be allowed to intrude on that particular dream world.

In St Austell and Newquay the 'big tourist towns' on the two coasts are separated by a 'huge rural expanse' in between. This purveyed the strong impression of an under-populated empty wilderness. Not a hint of the population growth suffered by the clay country villages in the last twenty years (the highest in Cornwall). These were conveniently airbrushed out to ensure the area stays ripe for colonisation. (Perfect for eco-communities in fact). In South East Cornwall we were informed that 'most of the population live in small villages and former fishing ports'. In the real South East Cornwall 40 per cent live in the three dormitory towns of Liskeard, Saltash and Torpoint. Another 20 per cent who live in Callington, Calstock and Looe might also be surprised to learn they're actually living in 'small villages'.

The level of research that went into these profiles could be bettered by a seven year old doing their first school project. It's illustrated by a sentence in the Camborne and Redruth profile: 'Camborne School of Mines is still a centre of excellence in its field'. This may be a bit of an enigma for those trying to hunt down this centre of excellence which in fact was relocated to the neighbouring Truro and Falmouth constituency some five years previously. Meanwhile, in Truro and Falmouth the BBC was puzzled by Truro's popularity as the 'number one destination for retail and leisure'. This was 'unusual' as it's not the biggest settlement in Cornwall. Only unusual that is if your idea of 'usual' is an English shire county.

This nonsense would be farcical if it weren't so serious. These dominant English stereotypes of Cornwall represent the place as some sort of underpopulated playground. Tourism is the only 'industry' they can see. Cornwall must be a deserted rural arcadia because it's not urban. Indeed, it's the opposite of urban life. In tourist playgrounds nothing much of consequence happens. The people who inhabit them have no history. They possess no politics. Political issues melt into air, scattered by the miasma of cringe-inducing nonsense that the BBC endlessly exudes. Information dissipates and all semblance of truth dissolves, replaced by an unreal cartoon Cornwall of happy tourists, contented retirees and invisible and uncomplaining natives.

As Cornwall in late July and August reached saturation point many years ago the aim is now to extend the tourism season all year round. Not content with forcing hordes of visitors on us for a few months every summer the plan is to extend this delight into other seasons, making the chances of finding genuine peace and isolation in Cornwall increasingly impossible. In 2005 tourists spent 25 million nights in Cornwall (SW

Tourism, 2005). This implies that on any average day there was an extra 68,493 more people in Cornwall on top of the actual resident population. Therefore, the population of Cornwall - 532,000 according to the 2011 Census - is in reality more like 600,000. Using the seasonal breakdown of occupancy rates (SW Research Company, 2010) I calculate this means the actual population fluctuates from around 560,000 in November-January to 650,000 in August. Which means we shall hit a million by 2100.

Let's sum up. The message should be pretty clear by now. The tourist industry reproduces a particular image of Cornwall as a playground for the English middle classes. It uses this imagery to encourage people to holiday in Cornwall. Holiday experiences then create the desire to live in Cornwall either part-time or full-time and increase the likelihood of moving to Cornwall or purchasing a second home here. It's hardly a coincidence that the onset of a mass catering industry in the 1950s was followed within ten years by population turnaround and the beginnings of mass in-migration. However, far from recognising its role in stoking up growth pressures, policy-makers have taken the deliberate political decision to exacerbate the problem of tourism by subsidising this sector. Because of the power of prevailing stereotypes in the media and elsewhere a vociferous tourist lobby is able to exaggerate its role and distort strategic planning in Cornwall.

To give some credit where it's due though, some of Cornwall's ruling elite did belatedly become aware that a continuing reliance on tourism is hardly the brightest of bright ideas. Directing EU grants towards higher education was one example of this, although even this aspect has still been overly influenced by traditional representations (and external institutional agendas – witness the University of Exeter's assumption that Cornwall is the best place to site its 'Environmental Sustainability Institute'). But the emphasis is on finding additions to tourism rather than replacing it and there is little explicit recognition of tourism's insidious role in reproducing unsustainable population growth. The cultural inability to escape dominant myths lies at the heart of this failure of policy. Unfortunately, over-dependence on tourism reproduces a colonised outlook in Cornwall. Our decision-makers are psychologically structured by habits of thinking about Cornwall that prevent them demanding either a properly fair deal or equal treatment with the other nations of these islands. And many, though by no means all, of the type of migrant attracted to the idea of living in a tourist arcadia appear to be particularly ill-equipped to challenge stereotypes.

From second (and third, and fourth, and ...) home owners to temporary residents

This is best illustrated by the ongoing second homes scandal. Second homes are a critical link between coming to Cornwall on holiday and becoming a permanent Cornish resident. They act to encourage a certain type of in-migrant and they feed off the up-market tourist sector. Yet until very recently the Council had to give a council tax discount – the minimum being 10 per cent – to second home owners. Even the *Western Morning News* thought this was 'indefensible' (2 May 2012) and the Local Government Finance Bill gave local authorities the chance to scrap it entirely, although not to add a surcharge. Scrapping it saves Cornwall Council around £2 million a year (*Western Morning News*, 23 May 2012). Unfortunately, a knock-on effect will be that the number of second homes will become more difficult to discover. It would be hoped therefore that the Council will take immediate advantage of this and not stop there but begin to demand much more forcefully to be given the right to levy a council tax surcharge on second homes. Of course, given present policy, it's more than likely that any extra income would just be ploughed into further housing projects, thus exacerbating the problems highlighted here.

But Cornwall Council has been a little ambiguous on the issue of second homes so far, committed as it is to a new Cornwall project that – wittingly or unwittingly – is bent on transforming the social characteristics of in-migrants, skewing them more blatantly towards the higher social groups. Make no mistake about it. Neither Cornwall Council nor its County Council predecessor tacitly condone this change; they positively welcome it. For example, they had no problem allowing companies selling second homes to advertise at the Council-owned airport in 2008.

In its Local Plan too, Cornwall Council strangely makes little fuss about the requirement to build sufficient houses to cater not just for in-migrants but for the growth in the second home market. Council tax figures suggested that there was a massive rise in second homes from 9,230 in 2000 to over 14,000 now. Even on official figures over half the properties in some parishes around the Camel estuary, and over a third in other places in south east Cornwall, on the Roseland and the Lizard, are used as second homes and holiday cottages. But these figures are presumably the minimum as, if owners were willing to forgo the council tax discount (small beer for most of them), their second home wouldn't show up as such, or they could describe their properties as holiday lets in order to get small business relief. And as holiday lets pay business rates they don't appear in the council tax listings.

Anecdotal evidence suggests the number of second homes may be higher than the official figures imply. At Coverack for example it was claimed in 2011 that 60 per cent of the houses were not lived in permanently (*West Briton*, 14 July 2011). A year and a half earlier in Manaccan, also on the Lizard, it was stated that 75 per cent of properties were second or holiday homes (*This is Cornwall*, 25 Jan 2010). In 2009 it was reported that the market for second homes had bounced back strongly. While general housing demand was still in the doldrums as a result of the recession, almost half of 'prime properties' in Cornwall were being sold as second homes (*Daily Telegraph*, 16 Sep 2009), fuelled by the spending of City boomers on asset speculation. (But there must be some mistake. Weren't we told in all seriousness that the rich only spend the extra money they're getting from tax reductions on creating jobs for the rest of us?) According to the *Daily Telegraph* Cornwall was a 'lifestyle retreat' and 'there's bound to be a market for Cornish cottages packaged for city dwellers'. 'Packaged'? And we're still assured by the planners that housing supply merely reacts to housing demand!

Second homes are one facet of a phenomenon that's fast producing doughnut Cornwall – a tasty outer band encircling a black hole. In the desirable coastal zone private wealth is king. New wealth in its gleaming four by fours, jostles with more traditional old landed wealth, sharing its desire for social seclusion and locking itself away behind burglar alarmed gates and high hedges. From these cherished havens the inhabitants of the zone of seclusion gaze unseeingly over the views that lie spread out before them. Besotted by property, they own their little spot of land and they want to own the view as well. So the peace of the zone of seclusion is punctuated by the spluttering of conflict as new wealth strives to make its fragile arcadia into a zone of exclusion as well. Nowhere more than Helford Village in 2008, where a preservationist society dominated by second home owners forced a judicial review of a planned jetty and roadway designed to help local fishermen land their catch (*This is Cornwall*, 21 Jan 2009). For second home owners Cornwall is a one dimensional picture postcard, a place to enjoy the views they've bought, unsullied by economic activity.

For most of us the effect of second homes on local communities is pretty plain. If second home ownership is allowed to get out of control then local shops, pubs and post offices close and the price of property rockets well beyond local income levels. The life is gradually sucked out of villages which become merely the charming lodgings for lifestyle mag journos on a freebie or superb sets for supremely unfunny TV sitcoms. Such as Port Isaac for example.

But the view from the second home laager is otherwise. Newspaper columnist, author of 40 books and Oxford chap A.N.Wilson claims that without second homes 'the county [sic] would die'. Although spot the difference, as *with* second homes Cornwall will also die. Wilson was lamenting having to put his seven bedroom property in Port Isaac on the market for £499,999 in 2012 (*Western Morning News*, 22 Jun 2012). Which is odd because the same Mr Wilson was bemoaning putting the same property on the market back in 2009 for £650,000 (and it apparently at that time only had six bedrooms) (*Country Life*, 25 Aug 2009).

But if the zone of seclusion is one extreme then urban inland Cornwall is the other. The two are intimately connected, locked together in an embrace neither can escape. Lifestyle Cornwall creates lifestruggle Cornwall. To make the zone of seclusion safe for wealthy incomers a project class of regeneration 'experts' toils unceasingly to legitimate obscene numbers of new houses in the Cornish core. More and more people – both Cornish and less well-off incomers – are herded into high density areas well away from the coast. As the zone of seclusion consolidates its views, it turns its back on the destruction going on a few miles inland. For its residents, temporary or permanent, inland Cornwall might as well be another planet. They drive through it; they may even stop in it to shop or visit its tourist 'attractions'. But it remains thoroughly alien. Meanwhile, in this hollow zone us zombies stumble around, shell-shocked survivors of the symbolic death of Cornwall.

The Council's Local Plan responds to the demands of doughnut Cornwall, trying desperately to reduce growth rates in the areas of Cornwall that are most likely to be sold off to new permanent residents or to second home owners. Not of course that the Plan is particularly explicit either about this or its accommodation of new second home owners. On the former it indulges in the blatant mistruth that it's continuing a 'dispersal strategy'. And you have to look pretty hard to find any mention at all of the latter. However, tucked away in the lists of laughable reasons provided to legitimate the Council's plans for excessive growth in each community network area, we find references to second homes. Well, not actually second home owners as such, but 'temporary residents'. This newly coined term serves to give them a status more equal to 'permanent residents'.

I can reveal that in *more than half* the community network areas (10 out of 19) competition from 'temporary residents' is admitted to be pushing up the numbers of houses we 'need' to build. In Wadebridge and Padstow the problem of second homes can hardly be ignored. Padstow is described as 'a popular second home location' and the planners admit the horrifying fact that in this district 'four out of ten homes are already occupied by temporary residents'. Does this therefore explain the curious fact that, despite being the one area in Cornwall which has no predicted population growth, there was still a 'need' for 1,800 more houses over the next 20 years? It would be nice to know how many of these 1,800 are earmarked for second homes. But sadly we're not told.

In West Penwith there is also 'a significant level of competition between permanent and temporary residents ... and the growth figure chosen will need to accommodate this level of competition'. Which really means that more houses will have to be built to cater for the second home market. A similar unquantified 'need' to accommodate second home owners appears at St Agnes, St Blazey, Fowey and Lostwithiel, Liskeard and Looe and at Camelford. In the last of these there is 'a great deal of competition'. At Helston and the Lizard 'households ... face higher levels of competition than on average ... from prospective second home owners'. While at Bude 'residents in this area face a great deal of competition for housing from the second and holiday home market and the growth level chosen will have to take this into account'. Meanwhile, at Hayle and St Ives 'there is great deal of competition from second home owners ... and the number of new houses developed will need to accommodate this aspect of need' (all quotations from Core Strategy CNA documents).

'Aspect of need'?? This strongly implies that the phrase 'housing need' tossed around with such abandon by the Local Plan and its apologists includes the 'need' to build second homes for 'temporary residents', not to mention all those unaffordable homes for new permanent residents. Obviously, this is not something Cornwall Council wants to go large about. Quite the opposite. But the next time you hear councillors and planners wittering on about meeting 'local need' remember that their definition of this includes second homes as well as in-migration.

In the last three chapters I've identified a whole Pandora's box of factors predisposing policy-makers and politicians to a million-people Cornwall and to unsustainable population-led growth. Some of them relate to the actions of individuals, their backgrounds and their inability to see the wood for the trees. Others were more structural, such as central government policy frameworks, the power of the developers' lobby, the stifling 'common-sense' of capitalism and deeply ingrained representations of Cornwall. All these go a long way toward explaining the slow emergence of organised opposition to the Council's growth strategy and the unbelievably feeble response of the vast majority of our elected representatives when faced by that strategy. A proposed level of growth higher than that in the majority of Local Plans being put forward in the South West region of England was met by hardly a whimper until the process of determining the Local Plan had almost reached its finale in the summer of 2012. Why was opposition so slow to emerge in Cornwall? To answer that question we need to turn to the specific political crisis we've undergone over the past decade or so, one that has quietly and almost unnoticed eroded our democratic rights in Cornwall and effectively made it much harder for concerted and organised pressure to be applied to the runaway train of unlimited growth.

Chapter 9

Cornwall's democratic deficit

We have discovered that Cornwall Council has a cunning plan. Unwilling to resist the pressures that produce the great sale of Cornwall it wholeheartedly endorses that sale and adopts a de facto policy of encouraging population growth and massive social engineering. Yet amazingly, this key strategy shaping Cornwall's suburbanised future is subjected to hardly any public debate. When it comes to the issue of the Council's million-people project Cornwall is like a one-party state. Policed by a monolithic but shambolic bureaucracy, certain issues are ruled off the agenda. The media's role decays to the point where it merely recycles press releases from the local state and private sector lobbyists. Elections become meaningless as policy never changes. The ruling consensus in favour of growth and the latest big idea is not up for challenge and the plans for a million-people Cornwall most definitely not up for discussion. In this chapter I describe how the democratic deficit has widened over the last decade and show how Cornwall has been a major victim of a more general attack on our democratic rights from the parliamentary class. I will then argue that dissent is marginalised as the will to resist appears to have leached out of the majority of our elected representatives. A healthy democracy rests on healthy political parties and the chapter is rounded off by some discussion of the state of political parties in Cornwall.

We are told that we live in a democracy, where the people are ultimately sovereign. Those whom we elect – our representatives – direct society to meet the goals we set. Or at least this is the theory. In the UK this rosy picture is already a mite contentious as technically the monarch is still sovereign and our unwritten constitution deems us subjects of the monarchy rather than citizens of a democracy. Furthermore, once elected, the notion of parliamentary sovereignty, enshrined in the 'Glorious' Revolution of 1688, means that Parliament can do virtually anything it likes. Add the growing influence of big money in the twentieth century as corporations and well-funded pressure groups skewed extra-parliamentary pressure towards the rich and powerful, and we have to be rather sceptical about the 'democratic' nature of 'our' government.

Parliamentary sovereignty combined with the greed of MPs and a Byzantine payments system to produce the expenses scandal of 2008. Parliamentarians had hidden behind a veil of privilege and secrecy to indulge in all sorts of scams to add to their incomes, such as avoiding paying capital gains tax, 'flipping' second home designations in order to maximise expenses, or redecorating their houses courtesy of the taxpayer. Fortunately for them, this corruption was revealed in the middle of a major economic crisis when attention quickly became re-focused on saving capitalism. As a result, while a few of the more insignificant players were thrown to the wolves, several of the worst offenders walked free and shamefully even continue to collect their MPs' salaries.

The coup of 2010

Their confidence restored after managing to escape the fully deserved guillotine, this parliamentary class quietly engineered a little-noticed coup in 2010 immediately after the election of the Tory/Lib Dem coalition government. One of the first things the Tories and their Lib Dem allies did was to push through legislation for a fixed term parliament, setting the date of the next General Election for 2015. As most major democracies across the world already have fixed term parliaments this might seem like a well overdue reform. About a century behind the times, but that's about par for the course in our ramshackle parliamentary monarchical democracy.

But how long would the fixed term be fixed at? The vast majority of parliamentary legislatures have four year fixed terms, even shorter in Australia and the USA. So do the devolved institutions in Scotland and Wales. As does English local government. The Tory manifesto of 2010 had made no mention of fixed term parliaments. The Lib Dems had, but the term they were proposing was four years. This was in line with a Lib Dem sponsored private member's bill in 2007 for a four year fixed term parliament.

So did the Tories and Lib Dems choose four years? Of course not. They unilaterally gave themselves a longer mandate, deciding that they deserved five years before having to face the people again. Hardly anyone seemed to notice this sleight of hand. Or care about it. But it was a significant change that at a stroke diminished our right to vote and insulated politicians from the ballot box for an extra year. The Government hid behind the fiction that British parliaments already had terms of up to five years. Yes – in theory. But in reality most British parliaments hadn't lasted anything like five years in practice.

Here's the average length of Parliaments in the UK since the arrival of a properly democratic franchise.

1918-1935	2 years 10 months
1945-2010	3 years 9 months

The ramifications of this election-reduction exercise don't stop at Westminster. Unlike most European countries where it is unusual or even unconstitutional to hold elections to authorities at different levels on the same day, in the UK it's quite normal. A General Election in 2015 would therefore coincide with the next Welsh Assembly elections. Unable to contemplate the obvious solution - having two different election days in the same year - Nick Clegg apparently offered Assembly Members the option of cutting their term by a year or extending it by a year. So what did they choose? They chose to extend it (*Daily Telegraph*, 16 Mar 2011). The Fixed Term Parliaments Act of 2011 duly results in the next Welsh Assembly elections coming in 2016 rather than 2015. This would in turn lead to a clash with the next scheduled Welsh local government elections. So what did they do? Extend the gap before the next council elections in Wales to five years as well, postponing them to 2017. Odd how those elected always extend their mandates but never reduce them!

So the Tories and Lib Dems at a stroke extended the gap between elections by a year and a quarter. Reducing the people's opportunity to vote in this way followed other moves by the previous Labour Government that effectively increased the possibility of rigging elections in the UK. In 2004 they made postal voting ridiculously easy at the same time as cutting the resources for local registration officials to police the electoral register. The result was, as a judge in Birmingham concluded, electoral fraud that 'would disgrace a banana republic' (*Guardian*, 5 Apr 2005).

Making fraud easier and cutting opportunities to exercise the vote has since been followed up by plans to introduce individual voter registration. The number of people not registered to vote in Britain has already doubled in ten years to an estimated 3.5 million. But this measure looks very likely to lead to a further reduction – estimated to be as much as 20 per cent overall and 35 per cent in more mobile and urban areas. But don't expect any action about this as those missing voters are more likely to be poor and dispossessed, exactly those who are being targeted to suffer disproportionately from the Government's austerity programme.

Cornwall leads the way (in abolishing elections)

But what's all this got to do with Cornwall? Other than illustrate how we are unfortunately imprisoned in a state where the parliamentary class treats the people with arrogant contempt that is. Well, Cornwall was one of those places (along with areas on the English periphery such as Northumberland, Durham and Cheshire) that proudly blazed a trail by abolishing one tier of their local government in 2009 and opting for a unitary local authority. Urged on by the then Labour Government, the Lib Dems at County Hall were again complicit in reducing our rights to vote. A distinctive pattern appears to be emerging here.

The unitary authority replaced district councils delivering local services with a more remote (for most) authority centralised on Truro and meaningless, unelected and disregarded debating forums that most people have never heard of which operate in newly created zones called community network areas. Again at a stroke of the legislative pen this cut our opportunity to vote in local elections by a half. Instead of local elections in Cornwall every two years we now have them only every four years. Which means those who run Cornwall Council can escape the judgement of the people for that much longer. The Cornish voter now has fewer opportunities to cast their vote than elsewhere and many fewer than a century ago.

Table 9.1 Opportunities to vote in a twenty year cycle (all levels)

Cornwall	13
Devon (non-unitary areas)	18
Wales	18
Scotland	18
English metropolitan areas	23
Brittany	19
Cornwall 1894-1914 (boroughs)	31
Cornwall 1894-1914 (rural areas)	21

Of course, there were other advantages to imposing unitary local government on Cornwall and effectively abolishing proper local government. By equating Cornwall with the local level (something rebranding the Core Strategy as the Local Plan nicely reinforces), unitarization undercut the campaign for a streamlined strategic Cornish assembly along the lines of the Welsh Assembly. The Cornish Constitutional Convention, which was campaigning for such an assembly, is now effectively dead in the water. Rather paradoxically, the establishment of Cornwall Council works to reinforce Cornwall's colonial status as an English county. Had the opportunity been grasped to demand unitary government based on sub-Cornwall districts (something that might have been far closer to what people actually wanted) the assembly campaign could have been re-ignited. The County Council is Dead: Long Live the County!

Cornwall leads the way (in reducing representation)

Elections are one opportunity we have to speak truth to power, to let those who take decisions on our behalf know what we're thinking. The combined effect of whittling away opportunities to vote has been to reduce that right in Cornwall from an actual 19 in the two decades from 1990 to 2010 to a miserable 13 in the next two decades, a 35 per cent reduction in our democratic rights. But defenders of this move to abolish elections might well point out that we can also exert pressure between elections – by lobbying our elected representatives. Except that we now have far fewer of them left to lobby. In 1972 in Cornwall we had a total of 854 councillors in Cornwall (ignoring the parish level which has pitifully few powers). That was one for every 451 people. In 1973 that was reduced to 329 councillors when district councils were invented, one for every 1,170 people. Now we have just 123 councillors, one for every 4,390 people. Rather oddly, as the population inexorably rises so the number of representatives falls.

How does this level of representation compare with other places? When we compare Cornwall with the other countries of Great Britain the answer is not very well.

Table 9.2 People per elected local government representative (Great Britain)

Cornwall	4350
England	2870
Scotland	3870
Wales	2270

If we widen this out further and compare it with other European countries then we see the true extent of Cornish under-representation.

Table 9.3 People per elected local government representative (Europe)

France	120
Germany	420
Italy	600
Spain	620
Netherlands	1700
UK	2900
Cornwall	4350

(source Game, 2009)

Given these facts, it comes as some surprise that intermittent calls are heard to reduce the number of representatives in Cornwall even further. For example the Labour Party's sole councillor Jude Robinson came up with a suggestion in June 2011 for how Cornwall Council could save some money. The answer, said Jude, was obvious. The Council was 'too big' and the number of councillors needed pruning by a fifth, thus increasing the number of people per representative to a staggering 5,500, or almost twice the number as in England.

Journalists jumped on this, pointing out how Cornwall Council has twice the number of elected members as the Welsh Assembly (123 as opposed to 60 Assembly members) 'despite having less power'. And not only that but it also has twice the number of councillors as Devon County Council. For them and for most of the local opinion-shapers this was plainly a scandal. Why do we have all these freeloaders? It doesn't require a degree in the bleeding obvious to see that we could save a whole shed-load of money by cutting back on their numbers. Jude's brilliant scheme to reduce the cost of this bloated administrative monster was put to other councillors. Liberal Democrat Leader Jeremy Rowe quickly agreed. Not to be outdone so did Independent Councillor Andrew Wallis. Only MK's Dick Cole correctly pointed out that this was all nonsense (Cllr Dick Cole's blog, 6 Jun 2011). Not that this affected the opinion of Radio Cornwall's Graham Smith, who had mounted a longstanding campaign on his blog to expose the huge size of Cornwall Council and the incredibly gargantuan number of councillors idling their time away in its cloisters. For Smith size clearly mattered as he seemed to take the number of elected representatives as a personal slight.

Our opinion-forming class in Cornwall seems ever ready to cave in to crass populism or powerful interests rather than seek out the facts and act on them. Unfortunately, their impeccable logic turns out to be the opposite. For a start what this bunch of shallowbrains didn't or wouldn't admit is that councillors' allowances came to less than one per cent of the cuts being proposed by Cornwall Council. So, implying that a cut of a fifth in that amount would solve – or even make a discernable dent in - that particular problem was frankly ludicrous.

More worryingly, they are apparently incapable of understanding that sub-state government works differently in different parts of the UK. Wales has local authorities (22 of them) in addition to its Assembly. Devon – outside Plymouth and Torbay – still has two tiers of councils. In contrast, Cornwall Council is the *only* level of local government in Cornwall. Cornwall Council is not an Assembly despite windbaggery when it was set up. Forget it. It's a unitary authority. A local council. Wishful thinking does not make it into a regional assembly. Selective comparisons with individual Welsh or Devonian government bodies are utterly spurious as One Council means ... one bunch of representatives. Who actually, as I have shown above, represent a lot more folk than their counterparts do in other places. In this sense they provide better 'value for money' rather than less. Instead of being over-represented we are greatly *under-represented* – a clear result of the democratic disaster that was the unitary authority.

In the Middle East the people in 2011 began to call for more democracy. Here Labour, Lib Dems and Independents unite to demand less representation and seem to see democracy purely in terms of its cash cost. So why not go the whole hog? Why bother with representative democracy at all? After all, we've already handed the planning system over to developers and rely on consultants rather than on genuine consultation. Moreover, Conservative/Liberal Democrat central government policy is clearly to cut local government funding so far that it's forced to privatise its services, thus effectively putting them beyond democratic oversight. To balance these trends requires a campaign for the restoration of democracy, one that will sweep away anti-democratic time-servers and install a more representative, more decentralised and more diverse and representative local democracy.

In March 2011 Cornwall Council announced its 'governance review'. This responded to a central government invitation to assess the effectiveness of its present decision-making structure. The review was given a very narrow choice; it could decide to revert to a committee system, stick with the present Leader and Cabinet system or come up with some sort of hybrid involving various balances of power between Cabinet and full council. It reported in December 2012. Astonishingly, the terms of reference for this governance review also allowed it to consider reducing the number of councillors. In the event it didn't, but when the review was discussed that didn't stop Independent Cllr Julian German moving an amendment to invite the Boundary Commission to cull local representation even further. Ironically, one of the 'principles' of the review was that proposed solutions must 'enhance democracy'. Which was a bit rich, somewhat akin to closing the stable door long after the metaphorical horse has bolted.

For more evidence of Cornwall Council's cavalier approach to actual democracy take a look at the minutes of their Governance Review Panel, available on their website. Note the lack of effort to consult with those to whom they are in principle answerable– the people of Cornwall – and their replacement with 'inquiry days' for 'stakeholders, partners, interested parties and town and parish councils'. (Aren't we all stakeholders in the Council?) Not to mention the 'Independent' Review Panel of three non-councillors. This comprised the Bishop of Truro, the Deputy CEO of Cornwall College and the vice-chairman of Cornwall Council's own Standards Committee, all three presumably chosen for their connection to institutions that have a vast wealth of experience of democracy. At the end of the day, not surprisingly, the Council's Governance Panel recommended a modified cabinet system, although MK's amendment to restore a committee system received strong backing at the full council debate on the issue (Cornwall Council full council minutes, 11 Dec 2012).

The quango-state of Cornwall

Declining opportunities to vote and the steady reduction of representatives to vote for or put pressure on is exacerbated by the presence of the quango-state. Deregulation and a neo-liberal approach did not actually lead to the minimal state admired by its proponents. Even, or perhaps especially, globalised casino capitalism needs a strong state to provide the context for its rapacious activities. Strong enough that is to guarantee a flexible and docile workforce (which is what the Tory/Lib Dem Government's austerity programme is largely about) and active enough to ensure that giant corporations do not fail, as we saw with banks in Britain and General Motors in the States. But not of course strong enough to confront the big energy-guzzlers and take the regulatory action needed to limit climate change to a hopefully uncatastrophic two degrees. The big state has therefore been replaced by the quango-state. This eases the handing over of democratically accountable functions and services to the private sector. Such services then become unaccountable, hidden behind a veil of 'commercial confidentiality'. Quangos and privatisation are integral to the neo-liberal project embraced by Tories, Labour and Lib Dem politicians alike since the 1990s. Its beneficiaries are the global corporations and a tiny elite of the super rich. Its victims include democracy (Crouch, 2011). A large chunk of our everyday life is now overseen by anonymous and unelected people meeting well away from the public gaze. We know that the invited personnel of the quango-state is generally male and middle aged but other than that its operations remain a closed book to most, as mysterious and secret as the inner workings of the medieval Vatican.

Moreover, the quango-state has its own centre and periphery. In Cornwall its centre is the Convergence Empire created by European funding. This currently has a budget of £70 million a year and draws in matched funding from other agencies and central bodies. This is more than ten per cent of Cornwall Council's annual £1.16 billion budget but unlike the Council (at least in theory) its decision-making processes remain opaque, inscrutably unimpressed and unaffected by any direct democratic influence. The latest available minutes of the Joint Local Managing Committee for the Convergence programme (14 Oct 2011 – ten months old at the time of writing) reveal that three Cornwall Councillors and one Cornwall Council officer attended (the latter representing Chief Executive Kevin Lavery). These were part of a group of 21, chaired by central government in the shape of the Department for Communities and Local Government and containing another six or seven people directly employed by central government, including at least one refugee from the former Regional Development Agency. However, the last Convergence Partnership Delivery Group Minutes available online - those of March 2011 - are now well over a year old as I write. Have there really been no meetings since then? We're not told and we have no way of knowing.

But even Convergence can be seen not as part of the centre of the quango-state but part of a vast sprawling periphery, that shadowland between the public and the private. Quangoland is part of the continuum of the secret (or at least hazy) state. The use of the Private Finance Initiative (PFI) for public infrastructure adds to it by conveniently removing large swathes of public spending from public scrutiny. And if parrot calls of 'commercial confidentiality' aren't sufficient reason to withhold information about spending taxpayers' money from the taxpayers then decision-making can always be kicked into the long grass by other procedural devices.

A classic example of this was Cornwall Council's Cabinet decision in April 2011 to turn the Newquay Airport Development Panel into an 'informal members' working group'. This, moved by Independent Councillors Hicks and Kazcmarek, slipped through hardly noticed as part of a general review of Cabinet decision-making (Cabinet Minutes 20 Apr 2011, CAB/243). It neatly meant that information about the Council's plans for the airport and discussion about the £3 million a year (and rising) subsidy, already restricted because of 'commercial confidentiality' became even less likely to seep into the light of day. Although this infringes what one might have considered was a basic principle of democratic government – that those who pay have a right to know how their money is spent and why – members of Cornwall Council's Cabinet realised that their first duty was to support their pet project which had become too big to fail. True, there is a Newquay Airport Consultative Forum, but the function of that body – whose minutes are available – seems to be for 'stakeholders' to consult on the management of the airport and report back to Cornwall Council's Cabinet. It's a bit like an advisory panel and, as one of its terms of references is 'to stimulate the interest of the local population in the achievements of the Airport', is hardly designed to cast a critical eye over it or demand more openness.

In March 2012 Newquay Airport, facing a drop in its income of another £900,000 because of plummeting passenger numbers, told Cornwall Council's Cabinet its subsidy 'must' increase to £3.54 million (*Western Morning News*, 22 Mar 2012). The Cabinet duly agreed, with Leader Alec Robertson saying the airport, despite suffering the largest fall in passenger numbers in the UK, was a 'critical piece of infrastructure'. While it was later revealed that some Cabinet members were warning that the subsidy could not be guaranteed for ever, good money has continued to be thrown away after bad (*Cornish Guardian*, 29 Mar 2012). Moreover, it was also admitted that the managing director of this airport, solely owned by Cornwall Council, received £125,000 including car allowance and pension rights in the 13 months to March 2011, despite passenger numbers collapsing by 19% over the same period (full council minutes, 17 Jan 2012).

While Cornwall Council is responsible for the airport it's no longer responsible for such things as social housing - transferred to housing associations or arms-length companies years ago - and is losing control over schools as these effectively transfer to central government control when they become academies. One might be forgiven for thinking that local government is now spending more money on fewer things and that perhaps therefore we don't need so many elected representatives after all. But what this steady erosion of democratic control is all about is the removal of potential pressure points on a system sliding away from public scrutiny and democratic influence. Put simply, our rights to lobby and apply pressure are being attacked at the same time as we're losing our opportunity to vote. The combination of centralist authoritarianism within the council as the Cabinet rides roughshod over decisions of the full council and the privatisation of council services, made inevitable by government cuts, is a perfect example of the contemporary relationship of government and corporate power and a symptom of democratic decay. Add in to this relative paucity of elected representatives and of elections in Cornwall the context of the quango-state and we have a yawning democratic deficit, driven by neo-liberal ideology and reinforced by financial stringency (as of course in the UK we're not prepared to pay for democracy).

Of course, reducing potential democratic pressure points goes hand in hand with centralising decision-making and allowing business 'stakeholders' a major role in that decision-making. The result is an increase in the ability of well-heeled private power to cosy up to politicians, as was seen in the intimate links between multi-national business and 'mainstream' politicians revealed in the Leveson enquiry.

In 2006 across the UK an army of quangos spent the equivalent of over nine per cent of GDP, more than all that spent by local government (New Local Government Network, 2008). A survey of the quangocrats who ran public bodies in 2008 revealed that 36 per cent of them lived in London. The geographical peripheries of England as well as Cornwall were seriously under-represented on state-wide quangos. Cornwall in fact came out of the survey as one of most poorly represented areas – along with places in the north of England such as Bradford and Bolton, Redcar and Rotherham. When it comes to influence on the state we are supposed to be part of, we have little. The quango-state is also a centralised state and merely adds to our lack of representation at the level of the state. It would also be interesting on the Cornish level to know where the managers and directors of all the new arms-length companies come from. In brief, how many are Cornish?

For example, in June 2012 the Cornwall Development Company was advertising for a Director of Development at a salary of £75,000 plus benefits. Job-seekers in Cornwall may not have been aware of the opening as the Company used GatesbySanderson, an executive recruitment services agency based in Leeds, London and Birmingham, to advertise their job. In any case it was plain from the advert that the CDC was looking to add to population in-migration. It promised that 'a role in Cornwall will bring you close to an incredible natural environment ... with its stunning landscape, rich cultural heritage and pioneering economic past, present and future. Cornwall is a unique place to live and work'. Hoary old myths were coupled with the opportunity to ensure that the 'physical place shaping agenda in Cornwall ... fully aligned with skills and business support' would 'drive economic, physical and social regeneration'. The CDC appeared unconcerned about using appeals to the traditional in order to help to trash the traditional. As presumably do its paymasters at Cornwall Council.

This lack of influence may go some way to explain the lack of resistance when the central state attacks Cornish rights, as it has been doing with increasing frequency and ferocity since the 1990s. This accompanies an abject failure to deliver fair treatment for Cornwall, let alone the special treatment our status as homeland to one of the UK's indigenous peoples warrants. Defeat after defeat seems to have ground us down and made us unable to get up off our knees. This political weakness remains a fundamental problem and appears to be part of the reason why our elected representatives have in the main been so utterly pathetic in the face of plans for excessive and unsustainable population growth. I'll return to their inability to oppose their own council's million-people plan later but first let's take the Devonwall constituency as a perfect example to illustrate our elected representatives' inability and/or unwillingness to defend us.

The Frankenstein frontier pact

It didn't take too long for it to dawn on people in Cornwall that an inevitable result of Nick Clegg's Faustian deal with the Tories and the Frankenstein's monster of the Parliamentary Voting System and Constituencies Bill was to deliver a parliamentary constituency that crossed the Tamar. For the first time since the 13th century, Cornwall's historic border was to be ignored. The significance of that act by the Tory/Lib Dem Government went well beyond the mechanics of parliamentary representation. It reinforced the treatment of Cornwall as a bog-standard English county. It was a resounding humbling of those who claim that Cornwall deserves special respect as the home of the Cornish people. By respecting the Welsh and Scottish borders but flouting the Cornish border, the English political elite showed their utter contempt for Cornish claims. Fortunately, this particular disaster has now been avoided. But not because of opposition from Cornwall or from its elected representatives. Or from any smidgeon of consideration for Cornwall's claims to special treatment. No, its demise stemmed from the unravelling of Nick Clegg's plans to reform the House of Lords. Introducing democracy into that particular unelected chamber (one of only two unelected second chambers across the globe – the other being Canada) was far too much for a large number of Tory MPs to swallow.

Before this climb-down was announced however, widespread opposition emerged, focused on a 'Keep Cornwall Whole' campaign. This gathered support from across the political spectrum and organised a rally of several hundred people at Saltash in late 2010. Cornwall's parliamentarians promised to move amendments to exempt Cornwall from the deliberately bizarre and arbitrary new rule that no constituency could deviate by more than five per cent from the norm (a rule that would have led to a major redrawing of boundaries every five years).

However, the protestors could hardly have anticipated the insouciant way in which the Government brushed aside Cornish claims. David Cameron came up with the memorable remark that 'It's the Tamar, not the Amazon, for heaven's sake' (*Daily Telegraph*, 6 Oct 2010). Content to holiday at Knightsbridge-on-sea (aka the Camel estuary) Cameron clearly had not an inkling of the historical or cultural claims for special consideration for the Cornish border. Meanwhile, Nick Clegg could merely patronise Cornish claims with a feeble and sneering 'joke' about Dan Rogerson's constituents in North Cornwall being 'delighted to know that they are citizens of England and the UK' (*Hansard*, 5 Jul 2010, col 23). For Clegg, the all important 'rule of thumb' was the need to equalise constituency sizes. In short, he was quite prepared to sell out Cornwall's historical claims in return for a half-baked referendum on the alternative vote which was promptly heavily defeated.

Clegg once described the Liberal Democrats as 'a party ... which has Cornwall sort of coursing though its veins' (Radio Cornwall, 31 Mar 2010). 'Sort of' sums it up well. When an amendment to ensure recognition of Cornwall's border finally came up for debate in the Commons on November 1st 2010 it was lost by 315 votes to 257. Fair enough; all six Cornish MPs, Lib Dem and Tory, voted for the amendment. However, only seven other Lib Dems supported it while 41 voted against. If 29 of those Lib Dem MPs had had the guts to vote for this amendment then Cornwall would have been excluded along with some other peripheral territories. Make no mistake about it; the Liberal Democrats have to shoulder their share of the blame for making the struggle to secure recognition for Cornwall's equal status as a nation of the UK that much more difficult. And then, when the Lords debated an amendment to exclude Cornwall from the provisions of the Act only 21 Lib Dem Lords could be found to vote for it. A massive 63 preferred to join their Tory friends to vote it down.

Cornish Lib Dem MP Steve Gilbert had played to the gallery on the banks of the Tamar in 2010 by promising the crowd gathered there that his job was 'to vote against the Government to keep Cornwall intact'. However, when it came to the third reading of the Parliamentary Voting System and Constituencies Bill, Gilbert voted for it and thus against keeping Cornwall intact. Tory MP Sheryll Murray had rightly pointed out that Cornwall had a 'unique and specific identity' in a speech in the

Commons in early September 2010. No matter: she voted for the Bill. Fellow Tory MP George Eustice had been upset about the alternative vote, which he didn't understand because of its complexity and sheer strange Europeaness. But he still voted for the Bill. Tory MP Sarah Newton hadn't said much at all about the issue. So she voted for the Bill. Lib Dem MP Dan Rogerson had equivocated about his intentions in September 2010 when being interviewed by Radio Cornwall. So it was no surprise that he voted for the Bill too. Finally, Andrew George, Lib Dem MP for St Ives had vehemently opposed the Bill. He had been sure that 'all Cornish Parliamentarians will stick together on this one.' And he was right. They did. Because he too voted for the Bill. Oh, and he voted against as well. This was apparently a subtle 'principled abstention'. So subtle hardly anyone noticed it.

Tragedy had descended into farce. To add insult to injury, while ignoring the Cornish case, Parliament had voted in the meantime to exclude the Isle of Wight from the provisions of the Act. The message was unmistakable – the Celtic nation of Cornwall now has less status than the English county of the Isle of Wight.

If our parliamentarians could only offer such meagre resistance perhaps our local councillors sent a clarion call that reverberated through the corridors of Westminster. 'Here's 20,000 Cornishmen [sic] will know the reason why' etc. They had the opportunity. The Boundary Commission's consultation invited responses to their eventual proposal to join north Cornwall with a part of south west England in a hybrid Bideford and Bude (note the order) constituency. The Keep Cornwall Whole campaign called on people across Cornwall to rise up and make their opposition known in the consultation. Many individuals did so. However, the response of those who were supposed to represent them was less forthcoming.

Of the 123 Cornwall Councillors just nine could summon up the energy to submit a response to the Boundary Commission, either written or orally at the two days of hearings at Truro in November 2011. These included one Independent (out of 31 at the time), one Liberal Democrat (out of 40), two MK councillors (from the four then on the Council) and a clutch of five Conservatives (from 47). The Conservative input may seem surprising. And indeed a closer inspection reveals that most of the Tories were primarily troubled by local issues. For example Patrick Lambshead, councillor at Newquay, wanted Bodmin and Newquay to be renamed Newquay and Bodmin. That said, three of the five Tories at least expressed their regret at the cross-border constituency even though it wasn't the main purpose of their submission. Even including them, just seven explicit expressions of opposition to the Devonwall constituency from a possible 123 was a pretty poor return.

Perhaps parish and town councillors, powerless but closer to the grassroots, would be more eager to express their anger at this supremely indifferent treatment of Cornwall as a bog-standard English county. Did a flow of outraged representations from parish councillors flood the Boundary Commission? Hardly, as the following table suggests.

Table 9.4 Written representations from parish and town councillors and parish and town councils to Boundary Commission consultation, 2011

from	number	People per submission
Somerset and Avon	56	29,000
Gloucestershire	38	15,400
Dorset and Wiltshire	76	18,100
Devon	38	30,000
Cornwall	38	14,200

At first glance this may suggest that the Keep Cornwall Whole campaign had indeed resulted in a slightly higher relative level of submissions from Cornwall (although not much higher than Gloucestershire or Dorset and Wiltshire and certainly not enough to ruffle any feathers at Boundary Commission HQ). But when we look more closely we find that not all the comments from parish and town councillors concerned the Devonwall constituency by any means. And if they did they weren't necessarily opposed to it.

For example, Martin Bell, a councillor at Port Isaac, wholeheartedly supported a Bideford and Bude constituency: 'claims about Cornwall's unique cultural heritage and strength of feeling against are in my opinion wildly exaggerated' (at http://consultation.boundary commissionforengland.independent.gov.uk/). The evidence suggests he was right. Over half of the parish and town councillors responding merely commented on local issues. Others seemed to be a mite confused to say the least. At Torpoint a town councillor stated that the Boundary Commission had been 'right not to cross the Tamar to create a Devonwall seat.' Similarly, the South East Cornwall Conservatives congratulated the Boundary Commission: 'we do most sincerely commend your decision not to meddle with the obvious geographical boundary between Devon and Cornwall, namely the River Tamar. To have done so would have had very serious consequences'. For some people the Tamar apparently stopped just below Launceston and Cornwall ended at Bideford!

This takes the concept of parochialism to its ultimate limits. Plainly, given these attitudes, there's not much point expecting our representatives at this level to stand up for Cornwall. A handful of councillors at Bude, a couple from Truro and one from St Agnes were the exceptions rather than the norm. In equally depressing fashion, when it came to the actual councils' formal representations to the Boundary Commission we find more than half of those making a representation just complaining about the names of the proposed constituencies or other local concerns. If they bothered to comment at all, that is. There are something like 213 parish and town councils in Cornwall. A grand total of 15 commented formally on the Boundary Commission's proposals. Of these eight didn't even mention the Devonwall imposition. They were much more concerned by the name of the proposed constituency in the south east of Cornwall or other local issues. Poor old Bodmin Town Council was worried about 'the size' of the Bideford and Bude constituency, but apparently unperturbed by the principle of it. Only seven parish and town councils could stir themselves to write a letter condemning the trashing of our historic boundary and our treatment as less significant than the Isle of

Wight. So congratulations are due to Pelynt, Roche, St Blaise, St Hilary, St Minver Highlands, Saltash, and Tresmeer. Tiny Tresmeer, home to fewer than 300, could rouse itself to protest, but only around three per cent of the other parish and town councils could. A truly horrifying indication of the spirit-less failure of our current elected representatives to represent the long-term interests of Cornwall.

Even those submissions to the Boundary Commission that did complain about Cornwall's treatment viewed the Devonwall constituency as 'the least worst option' (Saltash Town Council) or stated that balancing electorates between the two sides of the Tamar would somehow 'ensure fairness' (Cllr Alex Folkes, http://lansonboy.blogspot.co.uk/). On the contrary, a Devonwall constituency would hardly 'ensure fairness'; instead its very presence would have embedded unfairness. It treated Cornwall not as a unique territory with its own history, Celtic roots and indigenous native people. It trampled over our claims for recognition. It made future demands for devolved powers or special treatment that much more difficult by reinforcing our status as an insignificant and disregarded county at the tail end of England. The obvious alternative – if we were reluctantly to be coerced into this – was to demand a cross-border constituency weighted as far as possible towards Cornwall. But this of course was ignored. One could well be forgiven for concluding that the feeble response of our councillors and the disingenuous stance of our parliamentary representatives – pretending to stand up for Cornish rights but then voting for the legislation that reinforced our subordination – means we might as well give up the struggle.

Where has the sprit gone from our land?

Such weakness is indicative of a wider malaise and a debilitated state of resistance in Cornwall. As that excellent Cornish band Bucca asks, where, indeed, has the spirit gone from our land? They've sold our land and no-one seems to notice. Or care. The way we lay down and let the Tories/Lib Dems destroy any lingering significance of the border merely mirrors the lack of concern over continuing the disastrous growth drive of the past 50 years. If opposition to Devonwall was feeble, then opposition to the prospect of a million-people suburbanised Cornwall is almost invisible at the level of Cornwall Councillors. We've seen that the gang of three councillors at Bodmin (Lib Dem councillors Ann Kerridge and Pat Rogerson and Tory – then Independent – councillor Lance Kennedy) were in favour of high growth. Even the original 70 per cent growth rate proposed for Bodmin in just 20 years wasn't too much for them. From the minutes of the Planning Policy Advisory Panel of 4 August 2011 we can see that Cllrs Scott Mann (Con, Wadebridge) and Lisa Dolley (Ind, Redruth) favoured 52,000 houses, thus hiking up the growth rate of the past couple of decades. From the same minutes we also see that Cllr Dick Cole (MK, St Enoder) was desperately trying to slow down the march to a million by arguing for 40,000 houses. With the benefit of the latest data discussed in Chapter 1 we now know that even that figure, just 1,320 fewer than were built in the last twenty years, is far more than we actually need. Unfortunately however, as there was no recorded vote we don't know the views of the others present.

Similarly, when the full council debated the Local Plan in February 2013 councillors decided not to have their votes recorded, displaying a shameful preference for secrecy, especially as all votes in Parliament have been openly recorded since the eighteenth century. MK councillors have all gone on record supporting a lower figure than 42,250 and a slowdown in the current unsustainable growth rate, as did several others. Yet only 20 councillors could be found to vote for a more sustainable, although still not sustainable in the long run, 29,000 house target moved by Cllrs Biscoe (Ind, Truro) and Nolan (Lib Dem, Truro). And just 33 eventually voted against the figure of 42,250, out of a possible 121.

In November 2012, the pressure group *Our Cornwall* asked all 122 councillors (there was one vacancy at the time) for their views on the housing target. Just 31 could be bothered to reply. Of those none were willing to admit their explicit support for 49,000 although 11 declined to commit themselves. Meanwhile, five opted for 38,000 while 14 went for a target of 29,000 or lower. While this demonstrated some growing doubts about the Council's plans we must presumably conclude that the majority of the other 91 councillors were signing up to the Council's million-people plans. Their strategy seemed to be to say as little about the growth project as possible. With the exception of MK councillors and a few others, we had to look very hard indeed to find any spark of resistance to the unsustainable growth strategy from our elected representatives, let alone any spirited effort to provide a focus for opposition or encourage the production of a more sustainable alternative to the Local (Growth) Plan.

Quiescent councillors: moribund parties

If the majority of councillors appear to have abdicated their responsibility to represent a growing disquiet about the Council's growth strategy, that only reflects the attitudes of their political groups and parties. The health of a representative democracy lies in its political parties. Parties are energised and renewed in the periodic testing ground of electoral politics. But, as we have seen, in Cornwall our opportunity to vote has been severely curtailed recently. We must not be surprised therefore to find that our political parties in the main are unable to oppose the growth strategy that's been imposed on us with little or no public debate. At least one might have hoped that they would vigorously call for some democratic debate on population-led growth and its consequences even if they supported it. But sadly not. In fact, not one party bothered to submit its views to the initial consultation in early 2011 on the Core Strategy options.

It's not exactly surprising to find Conservatives on Cornwall Council backing the Council's mindless growth strategy. Since the days of Thatcher the pro-business pro-deregulation wing of Conservatism has won out over the one-nation style that might have taken the word 'conserve' in the party name a bit more seriously. The only thing the Tories seem intent on conserving these day is the right of a small minority to make and keep a lot of money. On the local level a few Tory traditionalists, when they think through the consequences, are horrified at the changes that are coming as a result of the million-people strategy. However, there was little sign of such awareness among the hard faced men and women who surrounded former Leader Alec Robertson as he led the drive forward on behalf of the property developers and the big supermarkets with little opposition from within his own ranks.

Then there's the Liberal Democrats. Traditionally the party of opposition to the Tories in Cornwall, that role has now been fatally compromised by their support of Tory policies in central government. At least we know where we stand with the Conservatives, whose policy seems to be to transform Cornwall into a suburban English county with a suburban English population. But when it comes to the Lib Dems, who knows? The party has always tended to run with the fox yet hunt with the hounds, for example playing the Cornish card at elections by loudly demanding a fair deal for Cornwall yet regularly and abysmally spurning the chance to stand up for Cornwall when in office. A local record of hollow and hypocritical stances is now plain for all to see in central government. Lib Dem claims about fairness turn out to be so much hot air in a climate of dismantling the welfare system, back-door privatisation of the health service and budgets that consistently take a higher proportion of the income of the poorest than of the richest.

Instead of listening to them bleating about 'fairness', let's look at the actual voting record of our three Lib Dem MPs on a number of key issues. All three voted to reduce security for social housing tenants (May 2011) and to cut education maintenance allowances (Jan 2011) while none of them could bring themselves to vote against doubling the period before an employee can claim unfair dismissal (Mar 2012) or the sale of public forests (Feb 2011) or the Police and Security Bill that extends the role of secret courts (March 2013). Dan Rogerson could also vote to abolish the Agricultural Wages Board (Oct 2011) and in favour of the Health and Social Care Bill (Sep 2011). So could Steve Gilbert who was admittedly the only one of the three to vote to raise university tuition fees (Dec 2010). The House of Lords carried five amendments ameliorating the draconian Welfare Reform Bill, trying to protect the disabled, cancer patients and the young unemployed from some of its more vicious elements. When these amendments reached the Commons and were duly rejected, Steve Gilbert's voting record was identical to that of Cornwall's three Tory MPs, voting against all five key amendments. Rogerson voted against four of them and abstained on one while Andrew George was more equivocal, voting for one, against two and abstaining on two.

In the House of Lords Lib Dem Cornwall Councillor Robin Teverson was indistinguishable from the Tories, voting against all five amendments. Former Lib Dem MP Paul Tyler also voted with the Tories on four out of the five. Meanwhile, the other former Lib Dem MP who's now comfortably ensconced in the Lords, Matthew Taylor, voted identically with Andrew George. It seems that effectively we have five Tory MPs in Cornwall therefore as, whatever they might say, Rogerson and Gilbert tend to vote solidly with their Tory colleagues. Only Andrew George has opposed some, although not all, of the Government's actions, rebelling on more than half the key votes.

Table 9.5 Cornish Lib Dem MP's voting records on twelve key votes

	For	Abstained	Against	Total	% in support of Government
Gilbert	10	2	0	11/12	92
Rogerson	9	2	1	10/12	83
George	4	3	5	5.5/12	46

This pattern – of talking the talk but only rarely walking the walk – is replicated locally. For instance, most Lib Dems on the Strategic Planning Committee ended up voting against Truro's eastern urban extension, which was good. Yet as we have discovered, some Lib Dem councillors are keen to see even faster growth and an earlier implementation of the grand million-people plan. Most of course just keep their heads down and say very little. And we mustn't let the amnesia that afflicts the political memory of the media lure us into forgetting the actions of the previous Lib Dem controlled County Council. For it was that body that gave us the waste incinerator disaster, that began to pour money into the black hole that is Newquay Airport, and that has to take the major share of responsibility for the attack on our democratic rights and devolutionary potential that resulted from foisting onto us an unwanted and centralised unitary local government. That council was also quite capable of signing up to the million-people plan with little apparent difficulty, supporting housing targets of 57,000 at one stage and offering little to counter the truly 'bonkers' population growth targets that the former unelected South West 'Assembly' wished to impose on Cornwall.

Andrew George and those Lib Dem councillors who think like him or who harbour pretensions to the progressive policies that the Liberal Party once espoused need to take a long, hard look at their party. From the outside it now looks awfully similar to Blair's Labour Party, captured and led by people who either practice the corporate politics that makes them virtually indistinguishable from the Conservatives or New Labour, or people who are too timid to challenge the corporate status-quo. They need to re-assess their support for a party that agreed a UK budget in 2012 that almost went out of its way to attack Cornwall – by imposing a pasty tax, regional wage rates for public sector workers (later withdrawn) and cuts in family tax credits (significantly not withdrawn). Now is surely the time to put Cornwall before career, leave the Lib Dems to rot in their advanced state of putrefaction and help build a movement that might begin to challenge the one party growth consensus that has Cornwall in its iron grip.

But who might they join with to do this? Where is the struggle to replace a million-people plan with sustainability and stability? It obviously can't be found among the Independents at the County Hall bunker. This group, shackled to the Tories, contains a bewildering variety of positions. These range from growth sceptics to former 'Cornish' Independents who have sadly undergone a transition from poacher to gamekeeper, to those – often the same – who wholeheartedly back the Council's million-people strategy. Or there's the Labour Party in Cornwall. As with the other 'mainstream' political groups, it's difficult to discern an actual Labour position on population growth. Of course, in Cornwall Labour is not 'mainstream' at all but a minority interest. Jude Robinson, its sole Cornwall Councillor before 2013, seemed to be in favour of lots of affordable homes. Saying that is about as politically risky as declaring support for Christmas. The Labour Party remains dumb when it comes to the number of unaffordable homes. But Cllr Robinson's support for 42,250 houses, together with Labour's past record of support for eco-towns and the Regional Development Agency's Regional Spatial Strategy, doesn't provide much hope for principled opposition from this quarter. And in September 2012 when Camborne Town Council discussed an open letter from *Our Cornwall* calling on an alternative to the million-people plans the sole Labour councillor voted against the letter.

Which leaves us with Ukip, MK and the Greens. To give them credit, Ukip has been fairly consistent in opposing mass housing plans in Cornwall. But the party is an exotic and acquired taste. While opposing 'unwanted housing developments' and supermarkets it also opposes wind turbines because it remains in a state of climate change denial. While wanting to 'prevent developers from concreting over the countryside' it appears to believe half of the houses that will be built will be for Rumanians and Bulgarians. While recognising that central government is taking money away from local councils it seems to think the money is then given to the EU and foreign aid. Its anti-devolutionary stance, its Europhobe obsession and its neo-liberal economic policies, which make Osborne's austerity cuts look very mild in comparison, make supporting Ukip akin to jumping from the frying-pan into the fire. From the opposite direction, the Green Party might also be expected to favour a stable-state population in Cornwall but seems not to want to take a high profile position against the Local Plan. Indeed, the Greens declined to support *Our Cornwall*'s call on the council to rethink its growth strategy in the autumn of 2012 and the sole Green Party councillor on Camborne Town Council joined with Labour to vote against supporting it. The Green Party's unaccountable silence when it comes to taking a public stance on Cornwall's population and housing growth contrasts with Ukip's enthusiastic backing of *Our Cornwall*'s campaign, a contrast that's very difficult to understand as one might expect the former to want to slow down climate change while the latter denies it's happening.

Only MK has consistently opposed population-led growth. Most MK councillors have been vocal in stating their opposition to the housing targets and the party was publicly condemning the Local Plan as unsustainable back in March 2012 well before a campaign of resistance began to catch fire (http://www.mebyonkernow.org/news/article.php?id= 30). MK is also the only political party with policies that provide the basis for restoring Cornish control over planning. It now has to overcome the difficulty of reaching out to the non-Cornish in the population and make its voice heard over the crass stereotyping and misrepresentation of the media (for a typical example see Robert McCrum's piece in *The Observer*, 24 Jun 2012).

But does the Local Plan, which is itself just a symptom of that dominant population-led growth ideology that grips our political leaders, need a new kind of politics? Is it too critically important to be left to the tribalism of party politics? And politics itself is about a lot more than Cornwall Council's growth strategy, even if the latter is one of the most critical issues we in Cornwall face. At least planning policy – unlike education or health – cannot in theory be fully privatised. Corporate interests and the developer lobby need a planning system, albeit a stripped down one with less bureaucracy, in order to provide some sort of legitimacy for their activities. Unable to privatise planning they concentrate on capturing the planners. Which they've succeeded in doing very well. Therefore, those opposed to the million-people scenario of unsustainable growth need to concentrate on capturing the councillors and projecting an alternative more sustainable view into the media. More and more people are beginning to wake up and say enough is enough. And more will inevitably join them as the scale of Cornwall's transformation becomes ever clearer. Now is the time to plan the best way to resist. Now is the time to demand that Cornwall Council's growth strategy is subject to some long overdue genuinely democratic debate. In my next and final chapter

I'll ponder this further and put forward some possible strategies of resistance.

Chapter 10

It's our Cornwall: Time to reclaim our land

We have seen in this book how Cornwall Council is determined to promote 'growth'. However, their definition of 'growth' turns out to be extremely narrow, effectively driven by housing and population. Prosperity, we are promised, is assured through housing. Unfortunately, this completely ignores the evidence of the past half century, during which time rapid population growth in Cornwall has patently not produced prosperity. If anything it has produced the opposite – the lowest wages in the UK and a fragile economy as the events of the past few years indicate. Moreover, research shows that even those in-migrants who arrive better off than the host community find their standards of living drifting down over the years (Williams and Champion, 1998). But, eyes fixed firmly on the future, the decentred growth apologists, many of whom are in restless transit, spending their lives in a placeless limbo, forget the past. Or are blithely unaware of it, intent on importing their one-size-fits-all solution. Regenerate! Grow! Suburbanise! Endlessly. But our future doesn't have to be sacrificed to this blinkered 'vision' with its limited horizons. There are alternatives to the developers' dream, of passive consumers in pursuit of the latest gadget that we don't need but are persuaded we want, as we 'sit isolated in overpriced new flats and houses. chained to soulless jobs by mortgages that drag across generations' (Simms, 310). The message of this final chapter is that other paths exist. I intend here to sketch out some alternative policy aims before beginning to explore how we might organise to achieve those policies.

Incapable of learning from the past, our growth gurus are also unable to properly visualise the future. The result of continuing the current growth rate is inevitably a population of nearly a million by the end of this century. If we continue the building plans proposed for the next 20 years beyond that point, more than half of Cornwall will be built on in just over two centuries time. And beyond that, continuing the present growth rate results in every single piece of land in Cornwall – from the tops of the tors to the shores of the sea - being urbanised by around 2310. That may sound like a long time but it's a heck of a lot less time than has elapsed since the civil wars of the seventeenth century or even the Tudor period. No doubt our growth gurus would ridicule the prospects of this level of urbanisation ever happening. But they refuse to divulge when, how or why they expect recent trends to change.

With no sense of history and no vision of the future other than promises of prosperity supposedly stemming from endless suburbanisation, ceaseless consumption and limitless profit-making, Cornwall's growth clique employs the Local Plan to mystify the public and suppress the truth. Cornwall's proposed population growth over the next two decades results almost wholly from in-migration. Well over three quarters of the proposed extra housing is to meet demand from housebuyers living outside Cornwall. But the Local Plan hardly mentions this. The status of Cornwall as the homeland of one of Britain's indigenous peoples provides us with a powerful potential reason for demanding special treatment. But the Local Plan ignores it. Somewhere near one in three of the houses built recently are not even used by permanent residents, whether native or newly arrived, but are snapped up for use as second homes and holiday lets. But the Local Plan fails to tell us how many and sanitises the problem by redefining second home owners as 'temporary residents'. The Council's own assessments conclude that continuing with current growth rates or boosting them to even higher levels will have serious environmental effects. But the Local Plan conceals this from us. Population growth on this scale is patently unsustainable. But the Local Plan asserts all growth everywhere in Cornwall is always sustainable.

As we have discovered, a perverted form of joined-up thinking lies behind the Council's strategy. Population growth feeds off and in its turn creates the demand for more supermarkets and more infrastructure. A mass incinerator at St Dennis needs a high and steady throughput of waste for another generation to be 'viable'. Roads have to be built at Bodmin, Camborne or Newquay to 'unlock' land so that more houses can be built to house more job-seekers who will chase the jobs created and competed for by more people who will need more roads to drive to the new retail outlets which will attract … and so on. And on. Into that dreary featureless dumbed-down dystopia mapped out for us by corporate neo-liberalism and those who are set to make money of this life-sapping vicious cycle.

All this can make a warped sort of perfect sense in terms of its own assumptions. You want more affordable homes. Then we have to build a lot more unaffordable homes. You want a spanking new sports stadium. Then we must have a new suburb to go with it. You want more jobs. So we must have more people, to create the demand for the goods and services that will produce those jobs. You want sustainability. Then we must embrace growth. You want to save Cornwall. Then we have to destroy it first. The self-referential logic in which the Local Plan and the Council is trapped can appear perfectly sane in its own terms. It is only revealed to be totally deranged when we step aside from it and view the bigger picture. We then recognise its terrible truth.

Those who embrace the Local Plan fail to consider its long-term outcomes or consequences or the viciously repetitive cycle it perpetuates. They lack any self-awareness or reflexivity about their actions. Far from taking us towards some desired end the means have become the end, taking on the attributes of a perpetual motion device. But just as perpetual motion devices are deemed to violate the first and second laws of thermodynamics so the growth cycle in Cornwall is physically impossible to sustain after a certain point. Growth has already gone a considerable way towards destroying the attractiveness and distinctiveness of Cornwall. However, there is an even deeper problem with the psychology of growth. By limiting its vision to the short term, by prioritising immediate gratification over long-term consequences, the growth camp adopts an infantile mindset, one that refuses to understand or consider the consequences of its own actions. In a very fundamental way, it lacks maturity.

It doesn't have to be this way

Even within the constraints of a system that elevates capital accumulation above all other gods it doesn't have to be this way. In the last decade Cornwall grew at a rate double that of most Welsh rural areas. Take Ceredigion in west Wales. In the 1980s and 1990s Ceredigion was experiencing counter-urbanisation pressures greater than in Cornwall, yet its growth rate of 13.7 per cent in the 1990s fell to just 1.3 per cent in the 2000s. Or take Cumbria, an area of England with quite a lot in common with Cornwall, for example distance from London, tourism, population distribution and older declining industrial areas. But when population growth in Cornwall in the 1980s was almost 10.6 per cent, in Cumbria it was just 1.1 per cent. In the 2000s in Cornwall it was still 6.5 per cent while in Cumbria it had risen – but only to 2.5 per cent. In the extended period from 1981 to 2011 Cornwall's population rose by over 25 per cent but that in Cumbria by less than 4 per cent.

Was this really due just to the presence of a National Park in Cumbria? That can't be the whole story as Devon, also with its National Park, saw a growth rate of 17 per cent, nearer to that in Cornwall. But why isn't our council looking as a matter of urgency towards rural Wales or to Cumbria for hints and pointers for devising a population stabilisation strategy? Does European funding, which presumes growth, actually stop them doing this? As we have seen, rather than look to places where population growth has fallen back to a more sustainable level, the last Council considered our growth rates of the previous decade to be too low and invited the British Property Federation to tell them how to overcome 'barriers to growth'. And that can only mean one thing - make the opposition to suburbanisation even feebler than it already is.

Despite its very low population growth Cumbria's disposable income per private household rose by 31.2 per cent in the boom years between 1999 and 2008. Cornwall's rose by 33.7 per cent even with the additional help of generous European funding (Eurostat, online at http://epp.eurostat.ec.europa.eu/portal/page/portal/eurostat/home/). This suggests that high population growth hardly correlates with rising prosperity in the way the Council simplistically asserts. West Wales saw its disposable income rise by 33.5 per cent - around the same as Cornwall - but with a population growth rate well under half ours and falling. The truth is that there is no automatic link between population growth and rising material prosperity. If the Cumbrian or Welsh countryside can be protected from the worst ravages of over-development and yet living standards do not noticeably suffer, then our current path of population-led growth is clearly not the only one available. Strangely, this suggests that reducing population growth to a more sustainable rate wouldn't automatically consign us to the dark ages.

Across the world, island societies perform best on the Happy Planet Index, a measure of well-being that takes into account more than just material wealth (Simms, 75). Cornwall is almost an island. Perhaps it's time we had more of an island mentality. Contrast the Local Plan's complacency about population growth with the Jersey Government's attitude for example. In 2006 Jersey established a Population Office to regulate migration while its Strategic Plan seeks to manage population growth and migration and states that 'a growing population will increase the pressures on natural resources and make it necessary to find ways to maintain our quality of life whilst consuming less and creating less waste … the challenge is to maintain a working age population which enables the economy to flourish and public services to be sustained without threatening our environment and way of life'. Exactly the same could of course be said about Cornwall. But isn't.

Faced by an even higher population growth than Cornwall – 12.2 per cent in the past decade – Jersey has decided to initiate a population and immigration debate and establish targets for limits on population growth by 2013. Action may include tariffs on immigrants of up to £5,000 (*This is Jersey*, 8 Jun 2012), tougher regulation of licences for non-locally qualified staff for posts not filled within the island and changes to the housing laws.

Whatever happened to the precautionary principle?

When the future is uncertain, as it is at present, the soundest advice would seem to be to stop and think. If you're unsure what's in store for you then destroying the assets you currently have looks like reckless behaviour indeed. Yet this is precisely what the Local Plan and the million-people growth agenda that lies behind it does. It cheerfully trashes the environment while simultaneously undermining Cornish claims for special consideration by carelessly colluding with or actively encouraging the extinction of those aspects that make Cornwall a special place. Inflexibly fixed on unflinchingly accommodating 80,000 and more people in the next two decades alone, it refuses to admit, let alone discuss rationally, the inevitable consequences of its own irresponsibility.

We have reached the point nonetheless where urgent action is required to reverse the inevitable consequences of current policies. The most sensible thing to do would be to adopt the precautionary principle. In the absence of evidence that population growth brings prosperity and the presence of evidence that it produces environmental degradation and unacceptable social and cultural engineering the responsible action is to be cautious. Slow down. Wait. Investigate all possibilities. Think long-term rather than short-term. Subject building proposals to some tests of viability. For example, will they increase or decrease pressure on the biosphere; will they lead to a more equal distribution of the benefits of economic activity; will they enhance or detract from the well-being of the people who live in our communities? Decide what is in the best interests of Cornwall and its current population rather than work ceaselessly to enable developers and corporations, most of them based upcountry, to make profits out of suburbanising our land and selling it to a new population.

The analogy of global warming is relevant here. Our local political and economic elite acts exactly like the global ruling class and their pet politicians, determined to ensure the world is fit for maintaining the wealth of the tiny group of super-rich who monopolise the bulk of our resources. The world's politicians cave in to economic power and look on helplessly as the need for corporate profits and an elusive quest for economic stability propels us inexorably towards disastrous climate change. Just as energy companies fund their literally well-oiled campaign to discredit the scientific consensus on climate change, so locally developers exert pressure on Cornwall Council to build more houses, shamelessly using the desire for more affordable houses and other infrastructure as a device to maintain the sustainability of their own profits. Developers and their mercenaries foster the myth that more houses are needed to house our people in need. This conveniently ignores the fact that finding somewhere to live is not a matter of simply building more houses but a question of how easy it is for people to get access those houses. These two things are not the same. But, busily doling out permissions for luxury coastal housing and second homes, this is not something the unholy trinity of planners, developers and councillors like to dwell on. Just as £ millions are spent on campaigns of disinformation from the climate change deniers so is money expended by Cornwall Council on greenwash designed to hide the inevitable unsustainability of its own unimaginative growth project. Just as 'business as usual' is bringing all of us to the edge of unpredictable and potentially chaotic change so 'business as usual' in Cornwall brings us to the brink of suburbanisation and beyond.

Therefore, to avert potential catastrophe at either scale, we have to re-assert the importance of the precautionary principle. Government, at all levels, has to start acting not merely in the interests of the propertied and wealthy but of everyone. However, it's one thing to say this, quite another to achieve it. Make no mistake; the odds are stacked against it. The system works to reward short-term growth policies not long-term precautionary principles. Nevertheless, here we do have an alternative. In order to embed the precautionary principle at the heart of policy-making, Cornwall Council's greenwash and management school gibberish has to be scrapped and replaced with another discourse – a discourse of genuine sustainability. In order to do that we have to discover a way to organise the growing upsurge of doubt and disenchantment about the direction in which the Council is taking us. Then we could let Cornwall shine as a real beacon of hope for the rest of these islands rather than cower like the tame lapdog of over-development which it has sadly become.

Three steps to sustainability

If policy-makers genuinely wished to see Cornwall setting an example by becoming a green peninsula it isn't enough merely to adopt a more responsible precautionary principle, only agreeing building projects if there were clear long-term advantages and benefits for Cornwall and its existing population. We need to go a lot further than that. Current policies of 'growth at all costs' have to be jettisoned and a policy framework adopted that actively seeks first to reduce the rate of housing and population growth and then to stabilise it. If this could happen in west Wales over the past couple of decades then it's hardly beyond the realm of practical politics to envisage the same thing happening here. The role of local government (or in our case ideally regional government) should be to do all it can to facilitate the process and replicate the conditions that make it possible.

Three steps are therefore required. They are
   1) identify the limits
   2) explore the policy
   3) apply the policy

In 1976 Cornwall County Council planners concluded that, in order to 'maintain the physical character of Cornwall' its ideal population capacity would be 430,000 (*Structure Plan Policy Choice Consultation Document*, 1976, p.76). At the time the population was around 400,000. It passed 430,000 in 1982, is now over 532,000 and still rising, clearly to the detriment of that 'physical character'. That one effort to quantify Cornwall's ideal population capacity back in 1976 was never repeated. As we have seen, even a population of 430,000 would now be greatly in excess of our biocapacity which stands at just 208,000. The idea that we can continue to pack more and more people into Cornwall while simultaneously increasing our demands on global biocapacity is fundamentally flawed. Sooner or later, the finite constraints of land area, food production, space for leisure activities, and aesthetic attitudes towards the built environment will demand a halt. We will have reached the limit.

But what is that limit? Moreover, what population would best sustain our environmental assets and maintain the Cornishness of Cornwall? If we wish to retain current levels of resource consumption and waste generation and live within even our global means we should be aiming at a population of just 208,000. (If we wanted to live within Cornish limits and be self-sufficient the population would have to fall to around 66,000!) Nonetheless, this provides us with the lower end of an ideal population size for Cornwall. In stark contrast, the Council was happily planning to accommodate a net in-migration rate of around 45,000 every decade. So they obviously regarded the limit as more than 637,000, the originally planned population for 2031. As I have repeated regularly (and monotonously) in this text, if current trends continue, that population hits a million soon after the end of this century. So is that the limit? Or is it even higher? Personally, I feel we're already well past the optimal population. Cornwall has become too crowded, too congested and too suburbanised for my tastes. But others may have different ideas. What we haven't done is to debate the limit. So the first step is to be more open about the longer-term consequences of current policies and initiate a public debate about the desirable population of Cornwall. There is a tendency to jump to the conclusion that stabilising Cornwall's population would demand a total halt to in-migration. This is far from the case. The growth in population results from an excess of in-migrants over out-migrants. If the number of in-migrants was reduced by just a fifth (or the number of out-migrants rose by just a fifth) then net migration would be in balance. In other words, if just one in five of the migrants who now come to Cornwall decided not to come, then population would stabilise.

Once we agree a limit then the second task is to explore policies that can contain population numbers to that level. Instead of colluding with the developers' lobby to explore ways of removing 'barriers to growth' policy has to shift to exploring ways of creating barriers to unsustainable growth. A key element here will be the need to evolve new and innovative policies towards the provision of housing, both within the market and outside it. But this will have to be coupled with identifying the planning tools required to control market mechanisms. Lessons have to be learnt from places where population is already stable like west Wales, Cumbria or, closer to home, Scilly. Examples could be sought in other European regions. But to do this policy-makers need to become a lot more outward-looking and less parochial and introspective. The banality of a planning approach that guarantees the stifling of Cornwall's unique character has to be challenged. Policy has to free itself from the influence of the corporate and developer lobby and become once again answerable to the people not the profiteers.

Ultimately, as we saw in chapters 6-8, the structural pressures propelling us towards unsustainable growth are extremely powerful. The psychological costs of admitting failure are too great, the comfort of the familiar breeds inertia and the economic lure of making money from the great sale of Cornwall is too enticing to forgo. Therefore, it would be foolish in the extreme to believe that population stabilisation and sustainability can easily be achieved within a system designed to encourage the opposite. Cornwall councillors would have to support and lead a campaign of critical resistance to, and education about, centralised policies. If they are trapped by such policies then they have a duty to make it plain both to the people of Cornwall and to the powers that be that hierarchical diktat leaves them with few options under the current rules. Instead of enthusiastic collusion with growth agendas designed to force us to accommodate unsustainable levels of in-migration the Council should explain to the people why it has to adopt an attitude of reluctant submission. This would be an interim position, while working towards the greater devolution of real decision-making powers over planning, housing and economic affairs. In turn, in order to obtain these, the Council would have to adopt a consistent position on Cornwall's special status, rejecting the humiliating and insulting 'county' designation imposed by central power and doing more to demand the proper respect due to a national minority.

The need to explore sustainable policies doesn't however stop with housing and planning. *All* Cornwall Council policies - from financial support for Newquay airport to the policies of VisitCornwall to subsidising the Eden Project to the inward investment efforts of the Cornwall Development Company – have to be assessed in the light of their potential effect on population growth. Thinking must be joined up to dampen the process of population growth rather than as at present to boost it. For example, current over-reliance on tourism is, as I pointed out in chapter 8, hardly conducive to the encouragement of a sustainable level of population. As it dominates the public discourse, tourism also acts to drown out other possibilities and presents an obstacle to imagining other, more rational, ways of organising our economy. Indeed, the shift since the 1980s towards a more up-market tourism and away from the sun, sea and sand marketing of previous decades may well exacerbate our problems by targeting exactly those groups with sufficient disposable income to enter the second homes market. This is also of course the same segment of the population that most profligately produces greenhouse gases and greedily gobbles up the earth's resources. A 'green Cornwall' stance that actively encourages such expensive lifestyles is clearly contradictory and logically has to be abandoned.

Having decided on the limit and explored policies that would work towards reducing population growth to within that limit the final step towards sustainability is to apply those policies. This is the point at which prescription is transformed into practicality. Action for real sustainability is inevitably political action. This in turn can be broken down into two aspects – political will and political organisation. In a supposedly representative democracy, we need representatives who have a clear, coherent sense of what is best for Cornwall and a determination not to be swayed from implementing the policies or exerting the pressure that will save Cornwall from suburbanisation. As I argued in chapter 9 the current democratic deficit in Cornwall means that we are very far from that state. There is clearly a long road to travel in order to transform our present sad situation and produce the critical campaigning representatives for which Cornwall and its communities are crying out.

The insufficient number of such active critical minds in our local government is indicative of a wider malaise and a debilitated state of resistance in Cornwall. Cornwall Council. The developers' lobby feeds off this apathy, getting away with the most outrageous deceptions, as we've seen, and ploughing on with their plans to sell off Cornwall. To some extent of course the very speed of this process saps our will to resist it. As soon as one unnecessary housing project is temporarily halted, another pops up. Small victories are inevitably followed by major defeats. Which is where I started at the very beginning of this book.

However, all is not lost. It doesn't have to be like this. There are alternatives. And there is still hope. Despite having been bludgeoned into meek submission by half a century of uninterrupted population growth and cultural engineering. Despite the lack of trust and the fragmented sense of community this remorseless process has created. Our hope lies with the people in our communities. It is no good looking solely to an enfeebled group of elected representatives to defend us. They've had their chance for 50 years and have comprehensively blown it. With a handful of honourable exceptions our present councillors have to either stand aside or be removed so that a proper challenge can emerge to rival the top-down suburbanisation agenda of that (in the main) unelected group that assumes the right to speak on our behalf.

I am deliberately resisting producing a menu of possible policy options here. The whole point of this book is to act as a warning. A warning that the current population growth strategy is flawed. When I set out to write it I did not intend it to be a manifesto or to contain a detailed list of less destructive alternative policies. I have faith that others can build on the general principles here and begin to flesh out an alternative set of policies. These may well include such things as taxation policies, second homes policies and new education and skills policies aimed at Cornish residents.

However, one essential requirement in order to resist the current 'logic' is devolution of power to Cornwall. We must be able to set our own planning framework that recognises our specific needs and deals with our particular and unique circumstances. Devolution must mean a lot more than the current Tory/Lib Dem Government's policy which is to devolve financial responsibility but in a way that ensures this creates an imperative to build, thus merely perpetuating the present vicious circle.

It's our Cornwall

As I keep saying, it doesn't have to be this way. If planners and councillors at Cornwall Council have been captured by the developers and their apologists, if those we have elected are enfeebled and unable to resist the million-people strategy, then it behoves those who can see through the great growth chimera to build resistance. The first thing we have to resist is despair or defeatism. We have to challenge the notion that 'we're never going to change things'. The one certain thing in our world is change. However, what we have to do is to manage change, not let ourselves be managed by it. It's argued that engaging in constructive protest and campaigning itself has a positive impact on well-being (Simms, 125). So improve your health: question the nature of your orders. At present, we see a flowering of local campaigns across Cornwall in reaction to the latest sell-off of our countryside and heritage. These are symptoms of hope, although too they remain isolated and unconnected and are picked off one by one by Cornwall Council and the developers. Moreover, the extreme parochialism of the local press and the Devonwallcentric nature of television often ensures that objectors may be unaware of similar actions in a town or village just twenty miles away. But it doesn't have to be this way.

Groups can come together and present a united front. The groundswell of interest in the *Our Cornwall* campaign and its open letter to councillors in the summer and autumn of 2012 indicated that a willingness to resist the Council's developer-led strategy is alive and well in Cornwall. Forty-five separate organisations, including a dozen parish and town councils, supported *Our Cornwall*'s open letter. The campaign took inspiration from a similar one in Wiltshire a year or two earlier which claimed that Wiltshire Council's plans would lead to 'massive estates on greenfield sites, more characterless car-based suburbia, more traffic congestion and pollution, declining town centres, damage to the environment and loss of agricultural land'. The secretary of one of the groups involved said she 'senses mounting resistance in all parts of the county to a plan that will dump a sprawl of urban extensions and industrial estates into the open countryside'. Wiltshire Council's response was also deeply familiar – the plan was 'based on the amount of people who will need housing by 2026'. But, as a former planning inspector and past president of Royal Town Planning Institute who was involved in the Wiltshire campaign stated, 'in economic and planning terms it simply does not stack up'.

Another template emerged in Herefordshire in 2009, one that linked local campaigns against development to political action and to councillors. In July 2009 a small meeting of eight people took place, arising out of opposition to plans for massive housing developments in the countryside around Hereford. At that meeting a group was formed calling itself *Herefordshire First* and members were recruited by word of mouth. In parallel, a campaign had been active in the city of Hereford fighting a proposal for a large supermarket to replace local markets. In January 2010 that campaign – *It's Our City* – merged with *Herefordshire First* to form a wider organisation – *It's Our County*. This group included a councillor on the local unitary authority. He persuaded two other councillors to join him to form a political group on the council in April 2010. By August of that year they counted five councillors in their group and a month later *It's Our County* was publicly launched. In the local elections of May 2011 the organisation put up 29 candidates for the 58 seats on the local authority.

Nine were elected and this became ten when the single Green Party councillor affiliated to the group.

It's Our County campaigns on four principles – independence and a commitment to putting Herefordshire first; honesty and transparency; sustainability, emphasising quality of life over rampant development; and localism, supporting what's right for Herefordshire rather than 'bog-standard solutions'. Cornwall first? Quality of life over rampant development? Cornish solutions not bog-standard solutions? There is surely a lot to learn from this. Incidentally, population growth in Herefordshire in the 2000s was just 4.9 per cent compared to Cornwall's 6.5 per cent! But, whether transferable to Cornwall or not, this example carries two important lessons. Firstly, it tells us that organisation doesn't happen overnight. It needs to be built patiently. Secondly, it shows the importance of lining up local councillors with local campaigners. In Cornwall our priority has to be to get councillors to end their current vow of silence and commit themselves on the growth issue. If they tacitly support the million-people strategy they should be forced to admit it and defend their position. If they oppose it then they must tell us what they intend to do to prevent it or work with communities to evolve a set of grass-roots alternatives.

Those who gain from the great sale of Cornwall need to be named and shamed. Hitherto, their project has proceeded largely unchallenged and out of the spotlight. But the greater transparency of data that the internet provides opens up new possibilities for monitoring and exposing this project, its policy-led evidence and its banal assumptions. That will be the first step to forcing a wider debate about the longer-term consequences of slavishly following a developer-led agenda. However, what we must avoid is a resort to the dead-end of nostalgia and preservationism. Cornwall has changed and there's no going back to the 1950s. What we have to do now is wrest its future back from the palsied grip of the growth clique and replace their narrow horizons with wider ones.

For instance, recognising Cornwall's distinct history and the presence in it of one of Britain's indigenous peoples provides us with yet another model for action. In Welsh-speaking Wales the group Cymuned was formed in 2001 to defend local communities from the threats stemming from demographic change. Cymuned activists deliberately adopted the language of 'anti-colonisation' rather than 'anti-immigration' to avoid being trapped in a discourse associated in England with racism. In Cornwall similarly. 'immigration' does not seem to be the most appropriate word when our 'immigrants' are of the same skin colour and have not arrived from Bulgaria or Romania but places a lot nearer home. Cymuned has explored policies that would create a housing market designed for locals rather than outsiders and policies to strengthen small, local businesses. This has been coupled with campaigns demonstrating against the predatory activities of estate agents, supermarkets and the like. The potential applicability of an action group like Cymuned in Cornwall was recognised early in the 2000s when a Kernow branch briefly emerged. It may be time to revisit this.

Whichever model or models of resistance are adopted, unless there is a change in policy we are on course to double the population of Cornwall by the end of the century. Despite the failure of the policy of population-led growth over the past half century, an elite besotted with housing and population still controls the debate and monopolises the media. The simple truth is that Cornwall, its countryside and its communities are being thoughtlessly sacrificed not for the elusive prosperity of its people, forever promised but forever deferred, but in the interests of landlords, developers and others who gain from accommodating the net in-migration of permanent and temporary residents largely from the south east of England. But there is hope. Their growth fetish is ultimately unsustainable. As the environmental and cultural contradictions of this 'policy' mount, more and more questioning the sense of continuing to sacrifice agricultural land and cherished countryside. Those who realise that the growth juggernaut cannot continue indefinitely and has to be replaced by a plan for a sustainable Cornwall remain under-represented in the stripped down, increasingly undemocratic corridors of local government. In the meantime, those who object to the mad merry-go-round of growth in their localities must join together to put pressure on elected representatives and the media. We have to alert the rest of the population to the future that has been surreptitiously mapped out for us. Time is short. But we only have one Cornwall - our Cornwall - to save.

Reference list

Cornwall County Council and Cornwall Council reports and documents

Annual Monitoring Report Planning Policy 2010-11, 2011

Can Do Cornwall: Helping to build a better future, 2011

Core Strategy Options Paper 1, 2011

Cornwall Environment Evidence Report, 2010

Cornwall: Our Strategy for a Greener, Sustainable, Low Carbon Cornwall, 2011

Equality Impact Assessment, 2011

Housing Growth Discussion Paper, v4, 2012

Housing Issues Paper, 2011

Local Plan Strategic Policies, 2013 (LPSP)

Newquay Cornwall Airport Draft Masterplan for Cornwall, 2008

Planning Future Cornwall: Our Preferred Approach, 2012 (PA)

Planning Future Cornwall: Community Network Areas, 2012 (CNA)

Planning Future Cornwall: Sustainability Appraisal, 2011 (SA)

Population and Household Change v.2, 2012

Quality of Life Survey, 2007

Structure Plan Policy Choice Consultation Document, 1976

2011 Census at a glance, 2012

Other references

Bishop, Simon and Tony Grayling, *The Sky's the Limit: Policies for Sustainable Aviation*, Institute for Public Policy Research, London, 2003

Convergence Office, *ESF Framework*, Truro, 2009

Crouch, Colin, *The Strange Non-Death of Neoliberalism*, Polity, Cambridge, 2011

Deacon, Bernard, *To fly or not to fly: A response to the Newquay Cornwall Airport Masterplan*, CoSERG, Redruth, 2009

Deacon, Bernard, Andrew George and Ronald Perry, *Cornwall at the Crossroads*, CoSERG, Redruth, 1989

Department for Communities and Local Government, *Council tax base, October 2011*, London, 2011

Department for Communities and Local Government, *Community Infrastructure Levy, an overview*, London, 2011

Department for Communities and Local Government, *National Planning Policy Framework*, London, 2012

Game, Chris, 'Place-shaping's difficult if you don't have a place: the toponymy of English shire government', paper presented to the Political Studies Association annual conference, Manchester, 2009

Husk, Kerryn, 'Ethnic group affiliation and social exclusion in Cornwall', unpublished PhD thesis, University of Plymouth, 2012

Jackson, Tim, *Prosperity Without Growth: Economics for a Finite Planet*, Earthsea, London, 2009

Lefebvre, Henri, *The Production of Space*, Blackwell, Oxford, 1991

Minton, Anna, *Ground Control: Fear and happiness in the twenty-first century city*, Penguin, London, 2012

New Local Government Network, *You've Been Quangoed*, London, 2008

Office for National Statistics, *The sub-regional value of tourism in the UK in 2008*, London, 2011

Parkhurst, Graham, 'Influence of bus-based park and ride facilities on users' car traffic', *Transport Policy* 7, 2000, pp.159-72

Peasgood, Alice and Mark Goodwin, *Introducing Environment*, Oxford University Press, Oxford, 2007

Perry, Ronald, Ken Dean and Bryan Brown (eds), *Counterurbanisation: International Case Studies of Socio-Economic Change in Rural Areas*, Geo Books, Norwich, 1986

Ross, Carne, *The Leaderless Revolution: how ordinary people will take power and change politics in the 21st century*, Simon & Schuster, London, 2011

Simms, Andrew, *Cancel the Apocalypse: The new path to prosperity*, Little, Brown, London, 2013

South West Regional Development Agency, *Economic assessments of South west Regional Airports*, Bristol, 2007

South West Research Company, *Cornwall Occupancy Rates 1993-2009*, Exeter, 2010

South West Tourism, *The Value of Tourism*, Exeter, 2005

Thomas, Charles, *The Importance of being Cornish in Cornwall*, Institute of Cornish Studies, Redruth, 1973

Willett, Joanie, 'Cornish identity: Vague notion or social fact', in Philip Payton (ed.), *Cornish Studies Sixteen*, University of Exeter Press, Exeter, 2008, pp.183-205

Williams, Malcolm and Tony Chapman, 'Cornwall, Poverty and In-Migration' in Philip Payton (ed.), *Cornish Studies Six*, University of Exeter Press, Exeter, 1998, pp.118-26

Index

www.ingramcontent.com/pod-product-compliance
Lightning Source LLC
Chambersburg PA
CBHW060337200326
41519CB00011BA/1963